The Sailing Out

Julie McDonald

The Sailing Out.

Iowa State University Press

Ames

Composed and printed by The Iowa State University Press, Ames, Iowa 50010

First edition, 1982

Library of Congress Cataloging in Publication Data

McDonald, Julie.
    The sailing out.

    I. Title.

| PS3563.C357S3 | 1982 | 813′.54 | 82–10065 |

ISBN 0–8138–1624–6

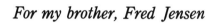

For my brother, Fred Jensen

NOTE

This book is not a memoir or a family portrait. The people in it were created to live between its covers and, the author hopes, for a time in the memories of its readers.

The Sailing Out

Don't sail out farther than you can row back.

DANISH PROVERB

1

I WAS BORN the year of the Crash—a few months earlier than Black Friday—but my farmer parents had done their crashing well before their urban neighbors and were well adjusted to the Great Depression by the time I arrived.

After three days of trying to be born in the farmhouse bedroom where my mother was attended by a physician with a powerful yen to go fishing, I yielded to the pull of impatient forceps. That's what gave me the square head that mocked my Aunt Kamille's prediction that I would grow up to look like Queen Marie of Roumania.

My first memories are of lying in the white-painted crib my father had made from banana crates, afraid to close my eyes in the dark. If I lowered my eyelids, the earth opened in great fissures as whirling, shrieking pinwheels came at me. Drugged by the hard work of the day, my parents slept just beyond my reach. The slightest cry would have brought one of them to comfort me, but I lay stiff and silent with my eyes opened so wide that my forehead ached.

As I grew older, another recurring scene was played against the backdrop of heavy, country night. The noon sun lit a rocky grotto where my parents laughed and talked while they spread a picnic cloth and passed food to each other: chicken, coffee with cream, and potato salad covered with slices of hard-boiled eggs that stared with big golden eyes. I ran to join them, but as I came close, the earth split into a deep chasm. Hungry and lonely on the other side, I backed away from the crumbling edges of the deep-cut earth into sleep.

In the morning I looked out the window and marveled that the yard was flat and solid as a table top, packed hard by a flock of pecking chickens, but the terrors of the night stayed with me until I went outside and tested reality with my feet.

When I came into the house, no one questioned my stomping ritual. All was well as the eastern sun poured into the kitchen through the window beside the cookstove. Daddy thanked God for the oatmeal and the scrambled eggs with their tiny green sleeves of chives. My dog Sofus stretched out in a warm square of light on the linoleum, thumping his tail whenever I looked his way. It seemed to me that Sofus particularly appreciated the dress I was wearing, my favorite. I loved the small print of pink tulips so much that I tried to wear the dress inside out when the right side got dirty, but Mom would have none of that. The tulips were clean to-

3

day, fragrant from the kiss of a flatiron pulled from the stove burners just short of a scorching heat.

Little Bo-Peep in the bottom of my cereal bowl was suffocating in oatmeal, and I ate the stuff to rescue her. She was grateful, and so were her sheep.

Mom was wearing a green headache band and the dress she had made on the sewing machine that said *Bismarck, Bismarck, Bismarck!* when she stepped on the treadle. She looked like a stranger in this new thing, and I squinted my eyes, trying to get her to look the way she always did. I pushed at time to see the dress old and familiar, fading and softening the stiff new material.

She served Daddy's eggs from the big frying pan on a back burner and passed behind his chair to take her own place, touching him as she went. His hand closed on her fingers.

"I know that foxy get-up is for Valborg," he said, "but I'm enjoying it too."

"Well, I don't want her to think I've gone to rack and ruin out here on the farm. Oh, Lauritz, I'm so nervous!"

"That's foolish. She's your sister, isn't she?"

"That's just it. We know exactly how to hurt each other."

"It beats all the way you Jorgen sisters take turns being mad at each other. When a Dane gets a mad on, it's a long, cold winter, and I'm glad the ice is breaking between you and Valborg."

"It's hard to know how to act," Mom said. "The longer a thing like that goes on, the worse it gets. Margaret, please mind me while your Aunt Valborg is here, and be nice to her. You can call her Aunt Val, I guess. That will be easier for you, and Mama says everybody calls her Val nowadays."

I tried to think how Aunt Val would look. Probably like Aunt Kamille, who lived in town. She would have grasshopper green eyes, a straight nose with a little bump at the bridge, and a high twist of molasses-colored hair. Maybe not, though. Mom and Aunt Kamille were as different as the kittens in a barn-cat's litter.

Aunt Val was coming from a place that sounded like the noise the bees made under the eaves of the shed: *Arizona, Arizona!* She was coming on a train, Mom said, and since I'd never seen a train, I supposed it would run on the road like our Ford and bring Aunt Valborg straight down the lane.

"You'd better get started, Lauritz. I'd hate to keep her waiting."

"Won't you change your mind and come to the station?"

Mom hugged her round, white arms. "No, Mama and Kamille will be there, and I'd rather meet her for the first time on my own ground."

"All right—as long as you trust me with a good-looking widow woman."

Mom laughed and walked to the Ford to kiss Daddy good-bye. She always looked away before the car turned out of the lane because she said

4

it was bad luck to watch a loved one out of sight, but I kept my eyes on the square black top until it sank beneath the Fiscus hill.

When Mom went into the house for a knife to cut some Austrian copper roses, I asked for a battered serving spoon to dig in the hard dirt near the back-door pump. The earth was stony, bending the spoon handle against the bowl. Sofus came to help, throwing dirt between his back legs with the furious scrabbling of his paws. When he stopped, looking back at me with his tongue lolling and dripping, I decided his trench was deep enough to bury the picture I had hidden in the back of the buffet drawer.

I was on my way to get it when Mom said, "Margaret, how did you ever get so filthy?" She put the roses on the stoop and swatted the dusty skirt of my dress until the tulips re-emerged, but that wasn't good enough. She said I'd have to change.

"No! I want to wear this!"

"Well, you can't. I won't have you looking like a pig and making Valborg think I let Davy go around like that when he was here."

Davy. He was Mom and Daddy's boy before I came. In the brownish snapshot I meant to bury, they had their arms around him. I had made a hole in his head with a pencil point one wash day when Mom shut me into the dining room to keep me out of the way while she hoisted big kettles of boiling water from the stove to the Maytag. Daddy wasn't with me that day, but when he was, he sat in the big armchair reading *Wallace's Farmer* and listening to the stock reports on the radio. I would climb into his lap and tie his hair into knots that wouldn't hold. When he was tired of such attentions, he would set me down, saying, *"Nuh, suh, lille pige,"* which meant something like "That's enough, little girl."

Sometimes I sneaked down to the barn to be close to Daddy, but he said it was a dangerous place and sent me back to the house. Usually I obeyed, but once I threw a tantrum and refused to go until Jess, the hired man who was in and out of the insane asylum at Clarinda, held out his hand to me and led me away. I loved Jess because he picked up my highchair with me in it and whispered to me. Mom asked me what he said, but I couldn't tell her. Jess didn't make words—just sounds that seemed to have colors and mysterious meanings.

When Daddy came back with Aunt Val, Mom ran out to meet them. She had been pulling the tulip dress off over my head when she heard the car. I pulled it back down and followed her. Mom put her arms around Aunt Val, and they both cried. I walked around them twice, trying to get a good look at this aunt who looked nothing like Aunt Kamille, Mom, Grandma, my dead Aunt Else, or the Aunt Laura who lived both far away and in the big album with dark gray pages.

When Aunt Val let Mom go, she grabbed me, and all I could see was the inside of her ear and a curtain of hair as red as the wood of Grandma's cherry buffet when the sun hit it. After the big squeeze, she pulled back, and I saw her twin-peaked mouth of barn-paint red.

"Pretty, pretty, pretty!" she said, lifting me for another hug. "Sweet enough to eat!" She held me so tight that the words vibrated in my chest and stomach. She had a chokingly sweet smell—nasty-nice like the scent of catalpa blooms.

"Valborg," Mom said, "don't spoil her rotten."

"Sorry, Pete, I forgot I was back among the Danes of Iowa—all pinched and proper. They're not like that in the Old Country."

"How do you know? You've never been there."

Daddy had been standing back, just watching, but now he said, "*I* know because I was born there. You're right, Valborg, we *do* change in America."

Aunt Val winked, and I was fascinated by that quick dip of an eyelid. Nobody else in the family did that.

"Well," she said, "are you going to keep me standing in the yard all day?"

Mom put three coffee cups on the table, but Daddy said he had to change his town clothes for overalls and go to the field.

"Don't work too hard," Aunt Val said, and as soon as he shut the yard gate, she kicked off her shoes and dug into a long, leather pouch decorated with colored beads. "Isn't that the nuts? I was dying for a weed all the way from town, but I just couldn't smoke in front of Lauritz." She lifted a burner from the stove and struck a sulphur match on its rough edge, blowing a shaft of smoke from her red mouth. Cliff Potter our neighbor made cigarettes from loose brown threads and little squares of paper, but Aunt Val's were perfectly round and came from a package.

Mom fanned the air in front of her face. "When did you take up smoking?"

"After John died. It was my way of thumbing my nose at *t.b.*"

Mom fussed with her headache band and played with the piping at the neck of her dress. Then she poked at the green diamonds in the goods of her skirt with one finger.

"Out with it, Pete, I know you're dying to ask about Davy."

"All right, how is he?"

"Healthy as a horse, with a negative *t.b.* test. You needn't have worried."

"Can you blame me? We loved him like our own."

"It wasn't your business to worry about him. Oh well, I can understand how you would—waiting so darned long for a kid of your own."

Reminded that I was present, Mom told me to go out and play. I chose the west porch, shaded in the late morning and close enough for me to hear the conversation inside. The day was too sunny for my taste. I preferred cloudy weather because all the pictures in my Mother Goose book had the look of a soft, gray day—one without frightening shadows.

"What brought you home, Valborg?" Mom was saying.

"A friend told me about some WPA mural projects. Thought I might have a chance, and now that my nursing career is over, I might as well paint."

"How can you be flippant about John's last illness? It makes you sound so hard."

"These are hard times, honey. Well, I'd better unpack. Do you think Margaret would like to help?"

I scuttled off the porch and got far enough away to come from a convincing distance when I was called.

Aunt Val was to have the south bedroom upstairs. Her scarred leather suitcase bulged with clothes, but I was most interested in a purple dress, peach-colored teddies, amber beads, and bright blue pajamas with a red dragon. Everything had Aunt Val's sweet, heavy smell, which meant they weren't new. Yard goods from the Golden Rule in Grandma's town smelled like medicine and couldn't be used until the store-bought smell was washed away.

Aunt Val dropped the amber beads over my head and marched me to the mirror. "See? Just like the Queen of Sheba." Then she tossed a pile of peach underthings at me and asked me to put them in the drawer. The swollen wood stuck, and she had to help me, saying, "Lots of things take two. Dear God, isn't it the truth?"

She went on rummaging in the suitcase, pulling out a picture I wasn't sure I wanted to see. Still, I didn't want to make her mad, so I looked. There were two boys, but I saw only one, Davy. The body was bigger, but the face was the same.

"He wanted to come with me," she said, "but he's at CCC camp building a park or something. He loves it. I doubt that Davy ever *will* come back here, but then—I thought the same thing about myself when I went away."

I didn't want Davy around, not ever, so I ran around the house three times with Sofus barking beside me. The circling was an obscure act of magic to insure the granting of a wish.

Aunt Val didn't stay as long as she planned, and it was all because of Jess. She found him in her room holding her clothes to his face. When she screamed, he tried to choke her, but I got there in time to stop him. All I did was say his name. He looked like someone just waking up before he went downstairs.

Two men came to take Jess back to Clarinda, and I didn't even get to say good-bye to him. When he started to yell and struggle, Mom took me into the downstairs bedroom and shut the door. In a little while, Aunt Val tapped on the door and came in with her cigarette and the little sauce dish she used for ashes.

"I feel terrible about this, Pete. If I'd just gone away quietly and hadn't said anything—," Aunt Val said. Her fingers moved to the red marks on her throat.

"It's not your fault," Mom said. "With Jess, it was only a matter of time."

Aunt Val sighed. "Well, Kamille's neighbors are driving east tomorrow, and I might as well hitch a ride to Iowa City to find out if my friend's contacts are worth anything. By this time next week, I could be painting the heroic American worker for the eyes of out-of-work Americans in a post office where they can't afford to buy a stamp.''

"Couldn't you apply by letter? *I* have a stamp, and living away from home will cost you money.''

"Thanks, Pete, but after what happened, this place gives me the creeps.''

Aunt Val left the next day in her purple dress with big white dots, but the south bedroom smelled like catalpa blooms for a long time after that. I'd go up there and sit on the bed to think about Jess. People talked about him after church on Sunday mornings. They said he was "funny in the head," "not quite right," "crazy." Whatever he was, I missed him.

When Daddy opened a letter and threw away the envelope with a stamp, I fished it out of the wastebasket. I didn't know how to write the way other people did, but I knew Jess could read the message in my wavy lines: "I wish you would come back. Nobody whispers to me anymore." I put my letter into the envelope and asked Mom to send it to Jess in Clarinda.

She turned her head away from me, biting her lips. Finally she said, "He won't be able to answer your letter, Margaret."

"That's all right, I can't read anyhow." I dredged up a phrase I'd heard somewhere and told her, "I just wanted to drop him a line."

Mom took my letter, but when I saw that it still was on the dining room table two days later, I took it to the mailbox myself. I wasn't tall enough to reach the box and had to go back for my little stool before I could deposit the letter and raise the metal flag.

Satisfied that I had put everything right, I began the endless wait for the return of the hired man.

2

WE HAD COMPANY for dinner every Sunday in that time when I knew that days had names, suspected that months did, too, but had no conception of years. We raised our own food, and nobody felt guilty about eating it, because we had all we needed and couldn't sell the rest anyhow. Aunt Kamille and Uncle Karl always showed up on Sundays with Marianne and Jack Russell, the children of my dead Aunt Else. To me, dead meant gone—simply not present—and since I never had known that aunt, I scarcely could miss her.

Daddy let Jack Russell set a line of gopher traps in the fields to get the bounty paid for gopher feet at the county courthouse, and I tagged along to check the traps. I hated it when the gophers were still moving, because then Jack Russell stepped on their heads. It didn't occur to me that he was making them dead—like Aunt Else—because their small bodies were still there, but I knew that he was inflicting pain.

"Don't you feel sorry for them?" I asked.

"No. Why should I? They're pests. Sofus, get away from that trap!" He slapped my dog on the muzzle, and if anyone else had done that, I would have attacked with feet and fists, but Jack Russell could do no wrong. I loved him.

His features were delicate to the point of girlishness, and he never would be a big man, Mom said, but he didn't seem to know that. He was quick to pick a fight, even though he lost them all.

"He'll never amount to anything," Daddy said.

"Now, Lauritz," Mom said, "the poor boy needs a father. Karl does the best he can, but it's hard to raise a boy in town. Maybe we should offer to take him."

I held my breath at the dazzling thought of Jack Russell coming to stay, but Daddy said, "Let him sow his wild oats in somebody else's ground."

Marianne hated the farm as much as her brother loved it. She was musical like her older sister Geraldine. Every Sunday she would say, "I can't believe that you chopped up the organ for firewood. If you hadn't, there would be *something* to do around here." Then she would flounce off to the window seat in the sewing room and stare out, vibrating with boredom until she looked like a pot on the verge of boiling its lid off. I wanted to see that lid blow, but I dreaded it, too.

"We've got new kittens, Marianne," I ventured. "Want me to show you?"

9

"No, the excitement might kill me!"

"Marianne," Aunt Kamille scolded, "don't be so nasty to Margaret."

"When do we eat?" said Marianne.

Aunt Kamille sighed and took me on her lap to tell the story of Little Black Sambo. I wondered if running around a tree for a long time would turn *me* into butter, and when we all sat down at the dinner table, I pushed the butter dish far from my plate.

"You set a wonderful table, Petra," Uncle Karl said. "Here's all this wonderful food, and just this morning I caught two kids stealing potatoes out of our garden and eating them raw—mud and all. I darned near got the spade and helped them, but we couldn't spare the spuds."

"Is it really that bad, Karl?"

With a mouthful of scalloped potatoes, he nodded and added a muffled, "Worse."

Aunt Kamille started to choke and had to leave the table. Mom found a square cut from one of Grandma's old tablecloths and wet it at the kitchen pump.

Watching her wring out the cloth until it looked like a white rope, I asked why Aunt Kamille choked and gasped that way.

"It's her old trouble. When she gets upset, the food won't go down. Kam always did bleed for the whole world."

When Mom got Aunt Kam settled on the bed and plastered the wet cloth over her eyes and forehead, I crept into the room to look for the blood, but I couldn't see any.

Aunt Kam lay very still, and the ladies in the picture on the wall above the headboard took no notice of her. They stood there in their white nightgowns as they always did, trailing their fingers along a stone wall and looking at nothing in particular against a sky too blue to believe. I wasn't sure, but I thought their names were Maxfield and Parrish. They weren't much company for Aunt Kam, and I thought that maybe I should stay, but I couldn't. I could hear Marianne excusing herself from the table.

She discouraged my tagging along on her restless wanderings, but she couldn't stop me from stalking her. The kitchen screen door slammed, and I could hear Mom swatting the flies Marianne let in. Town folks always opened the door too wide.

I used the parlor door where flies were less likely to settle and made it to the windbreak unseen by Marianne. I even got ahead of her, watching the wind make a red-gold flag of her hair and mold her dress tight to her body as I hid behind the sticky trunk of an old pine. She looked a little like Maxfield and Parrish—but crabbier. I could have reached out and touched her as she passed, but I didn't dare.

At the stock-watering tank she stopped and ran her fingers along the wet, green fur under the water. I knew just how it felt and smelled—slimy and sort of delicious and awful at the same time. I wasn't supposed to put my hands (or anything else) in the tank, because the livestock didn't like the smell and taste of people, but sometimes I did it. Marianne sniffed at her fingers and wrinkled her nose, wiping her hand on the outside of the tank before she walked on.

At the south pasture she slipped the baling-wire loop off the post, squeezed through without moving the bottom of the gate, and put the wire back. Town folks sometimes forgot, and that was what I was hoping for because I wasn't strong enough to pull the loop off. I could climb the fence, but then I'd be in the open. I risked it, stinging my soles in the jump to the ground. So far, so good.

Marianne walked toward the creek, pulling her shadow behind her. I wanted so much to come close enough to step on that shadow. Running to narrow the distance between us, I whispered, "Don't turn around. Please don't turn around."

She reached the bank of the creek and started down. First her feet disappeared, then her legs and hips. The thought of following her into that deep cut in the earth terrified me. I stopped. When her shoulders and finally her bright hair vanished, I forced myself to the edge to look down. Marianne clung to a small tree growing sideways from the bank to steady herself as she took off her shoes and stockings to wade in the shallow, brown water.

The creek looked so much like my waking nightmares that I scrambled backwards, sending a slide of dirt clods down the incline to bounce off her bare legs. She gave me such a look of rage that I closed my eyes against it, lost my balance, and fell, bringing a heavy section of the bank down with me.

Marianne snatched the back of my dress to keep me from the water and screamed, "Now look what you've done! How are we going to get back up?"

With dirt in my eyes and mouth and her anger in my ears, I tried to curl up in a ball and wait for the earth to finish swallowing me. This time, I'd have to endure the part of the nightmare that had never happened because I usually fell asleep.

"Oh, get up!" She grabbed my wrist and jerked me to my feet. "You aren't hurt. Take your shoes off because we'll have to walk close to the water until we find a place to climb out."

"I can't. They're tied in knots."

Snorting with exasperation, she knelt to work at the knots while I inspected the pale pink part in her hair and enjoyed the flowery smell of the soap she used. All we had was orange Lifebuoy, and that didn't smell good.

We carried our shoes, walking until our feet were big mudballs that looked like the bottoms of the rotten fenceposts Daddy pulled out of the ground. Every time Marianne found a foothold, it crumbled under her weight. I was glad. As long as we couldn't get out, she couldn't send me away.

"You try," she said. "You're not as heavy."

11

Wanting to prolong this captive companionship, I told her that I was tired and would have to rest awhile first.

She groaned and sat on a rotted log, dropping her dusty town shoes in her lap. The mud had dried rapidly on our legs, changing their chocolate-dipped look to that of old linoleum. Marianne pulled her skirt high and chipped away the brown crackles with her polished fingernails. The nails weren't long (too much piano playing), but they were pretty. In an over-bold move, I reached out to touch them, and she absently repulsed me.

"Do you think we're still on your farm? Oh, what would *you* know?"

I didn't know, and I didn't care. It was quiet and warm between the deep banks—cozy as a chicken incubator. Quivering blue dragonflies skimmed the brown water, giving me something lovely to look at. It was good, too, that for once, Marianne couldn't run away from me.

She was more restless than ever, though. Poking at a column of bubbles rising from the water, she thrust a stick into the mud and brought up a slimy, brown crawdad. I wanted it, but she threw the thing away in disgust and walked on, ignoring me until she saw the roots of a small tree clawing the air halfway up the bank.

"Come here. When I boost you up, grab those roots and scramble."

She lifted me, hands in my armpits, and I was so overwhelmed by her unaccustomed touch that I simply hung there savoring it.

"Take hold, dummy!"

Her arms trembled with the strain of my weight, and as I caught the roots, their support was gone. I was hanging by my hands.

"Dig your toes in. Pull!"

I did what I was told, uprooting the sapling and falling back on Marianne. She rolled halfway into the water and struggled to her feet, furious.

"Just look at what you've done to me!"

I looked. Creek water had darkened and dulled her hair and the bright flowers of her dress were mud-stained, but I still admired her.

She put her hands to her mouth to yell for help, and I joined in, but when we stopped for breath, there was nothing but thick, Sunday-afternoon silence. The stream moved along sluggishly and the slant of the sun had altered, completely shadowing the water. Soon it would be dark. Pinwheels would scream and whirl before my eyes. My hand crept into Marianne's, and she let it stay there. She shivered in her wet dress.

"We've tried everything else, so I guess we'd better pray. Kneel down."

Cold, slippery mud cupped our knees as we steepled our crusted hands for Marianne's petition. "Dear God, get us out of here!" She wasn't asking, she was telling. When she struggled to her feet, she started to cry.

"What's the matter? Don't you think He will?"

"Someday they'll find our bones," she said with a sob.

I felt the knob of my wrist through the skin and wondered how it would look when somebody found it. Like the rabbit bones Sofus found in the timber, I supposed.

Marianne touched her lips with the tips of her fingers and sobbed even harder. "All wasted!"

I threw a stick into the creek and watched it move slowly on the water. If the stick stayed in the middle of the stream until it was out of sight, it would mean that someone would come for us right away. When the stick drifted to the far bank, I changed the rules because I was really ready to go home. The banks seemed higher now, and the cut between them was filling with cold, bluish-tan twilight. Mom would be touching a match to the wick of the kerosene lamp in the kitchen.

Marianne decided that we should have gone the other way, and we started back, walking in our own footprints. The only sound was her sniffling and the sucking noise as we pulled our feet from the mud. Once I thought I heard someone calling my name, but Marianne couldn't hear it. She told me this was no time to get funny.

Then she heard it, too. We tried to answer, but we were too hoarse to make much noise. Fortunately, she could whistle. Sofus soon was above us, his golden coat blazing in the late sun that couldn't reach us. He almost stood on his head scrambling down the steep bank to jump and whine and lick our faces. I hugged him, drawing comfort from his sun-warmed coat, and even Marianne, who never liked him, said, "Good dog! Good boy!"

Daddy and Uncle Karl followed the dog, asking if we were all right and thanking God. Jack Russell was there, too, and he yelled at Marianne, "You're lucky the kid's O.K. If anything happened to her, Aunt Petra would have your hide! You could have got out, you dope! Why didn't you make a run for it and take that bank like a fly on a wall?"

"Just come down here and try it yourself, smart aleck!"

Jack Russell flopped on his belly and the men held him by the ankles, lowering him until he could reach our hands. They pulled me up first, then rescued Marianne.

Daddy buttoned me inside his overall jacket and carried me. Half-hypnotized by the even jar of his long steps, I looked over his shoulder at the creek with a feeling of triumph. It had tried to swallow me but failed.

Mom was lighting the lamp in the kitchen. She blew out the long wooden match, turned the wick up to make a fat orange tongue of flame, and hugged me hard, mud and all.

Aunt Kam sat in the kitchen chair beside the cob basket looking pale and stern. She told Marianne to clean herself up as well as she could and they'd go home.

"No, Kam," Mom said, "please stay for supper."

"If we expect to get any, we'd better," Jack Russell said, and they stayed, but Aunt Kam choked again and couldn't eat anything.

Marianne put on one of Mom's dresses, so big on her that it looked like a gunny sack tied with a rope. She didn't talk at all, but she ate: three pieces of cold chicken, lots of potato salad, and a big piece of burnt-sugar cake with two glasses of the milk she usually refused to touch because it was "right out of the cow." She didn't want to go home until it was good and dark because she didn't want to be seen in Mom's dress.

When they did go, Daddy carried me out to their car in my pajamas to say good-bye. Leaning from his arms, I tested what I supposed to be a new relationship with Marianne by touching her wrist through the open window.

"You get to take your bones home, Marianne," I said.

She pulled away and wouldn't look at me.

"Don't be such a snot, Marianne," Jack Russell told her, leaning across her lap to tickle me. "So long, Snooks."

Exhausted but fighting sleep, I begged to stay up, but I landed in bed. When my eyelids dropped of their own weight, I held my breath in the familiar terror of anticipation. The soft, black void caught me by surprise—no fissures, no whirling pinwheels—just slow exhalation and sleep.

3

GRANDMA LIVED ALONE in a dark blue house in Harlan, and when anyone needed her, she came and stayed for as long as her houseplants could get along without her. Before Mom and Daddy went to the stockyards in Omaha to sell cattle, they brought her to the farm to stay with me.

"What was your name when you were little?" I asked her.

"Amalie, the same as it is now."

"Nobody calls you that. You're either Mama or Grandma."

"That's so. I guess I'm the only one who really knows who I am, and sometimes *I* forget."

Grandma wore her dresses to her ankles and covered her skirts with long aprons tied at the waist. Her hair was gray with yellow streaks, twisted into a high knot held with a tortoise-shell comb. She smelled like growing things in the garden, and her hands were spotted with brown.

I found out how hard those hands could be. Mom always let me play in the flour when she baked, but when I poured out my small white mountain while Grandma was stirring dough, she shook her head and scooped it back into the cannister. It was also my custom to grab one of the long, black breadpans before they were greased for a "ride in the Ford" on the linoleum, but when I did that, she tumbled me out and gave me a good swat. I was too surprised to yell.

By the time the bread was set to rise, giving off a yeasty fragrance from the top of the warming ovens, we were friends again. Grandma showed me the dances of the Old Country, lifting her skirts to display footwork that seemed too flashy for tan-lisle ankles and tightly laced oxfords. She told me about keeping the sheep on the moors, and I imagined her carrying a crook prettied up with a blue ribbon like the one carried by Little Bo-Peep in my oatmeal bowl. When I asked her if hers had a bow, she just laughed.

"It's time to gather eggs," she said. "Take the brown pan."

Collecting the eggs was an adventure. The easiest way to do it was to yell and clap, putting the hens to squawking flight, but Mom didn't like me to treat her hens that way. I had learned to reach a sly hand under an angrily-puffed breast, grasp a warm oval, and get out fast. If my timing was off, a sharp beak raised a bead of blood on my hand, but that only happened when I allowed myself to be distracted by the menacing clucking. I was looking forward to the day when my hand would be big enough to grab two eggs at a time, cutting the occasions of risk in half.

I hated the nasty, feathery smell of the henhouse, and I tried to make one deep breath of fresh air last as long as possible. It never worked, because I had to pause to let my eyes adjust to the dimmer light. It was important to see well enough to avoid the snails of chicken filth on the floor. I could hold my breath only so long, and I had to choose between smelling it and stepping in it.

I filled the brown pan without getting pecked, but the hens were really letting me have it in chicken language. As I started back to the house, I saw Grandma smiling at me through the kitchen window. I waved, indicating that I'd be in as soon as I visited the backhouse.

This functional shack stood near the windbreak of pines. The wind made sad sounds in the trees as I edged onto the small hole cut especially for me between two larger ones. The edges of the big holes were worn smooth, but mine was too new for comfort. To make myself forget the biting pressure, I dropped an egg down the hole beside me and listened as it broke with a dull, plocking sound far below. I tried one in the other hole, and the sound was slightly different. By the time I had made use of a page of saws and hammers from a Montgomery Ward catalog, the brown pan was empty.

Knowing that Grandma would be mad because she was waiting for the eggs to make a cake, I went back to the henhouse to urge the biddies to lay more, but they slid the membranes across their mean-looking eyes and ignored me. I clapped my hands to scare them off the nests, but the straw hollows were empty. I choked in the feather-filled dust, realizing that I was in real trouble.

Sure enough, Grandma was knocking on the windowpane with her wedding ring, reminding me that she was waiting. I walked slowly to the house with the empty pan behind my back.

"Well, where are the eggs?"

"They aren't laid yet."

"What? I saw you carrying a full pan to the backhouse."

So she had. I cast about for another explanation. "Sofus knocked me down and broke them." As I spoke, I realized that my entire route was visible from the window.

"I don't see any shells," Grandma said ominously. "Let's try once more."

"A big snake came into the backhouse and swallowed them—every one of them!"

"Margaret, come here."

Grandma's hands moved quickly to her apron pocket, and I saw a small glint of gold. I stood before her, interested and a little scared.

"Stick out your tongue."

My impulse was to clench my teeth, but I didn't have the will to go against her. I did what I was told and felt a painful prick. I couldn't believe what had happened to me until she brought the tiny, gold safety pin between her thumb and forefinger close to my eyes.

"See? This is what happens to tongues that tell lies. Remember it."

I was too shocked to cry. Hiding under the kitchen table with Sofus, I tried to decide whether I was mad at Grandma or not. Mom would have taken me on her lap and told me how disappointed she was that I hadn't told the truth, and I would have climbed down with a gnawing feeling of guilt. Now, as I sucked a salty pinpoint of blood, I had a different feeling. I had paid for my lies, and I didn't have to think about them anymore. The relief was like that of the moment when pain stops, and I felt the full joy of it when Grandma's hand reached under the table to offer me a tiny ball of pie crust dough.

"Since we can't have cake, it will have to be pie," she said, and I watched the full bell of her gray plaid skirt swing energetically as she used the rolling pin on the table above me. The air was clear between us.

Grandma also came to us every Christmas and stayed for a week. One morning I woke early to dull, gray light and found myself in the unfamiliar softness of my parents' featherbed. While I was trying to understand why I was there, Grandma lifted her night-capped head from the other pillow.

"*Goddag, lille pige.*"

Sometimes she spoke to me in Danish, which I didn't understand, but I knew that this short greeting amounted to "Good morning, little girl." I asked where Mom and Daddy were and why we were in their bed.

"I came in to keep you from waking up alone, and then I decided we might as well keep each other warm."

"But where did they go?"

"To town. Jack Russell had an accident—the Studebaker skidded on the ice and hit another car."

"Did he get hurt?"

"Not much, but Vivian Corley was killed."

I pondered that information and felt a nasty thrill that I had no intention of sharing with Grandma. Jack Russell had brought Vivian Corley to see us once. Her dark brown hair was in finger waves, and she had a dent in her cheek when she smiled. When anyone talked to her, she answered without taking her eyes from Jack Russell's face. When I stepped between them to block her view, she leaned half off her chair to see around me.

"How do you like my girl?" Jack Russell asked me.

"*I'm* your girl," I said, and everyone laughed—even Vivian Corley. I glared at her, pretending my eyes were magnifying glasses to catch the sun and burn holes in her, rather than in paper. I concentrated on the burning so hard that I saw the pattern of the parlor wallpaper through a hole in her forehead just below the dip of a finger wave.

Our telephone ring, two longs and a short, shrilled and brought me back to the present. Grandma jumped out of bed to answer, leaving me alone and terrified. Vivian Corley seemed to walk toward me with a hole in her forehead. I moaned, diving under the covers, but new terrors

1 7

awaited me in the darkness there. The cracks in the earth, missing since my creek-bed adventure with Marianne, were back in full force.

When Grandma came back to bed, she misunderstood my suffering and tried to reassure me. "Don't cry, Margrethe." She said my name in the Danish way. "Jack Russell only broke his arm."

We went to town the day of the funeral, and I begged to see Vivian, but they wouldn't let me. I'd never know whether I'd really burned a hole in her forehead.

During the services I was to stay with Marianne at Aunt Kam's house, a rare privilege I couldn't appreciate under the circumstances. While everyone was getting organized to go, Jack Russell clung to the colonnade between the dining room and the parlor with his good arm. His broken arm looked like a big plaster chicken wing until Uncle Karl hid the sling under a shirt and the dark goods of Jack Russell's best suit.

Aunt Kam tied his necktie, saying, "I think it would be a kindness to the Corleys if you stayed home."

"I have to be with her as long as I can."

Aunt Kam sighed and helped him into his overcoat. Her eyes were the yellow-green of a dying plant, the color they took on when she was troubled. In happier times they were greener.

Jack Russell went down the walk like an old man, supported by Daddy and Uncle Karl. Mom and Aunt Kam followed, picking lint from each other's dark coats. They would stop for Grandma on the way to the funeral parlor. The worst thing, they said, was having to drive the fatal Studebaker.

When they were gone, Marianne went to the piano and played something loud. When she was tired of that, she talked, but *not to me*.

"Vivian wanted a navy blue dress the worst way, but her folks said young girls should wear color. Mrs. Schack from the funeral parlor went to Fern's Fashion and bought the dress Vivian wanted. It had a white lace collar, and I was crazy about it."

"Does she have that dress on now?"

Marianne glared at me. "Of course, you imbecile, that's why Mrs. Schack bought it."

"Did you see her?"

She whirled and grabbed my shoulders, sinking her nails. "You morbid, little monster! I don't even want to *think* about death. I only know about the dress because everybody at school was talking about it."

"I'm never going to get dead," I said, ducking out of her painful grasp.

"That's what *you* think! You'd better get out of my sight before I rub you out personally."

"What does that mean?"

She gave a snarling imitation of what she said was "George Raft and Edward G. Robinson mixed together." I didn't know who they were and didn't dare to ask.

Leaving Marianne in the parlor, I headed for the dining room to look for Punkin, Aunt Kam's sixteen-year-old tomcat. He was asleep in the window seat, and when I touched the furry frown between his ears, he stiffened and made a noise like a storm blowing up.

"Leave that cat alone!" Marianne yelled.

I would in a minute, I thought, but not until I pulled his tail to let him know what I thought of his attitude toward me. He yowled, raking my forearm. The dull, old claws made a triple trail of blood that called for further retaliation. I snatched up a doorstop shaped like a dog and brought it down on his paw. When he screeched and fled, leaving a snowfall of white and yellow hair in the block of sunlight he had vacated, Marianne snatched the doorstop from me and twisted my arm.

"What are you trying to do, kill him? Here Punkin, here kitty, where are you, angel boy?"

Punkin answered from the kitchen in his cracked, old voice, and she ran to him. I could hear her cooing and making kissing noises, and when she came back with the sagging, shedding cat in her arms, she said, "Aren't you ashamed to hurt this poor, old thing?"

"Yes, but he hurt me first." I showed her my arm. "Now we're even." If she had shown any interest at all, I could have explained that I dealt with a bump from a piece of furniture in the same way. I kicked it back, and that was that.

Aunt Kam kept a stack of *National Geographic*s on the bottom shelf of the library table, and I became so engrossed in pictures of the Sphinx and the Pyramids that I gave Marianne no more trouble.

When they came home from the funeral, Mom asked if I had been a good girl. Marianne rolled her eyes and went to her pink and green bedroom, shutting the door with a bang. I yearned to go into that room and look around, but I never dared.

I looked out the front window and asked, "Why is Jack Russell standing out on the porch?"

"He wants to be alone," Aunt Kam said.

Mom said, "Maybe you should have let him stay at the cemetery."

"What would people think? It's bad enough already—everyone poking each other and whispering—you'd think he was a murderer or something."

Uncle Karl sighed. "I guess that's what the Corleys *must* think. Maybe they have a right. Jack Russell drives like a lunatic. I only gave him the car keys because I remembered what it felt like to be too young and poor to own a team and buggy when I wanted to go courting."

"What's a murderer?" I asked.

"Shhh!" Mom said.

Daddy explained, as he always did. "A murderer is a person who kills another person."

"Oh," I said, "then Jack Russell isn't one."

"Out of the mouths of babes!" Aunt Kam said, and they all started to

1 9

talk about something else before I could finish what I was going to say. *I was the murderer. I was the one who burned a hole in Vivian's forehead shortly before she was dead.* I could see that they didn't want to hear about that, so I put on my coat, hat, and mittens and went out on the porch. Jack Russell was sitting on the rail, trying to strike a match with one hand. The hand shook.

"Hold the book for me while I strike it," he said.

I took off my mitten in the hope of touching him. Until the match flared, our flesh was joined, and his face came close to mine when he bowed to light his cigarette.

"You've still got me," I said.

Jack Russell choked, threw the cigarette into the snow, and put his hand over his face.

"Was her dress nice?"

He groaned, turning away from me, and I grabbed at the empty sleeve, trying to bring him back.

"Jack Russell, please tell me—was there a hole in her forehead?"

"Oh God!" he blurted, then leaned over the rail to throw up on the snow.

4

AS THE WINTER WORE ON, we settled into a lulling routine bounded by morning and evening chores. Daddy was in the house more, reading and writing figures in a book with lines. Sometimes he read to me, and I tried to match words I could hear with marks I could see.

I asked Mom to read "Goldilocks and the Three Bears" and "The Little Match Girl" until I memorized enough to believe that I was reading with her, but sooner or later, we got to the point where I had to drop out and listen.

When nobody had time to read with me, I made squiggly lines on paper, usually the back of a calendar month that had passed, and called it a story. When I could sneak Sofus into the house, I read my stories to him, but he was a farm dog, and Daddy thought it would ruin him if he spent time indoors.

The parlor and the upstairs rooms were shut in winter. We were together in a small space that had the closed-in smell of cobs for starting the kitchen stove, kerosene for the lamps, onions for the Danish meatballs called *frikadeller,* orange Lifebuoy, and manure on barnyard boots.

The downstairs bedroom was warmed by the dining room wood stove only at night. When Mom opened the door a few hours before bedtime, it had its own smell: feather pillows, a whisper of 4711 from Mom's hand-kerchief drawer, and a faint reminder of the white enamel chamber pot that spared us dark, cold trips in the night. Maxfield and Parrish couldn't smell anything. Their perfect noses remained unwrinkled behind the glass that locked them into their own world of bluest skies and palest stone.

A visit from the Watkins salesman was a big occasion for us. Mom said she couldn't afford to buy much, but she always tried to make some small selection from his case of bottles and boxes to insure a return visit. When the Watkins man hit the neighborhood, the word went out on the party line, and she checked her cupboards.

"Vanilla, maybe?"

"Petra, you have three bottles on the shelf," my dad pointed out.

"Well, I can always use vanilla."

The Watkins man must have had a name, but nobody ever used it. His black Ford was exactly like everyone else's, but it seemed to have a special shine when it came down the lane. The Watkins man climbed down, reached inside for his case, and took a quick look around to locate the dog before he walked to the welcome he was sure to get.

Mom let him show her everything before she said, "I guess I could use a bottle of vanilla."

"You must bake up a storm, Mrs. Langelund. I seem to remember selling you a bottle the last time I was here."

Mom turned pink and said nothing. We watched him rummage in the case for the vanilla, then hesitate and put his hand on something else.

"Tell you what I'm gonna do." He pointed at me. "This young lady here deserves the best, isn't that so?"

"That's so."

"Now, Mrs. Langelund, I know you're a good cook and a good mother, but scientific ree-search has figgered out that three squares a day might not be all we need to stay healthy. I realize that you know me as the Watkins man, but I have two or three items from other companies besides. You want this young lady to be as healthy as possible, don't you?"

"Of course I do."

"Then let me tell you about these capsules that spark the appetite, build up the blood, and keep that old body motor runnin' smooth."

The capsules were long and green—shiny in their gelatin casings— and Mom was afraid I couldn't get one down. She said they looked like horse pills.

The Watkins man laughed and said she was mighty sharp to say so because they contained a compound of pure alfalfa and a secret ingredient. He was willing to bet money I could swallow one, offering it to me in the palm of his hand. I got it down, and Mom bought a box.

A few days later, I took a handful of the pills outside, pulled the capsules apart, and poured the green powder down the tongue of my coaster wagon. It sure did smell like alfalfa.

Mom was on her way to the henhouse when she saw the pile of green powder on the ground. She let out a shriek. "Margaret, what have you done? Those pills cost a lot of money."

I explained. "The Watkins man said they would keep the motor running smooth."

"But your wagon doesn't *have* a motor."

"Neither do I," I said, mildly surprised that she had so much trouble understanding me.

"All that money down a wagon tongue," she said with a groan. "I should spank you."

From her tone I knew she wouldn't, but when she went to her hens, I sat in the wagon and wondered about the stuff called money. Once in a great while, someone gave me a penny. That was money, but I didn't get too excited about the brownish bits with faces on them. Pennies were no more interesting to me than the suckers with wooden handles the storekeeper gave me when we bought groceries in Fiscus. The suckers never tasted as good as they looked, so I left them in their cellophane, sticking them into a cup until I had a bouquet.

One of the high points of my week was the arrival of the *Des Moines Sunday Register*. It was rolled tight and banded with brown paper that had to be slit with a paring knife. The sharp smell of ink filled the kitchen as Mom pulled out the colored comics and gave them to me. When the rest of the paper had been read, Mom used it to start fires in the stoves, but she never touched a match to the comics. They were mine to be kept in a stack and enjoyed forever.

One April Friday I came upon a real treasure, an "Andy Gump" that had been used to line the silver drawer. It had been covered over with a drab black and white page that I tore when I was putting forks away. I eased it out carefully to keep Andy and his friends in one piece.

I found Mom dusting and pinching dead leaves from the potted fern. I didn't think that she'd stop and read to me, but when I asked, she shoved the dead leaves into her apron pocket and sat down.

"It's such a heavy day that I just can't make myself work."

I loved the clear, gray light with no shadows under a soft, pressing sky. Morning and afternoon were all the same, and change did not threaten. Andy Gump, whose mouth was down in his neck, and Min, whose nose looked marvelously pinchable, lived in a place where every day was exactly like this.

"Oh, Min!" Mom read to me. It didn't sound quite right. She tried again and did better. I never heard what came next, because a voice from outside was yelling Mom's name.

"That sounds like Cliff Potter," she said, dropping the funnies to go out and see what he wanted.

I stayed in the big chair, trying to puzzle out the words in the balloons above the heads of Andy and Min. Mom had turned on the radio when we sat.

It had warmed up enough to deliver a musical phrase that filled me with melancholy, some men singing, "driftin' along with the tumblin' tumbleweed." I wasn't allowed to touch the radio knobs. The only way to escape the song was to leave.

I grabbed a sweater and started outside, shoving one arm into a sleeve as the kitchen door banged behind me. The other sleeve dangled, forgotten, as I stopped and stared.

Mom seemed to be struggling with Cliff at the gate. She was crying. Then Anna, Cliff's wife, came running down the lane. That was something to see. She was a big, fat woman, and she was moving fast with her arms wide open. Just before Anna got to the gate, Mom broke away from Cliff and ran toward the windbreak.

"Mom," I yelled, "wait for me!"

She didn't seem to hear me, and when I tried to open the gate to follow her, Cliff yelled at me to get back. The yard was filling with cars screeching to stops. Men got out of them and ran to the field. I wanted Sofus, but he didn't come when I called. Nobody paid any attention to me. They were pointing at a thin finger of smoke rising from the creek where the bridge was. I couldn't see the bridge for all the men standing around, but when some of them clambered down the bank, I spotted Sofus's golden coat. He was lying there, looking down.

I finally got the gate open and started to run toward the creek, but the preacher caught me and carried me back to the house. I kicked and begged to be put down, but he paid no attention. He was making his Sunday sounds: "Oh Lord, show Thy mercy in this hour of grief." He put me over the top of the fence without bothering with the gate and went toward the trees where Mom was. Dr. Gus from town ran after him. Then Anna Potter took me inside and gave me a red sucker I didn't want. I was adding it to my bouquet when Dr. Gus and the preacher brought Mom into the house. She was quiet now and she didn't seem to hear anything. They put her to bed, but it wasn't night.

When Grandma came, all the strange people went away. She fixed me a bowl of bread and milk and told me to be quiet because Mom was sleeping.

"Will you finish reading 'Andy Gump' to me?"

She started, but then she said she didn't have the heart.

"Aren't you going to fix supper for Daddy?"

"No, Margaret. Your daddy doesn't need any supper here because God has taken him home. Get ready for bed, and I'll hear your prayers."

I started to protest, but thought better of it. I thought while I was putting on my pajamas, and when I knelt beside the bed in the upstairs room I would share with Grandma that night, I said, "God, send Daddy back!"

"You mustn't ask that."

"Why not? That's what I want, and He'd better do it, too."

Grandma sighed and told me that nobody bossed God around. She decided to come to bed, too, even if it was too early for big people to go to sleep. I escaped the terrors of the dark in her arms.

The next day Mom was up and walking around, but she didn't seem to be awake. Uncle Karl came to drive us to town, but I didn't want to go because I thought Daddy might come back while we were away. The green Studebaker Jack Russell had wrecked still moved, but it looked like a tin can stepped on by a horse. Uncle Karl made me get into it.

In town we stopped at a big house where the lights were held up by ladies that looked like Maxfield and Parrish. Even though the sun was shining, the lights were on under shades that gave the room a blue-green look. Flowers that looked as stiff as wheel spokes in their baskets were everywhere. They smelled cold.

A lady came to meet us and whispered to Mom. When she pointed to a long hall, Grandma took my hand and said, "I'll take her, Petra."

The hall seemed to go on forever. I asked, "Does God live here?"

"Yes and no. Come."

I certainly was surprised to see Daddy lying in a bed with a pink spread pulled to the middle button of his church suit. Obviously God hadn't understood me. I had told Him to bring Daddy back to the farm, but he'd made a mistake.

2 4

"Can I wake him up?"

"No, Margaret." Grandma closed her eyes for a minute and pinched her lips together hard.

Then we went back to Mom, and the whispering lady gave me a sucker—a green one. I thought about how I'd have to straighten this business out when I talked to God again at bedtime.

We had supper at Aunt Kamille's. Marianne invited me into her pink and green room for the first time ever and let me play with her jewelry while the women were doing the dishes. She even gave me a small compact filled with Lady Esther powder. The lady on the top of it wore a blue dress and had white curls piled high on her head.

"I'm sorry about your dad," Marianne said. "I always liked Uncle Lauritz."

"I'll get him back."

"What? What did you say?"

"I'll get him back. I asked God, and He sent him to the wrong place, but when I—"

"Margaret, hasn't anybody told you what this is all about? Your dad is dead—dead like Vivian Corley."

"No! I already saw him sleeping."

I threw the alluring compact on the bed, rejecting gift and giver, and it was a long time before I would believe that Marianne was right.

5

WHEN DADDY didn't come back to do his work, Mom put on overalls and went to the field. Somebody had to take care of me, so Grandma locked her blue house on Willow Street with a skeleton key and came to the farm to live with us.

Mom taught herself to drive the Ford. Starting it was easy. She turned the crank and jumped in to take the wheel, but when she had circled the barns and the corncrib until she was dizzy, she couldn't make it stop. She shut her eyes and ran the car into the haystack, where it chugged away until Cliff Potter could get there to turn it off. After that, she could drive. I wasn't thrilled with that development because I always got carsick after riding much more than a mile—more so when I smelled the gas she bought from the single pump owned by the Olsen Brothers Trucking Company in Fiscus. The top of the pump resembled a jar of orange pop. Each time I saw it, I marveled that it could look so good and smell so bad.

Daddy left before the corn was planted. Mom wasn't sure she could do that, so the hired men came, one after another. I was hoping for one as nice as Jess, but I always was disappointed. The first hired man was dark and hairy, somebody from far away. He grabbed Mom in the barn and tried to kiss her. I saw it from the hayloft, where I was playing with a new litter of kittens. Mom spat in the straw and scrubbed her mouth with the back of her hand. That surprised me, because when I tried to spit the way men did, she told me ladies didn't do that.

"Aw, c'mon, Miz Langelund, you're too much woman to go to waste."

"I had a man," she said, "and he was man enough to last me all my life. Put your things together and get off the place. I don't want to look at you again."

"Guess it's true what they say about Dane women—they'll freeze your balls off!"

Mom seized the pitchfork, and he backed toward the door.

"Now don't get excited, I'm goin'—I'm goin'."

Once outside he didn't move very fast. I watched him through a wide crack in the barn boards. When he got to the hog house, he turned around and touched two fingers to the bill of his greasy cap. Then he jabbed his middle finger at the sky and headed for the house. Below, Mom was leaning against a manger with her shoulders shaking. I heard her say, "Oh, Lauritz, I *do* need you."

Another of the hired men had a shiny, bald head that turned pink as a slice of ham when he was out in the sun. Mom finally gave him Daddy's old hat to wear. One hot July noon he was sleeping under the trees with his mouth open, crumbs from his dinner caught in the stubble of his beard. I couldn't resist tickling the washboard roof of his mouth with a foxtail weed. He woke with a roar, broke a switch from the spirea bush, and laid into me.

Mom saw the whole thing from the window and sent him away. I was glad to let her deal with him, because I no longer had confidence in my own magic—the small rituals I'd been trying since God disappointed me about bringing Daddy back. I'd done everything from touching fence pickets in a special order to burying and resurrecting box elder bugs, but nothing helped.

Daddy was under a mound of dirt in the Harlan cemetery next to Aunt Else and Uncle Soren. We went there to pull weeds and plant flowers on the graves. Daddy's was a brown hill, but the others were flat like gardens. Mom's daddy was buried under a big, old pine that he had planted himself when it was small enough for him to carry on his shoulder with its roots in a gunny sack.

"He's in that tree now," Grandma said, but I never could see him. When I backed away for a better view, Mom told me to watch out for the poison ivy that laced the hedge with glossy green.

After that long summer of many hired men, Mom walked me to the one-room school taught by Miss Eleanor Olsen. I carried a new metal lunchbox that made me proud.

"Take a good look around you so you'll remember the way," she said. "Tomorrow you'll go alone."

We passed the Potters' farm, and Anna waved from the window. At the Denkmans' corner we turned south. Clifford Denkman had helped Mom with the field work between hired men. I liked him and his jolly, messy wife, Ruby, but their son Virgil was, as Grandma put it, "another kettle of fish." As far as I knew, Virgil was incapable of speech. At church suppers he loaded his plate and took it to a corner, turning his back on everyone while he ate so fiercely that I was reminded of the Angus bull that tossed its head, pawed, and snorted when anyone approached its pen.

I was hoping that Virgil wouldn't be at my school, but Mom told me he would.

"This is his last year. Just keep out of his way."

Between the Denkmans' corner and the school was the Larson farm with an inviting lane that poured downward from the road to an arched gate laced with morning-glories of eye-stabbing blue. I could imagine Shirley Larson moving comfortably around the kitchen of that square, white house. She was one of my favorite church ladies; the Shirley who, with Goodness and Mercy, would follow me all the days of my life.

As we came to the schoolyard, my stomach tightened. I'd never seen so many kids running and yelling in one place. I knew some of them from

Sunday school, but we exchanged no sign on this new ground.

I also knew Eleanor the teacher, but Mom told me I'd have to call her Miss Olsen now. I wasn't sure I could remember that until I saw her come out of the school with a bell in her hand. Her hair was finger-waved, and her body looked like a vase in a dark plaid dress. She was no longer Eleanor, who wore overalls to help her trucker brothers load oats. This stranger was Miss Olsen the school teacher.

Mom disappeared without saying good-bye, and Miss Olsen said she'd show me my desk. I slid into the smooth, dipping seat and ran my fingers over the curly, iron grillwork at the sides. I couldn't read the words cut into the desk top and blackened with pencil lead, but I was confident that I would be able to read anything by the end of the day. That was what I had come to learn.

I was disappointed that I still couldn't read by the time Miss Olsen rang the hand bell and said, "Recess, people," but I wasn't surprised. She didn't stay with us long enough to show us how to do it. She wrote "A, B, C" on the blackboard, and told us to learn that much while she worked with the bigger kids. When I said, "A, B, C, D," she gave me a funny look and said I had to put up my hand when I wanted to talk.

I stood aside when everyone rushed to the door for recess, winding up last in line for the swings and teeter-totter. Next time I'd know better. While I waited for my turn, I watched Virgil Denkman climb the pole to the top of the swing frame and hold the chains, keeping the kids in the swings from pumping high.

"Virgil," Miss Olsen said, "get down from there this minute."

"You gonna' make me?"

I listened, amazed. It wasn't Virgil's surly defiance that struck me, it was his voice. He sounded like Daddy. I ran beneath the frame to hear him better, but Miss Olsen picked me up and put me to one side.

"Virgil," she said, "you know what happened when you were sassy to me last year. Do you want me to have another talk with your father?"

He shook his head like the Angus bull and slid down the pole, hulking off toward the trees near the boys' outhouse. I followed him.

"Virgil—"

"Get away from me, you little shit!"

Delighted with the vocal timbre I had missed with an almost physical pain, I didn't care what Virgil said as long as he went on talking. I'd never heard the word *shit* in my entire life and wasn't concerned with its meaning.

"Talk, Virgil."

"You shut up and leave me alone, or I'll take you in there and ram you down headfirst."

"I didn't know you *could* talk," I said, greedy for any sound he might make.

He wheeled with a roar and knocked me down, jarring me so hard that I saw colored spots before my eyes. I held my breath, fighting the fierce urge to hurt him back. Virgil was not a chair that bumped my shin or a cat that scratched my arm. Getting back at Virgil would start an unending cycle of pain. Besides, I didn't want to make him even madder. I needed to be near him to hear him speak.

For several days I dogged his steps, delighting in his spoken abuse, but the arm-twisting was too much. I made the mistake of telling Mom. When she came to school with me and sat there all day, Virgil left me alone and didn't say a word. It was terrible.

Even when I was on my own again, Virgil acted as if I weren't there—until I made it impossible for him to ignore me. I was scared to put dirt in his lunch bucket, but I did it, and I made sure that he saw me do it. Unfortunately his reaction was silent and physical. His big hands twisted the skin of my wrist until it burned like fire and nearly tore. Having pondered boundaries—where the thing that was "I" met the rest of creation—I knew that I must not let Virgil touch me again. It was too humiliating. However, I still meant to have what I needed from him—the sound of his voice.

On the way to school the next morning, I went down the Larsons' lane, ducked behind the blue blaze of morning-glories, and found a hiding place in the bushes. After what seemed like a long time, Virgil and two other boys came along. They were talking. I ignored the words and soaked up the sound of his voice, wanting it to go on forever, but it was fading with distance. How could I hang onto it?

"Virgil Denkman is a big dummy!" I yelled.

"Where are you, you little shithead?"

"Boy, is she ever stuck on you, Virg."

I couldn't see whether they were coming back, because I was down on my stomach to keep my light dress from showing through the bushes. I chewed my knuckles because my nails were too nasty to nibble. Mom had put saffron on my fingers to break me of nail-biting, and the awful taste simply wouldn't wash off.

"I'll catch her at recess and pound her," Virgil said. "Can't do it now 'cause there's Old Lady Olsen with her goldarned bell."

That meant I'd have to run into the open immediately or be late, and if Virgil saw me, he wouldn't wait until recess to pound me. I decided I'd rather be late. However, I had still another option. Why go to school at all? I could stay with Shirley Larson all day and yell at Virgil again when he went home.

Shirley was stirring something in a bowl when I peered through the screen door. When she felt my eyes on her, she looked up.

"Why, Margaret, you sure did give me a turn," she said. "I *thought* somebody was at the door, but I was looking too high. Isn't it time you were in school?"

"Miss Olsen sent me home." The lie came easily because that sort of thing did happen. Miss Olsen had sent Maxine Werley home because she wet her pants, but I certainly wasn't going to offer that reason. I added,

"She said I needed quiet." That was what Aunt Kam had to have when she choked.

Shirley motioned for me to come in. When I had shooed the flies and edged through the door, she felt my forehead with a hand warmed by wielding the big wooden spoon.

"You don't look sick to me, but if Miss Olsen wants you to go home, I guess I can run you over when Klaus gets back with the car."

"Oh, I can't go home. Mom's in the field and Grandma's sick."

"Mrs. Jorgen's sick? How come I didn't hear about it? I listened in on all the rings yesterday and today."

"Oh, we don't talk about it. It's just a thing she has."

"My, my. Well, in that case, I guess you'd better stay here and keep me company. When you have nothing but boys, you spend a lot of time alone in the kitchen. It's nice to have a little girl to talk to when you're baking."

It was a good morning. I scraped batter and frosting bowls, played the piano in the parlor, and picked some early asters. When Klaus came from the field for his noon meal, he asked what I was doing there, and Shirley repeated my invention.

"Hadn't you better call Petra?"

"Let her have some peace, poor woman. I'll talk to her when I take Margaret home."

It was good to sit at the table with Klaus, breathing in his mannish smell and watching his big hands cut and spear the food. I even liked the dirt-filled wrinkles that criss-crossed the back of his neck.

"How you gettin' along in school, Margaret?" he asked.

"Fair-to-middlin'," I said, aping Cliff Potter's tone when he didn't like something but didn't want to say so. "Can I go to the barn with you?"

"Nope, I've got no call to go to the barn until milking time, and you won't be here then."

"Klaus, it wouldn't kill you to show her around a little while your food is digesting."

"She's seen barns before, and there's nothing special about ours, but—if you say so. We'll go after I get the market report."

I told Klaus that he didn't have to take me. I'd changed my mind. If Shirley had to make him do it, we wouldn't have any fun. I'd already figured out that sometimes you lost when you won.

All afternoon I watched the angle of the sun carefully, trying to match the remembered slant of light at the hour when school was let out. I couldn't read clocks, and I didn't want to ask Shirley the time.

"You're antsy as a pup on hot tar," she said. "Want me to drive you home now?"

"Oh, no, pretty soon I'll start walking."

"But I was going to talk to your mother—"

"She's too busy to talk today."

When the light looked right, I said good-bye. Shirley watched from the door, forcing me to walk up the lane to the road. As soon as she turned away, I doubled back and hid in the bushes. The little kids came past, and after what seemed like hours, Virgil came. Alone and mute, he zig-zagged to kick clods on both sides of the road.

"Virgil!" I called in a high falsetto.

"Who's there?"

Afraid to speak because he was so close, I cackled like a hen.

"No goddam chicken can say my name," he muttered to himself, "and it ain't the Langelund kid because she's home sick." He shrugged and walked on.

When he was out of sight, I cut across the fields to go home. Keeping to the road past the Denkman farm was too dangerous. The short-cut also allowed me to dump the contents of my lunchbox in the backhouse, circle back to the lane, and make a normal entrance to greet my extremely healthy grandmother. I had told Shirley some of the truth, at least. Mom really was in the field.

The next morning I repeated the taunting of Virgil from behind the bushes and reappeared in the Larsons' kitchen. Shirley was testing the heat of a flatiron with a dampened finger. It hissed satisfactorily.

"What, again?"

"Miss Olsen talked to Mom. I'm supposed to ask if I can stay here to-day, too."

"Of course you can, but I can't imagine why Petra doesn't ring me up about it."

"The line's always busy."

"Well, I guess! Ruby Denkman has been talking to her cousin Emma since breakfast. She had the nerve to say, 'Isn't that right, Shirley?' I didn't say a word—just pressed the hook down real slow."

We had some nice times, Shirley and I, for almost two weeks. Then Miss Olsen's car turned down our lane, and it was all over. I wasn't spanked, but there are worse punishments. If I had gone to school instead of staying with Shirley all those days, maybe we would have stayed on the farm, and I could have been a 4-H girl. Mom got so upset about what I did that she got an auctioneer to sell all the animals—even Sofus—and the tractor and the manure spreader. We went to live in Grandma's dark blue house in Harlan without any animals, and I never heard Virgil say another word.

6

GRANDMA'S HOUSE once had been a pretty sky blue, they said. The whole outside was the color people put on porch ceilings to discourage bugs. Somehow they stopped believing that bugs didn't like sky blue, and she got the paint cheap. By the time we moved in, the shade had weathered and darkened. It was almost the color of a night sky. I liked it until I heard Mary Lois Engle tell somebody that I lived in a "dumb, black house."

If I had stayed in the first grade, where I was placed when I came to Laurel School from the country, the opinions of Mary Lois Engle would have meant nothing to me. However, the first grade teacher decided I was "not adjusting socially" and put me back in kindergarten, where Mary Lois held sway. Everyone said Mary Lois looked like Shirley Temple. She did have the sausage curls, but the Temple dimples appeared only when she poked her cheeks with her fingers.

Joining Mary Lois's fan club was my first herd experience. I loved it until the day when she took my hand with a great show of friendliness, turned up the palm, and shrieked, "Margaret has lines in her hand!" To point up my deformity she displayed her own butter-smooth palm. If she had approached me with indifference or even hostility, I could have borne it, but to find treachery in a soft hand clasp and a smile was more than I could stand. I snatched up a soft-lead pencil and defaced that perfect palm with a slashing stroke. Miss Sheriff deprived me of recess, thinking this was punishment.

Actually, it wasn't. I never knew what to do with myself on the big graveled playground. The older kids played crack-the-whip, hitting as many bystanders as possible with their chain of bodies. The younger ones jumped rope or played jacks. I simply backed into the high, wire-mesh fence and waited for the bell that started a frightening avalanche of yelling and shoving kids.

It was better inside. Miss Sheriff, suspecting that I'd had reasons for my treatment of Mary Lois, read me the story of the little engine that could and encouraged me to draw some pictures. I decided to do the windbreak on the farm. The brown crayon was missing from my box, so I used black. The bell rang and the kids came in, but I went on coloring.

Mary Lois leaned over my shoulder, breathing the tantalizing scent of jawbreakers from Mrs. Fenton's candy shop into my nostrils. "Tree trunks aren't black," she said.

"Mine are." I pressed the black crayon so hard that it broke.

"Sometimes they look black after a rain," Miss Sheriff said charitably.

Then it was time to rest on the little rag rugs we all had to buy and keep at school. Grandma wanted to send a hooked rug she had just finished, but I held out for a cheap, factory-woven rectangle like everyone else's. I lay on my side and picked at the red cleaning compound between the floorboards, reveling in the possession of a small island just like Mary Lois's. She slept on hers, but I thought on mine.

Living in town was strange. The nights never were black because of lights on high poles at every corner. Nobody brought a lunch bucket to school. Nobody listened to the market reports on the radio. Nothing (except the red cleaning compound) smelled like anything in particular. Mom seemed different in town too. Her skin, browned by working in the fields, had faded to the color of a piano's white keys. Her eyes looked as if she had rubbed beneath them with sooty fingers, and most of the time, they didn't really see me.

She had that faraway look when I came home from school and told her, "I have lines in my hands."

"What did you say, Margaret?"

Something was wrong with her ears, too. She never heard me the first time I said something. I repeated it.

She kissed both palms and said, "We all do."

"Mary Lois Engle doesn't."

"Then she must be terribly fat."

"No, she looks like Shirley Temple."

"You look like you, and that's better."

I wasn't too sure about that. The mirror above the kitchen washbasin reflected white-blonde hair, a tilted nose that I tried to straighten by holding the tip down, and eyes the color of a blue dish Grandma had brought from Denmark. I never could really catch myself in the mirror. My eyes were too busy to see the thing that lived behind them—whatever it was I saw in other people's eyes.

When Grandma came in with a dishpan full of grapes, I stopped trying to catch that elusive thing in the mirror, and helped her wash the clusters for use in making jelly. She was unchanging, and when I was with her, I had a sense of myself that was familiar and comfortable.

"Wipe your hands and have a cinnamon roll," she said.

I unwound the coil of springy, fresh-baked dough, and licked the sticky gouts of sugar, butter, and cinnamon from its length, particularly savoring the raisins.

Grandma laughed. "Land, I don't know why I bother to roll them up. Shall I make them in strips next time?"

I shook my head. Uncovering the hidden sweetness was the good part—that and the delicious risk of breaking the coil.

While the grapes simmered, their sweet, fruity fragrance filled the kitchen, and Grandma sat down with a book. The clock ticked tranquilly and the warm sun of late afternoon slanted through the south windows. In a house without men, there is no sense of hurrying. Watching someone read grieved me. Even the town school hadn't taught me to read yet.

"What does your book say, Grandma?"

"Happy families are all alike; each unhappy family is unhappy in its own way."

Mom turned from the window. She had been staring into the street, where nothing was happening, but that didn't seem to matter. "What in the world are you reading, Mama?"

"*Anna Karenina.* When we first came from the Old Country, I read parts of it in the Danish newspaper, but I came in at the middle. I always wondered what went before, and after all these years, I finally got it from the library to find out. This Anna in the book sailed out farther than she could row back. I know that, because I remember the ending."

"If I knew the ending, I don't think I'd go back to the beginning."

"We always know our ending," Grandma said. "It's like a little house you glimpse through the woods. You see the house, but the trees hide the path. Now I can go back and find Anna's path."

"What *was* this Anna's ending?"

"She threw herself in front of a train."

Mom made a sound like a whimper, pressing her knuckles to her teeth. "Even worse than Lauritz—and by choice?"

Grandma closed her book on a crocheted marker. "Petra, there's no use in my telling you not to think about his death. Go ahead and think about it as hard as you can until you're sick of bringing it to mind—then you'll turn to life again. This Anna in the book didn't look at death hard enough until it was too late."

Mom sat down at the table, covering her eyes with one hand. "Oh, Mama, I did think about death when I was little. I was so afraid that *you* would die that I tried to get mad at you and not need you, but I never thought about Lauritz dying. Now it seems that I'll be walking through a long, gray tunnel until I can be with him."

"I know, Petra, but it's children who bring us into the light. I remember hearing Mme. Schumann-Heink sing at Chautauqua. Her voice was so deep and beautiful that I can't find words to tell you about it. God gave that voice to only one woman in all the world, in all time, and it was almost lost in one minute—but her children saved it. Ernestine Schumann-Heink rowed back because of them. She meant to do the same thing as Anna, taking the children with her, but when she saw them holding hands—ready to jump with her—she couldn't bear it."

"I could never *think* of such a thing," Mom said, pulling me onto her lap. I hated to be held, but I decided that this was no time to show it. Her arms tightened around me, the clock ticked steadily, and Grandma stirred the grapes with a big wooden spoon.

"Do you think it's true, Mama?" Mom said. "That each unhappy family is unhappy in its own way?"

Grandma gave a little snort and said, "Not each. Even the devil can't manage *that* much variety."

"Are *we* unhappy?" I asked.

They both looked at me with the crooked smiles that stay in the mouth and never get as far as the eyes. I knew they weren't going to answer.

Were happy families all alike? We weren't like anybody else. Grandma put a card in the window for the iceman and lit lamps that had pleated, silver reflectors at dusk, but other houses had white boxes that made ice and electric lights. They also had barrelchairs covered with prickly plush and big radios with church windows of cloth where the sound came out.

At Christmas our tree was lit with candles placed in metal holders that were shaped like fish. Grandma thought it was wrong to put up the tree before Christmas Eve, but Mom persuaded her to do it earlier. For a few minutes each evening the week before Christmas, the tiny tongues of flame blazed. A bucket of water stood nearby—just in case.

By this time, I had made a special friend, Lotus Hess, who lived west of us on Willow Street. Her father was dead, too, but she had grown-up brothers and sisters, and she was the aunt of a kid almost as old as we were. Lotus didn't mind the lines in my hands, and she loved our tree with candles. We were blowing at the flames just a tiny bit to make them bend when Mom said something that made me prick up my ears.

"I've bought a house."

"I wondered how long it would take," Grandma said.

"You're not mad, are you? I mean, I guess I might have talked it over with you—"

"Why should I be mad? I'll miss you, but I'm glad that you're ready to live again. Two grown women don't fit under the same roof no matter who they are or how much they love each other. Where is the house?"

"Just south of Willow on Tenth Street—across the street from Kamille."

Lotus whispered, "That's just around the corner from us."

Mom said we had to blow out the candles because we were going to take a walk. She wanted to show me something. We walked Lotus home and went on, looking at the colored lights in all the windows until we came to a dark house. It was white, and the placement of the front door and two upstairs windows gave it a look of surprise.

"This is our new house, Margaret."

"Does it have electric lights?"

"Yes, and you'll have a room of your own."

Thinking that now we'd be one of those happy families that are all alike, I let Mom take my hand. Usually I pulled away, but I was feeling oddly dizzy, as if I had blown too hard on the tree candles. It began to snow.

By morning, I was convinced that every snowflake that fell on my face had left an itchy blister. It was chicken pox. How could you get such a thing in town where there weren't any chickens? It was December 24, the day the Danes call "Little Christmas," and I felt too sick to set a dish of porridge on the window sill for the Christmas elf. Grandma hid a lucky almond in the pudding we had for supper, but none of us found it in our dish that Christmas Eve.

In Denmark most of the celebrating was done the night before Christmas, Grandma said, but after the family came to America, the gift opening was postponed until Christmas Day. Grandpa thought the delay would build character, and Grandma believed that anticipation is greater than realization.

We had our realization in Grandma's back bedroom. Mom was so worried about me getting a chill that she made me stay under the covers while she opened my presents for me. Grandma had knitted me some red mittens in her tight, even stitches. Mom's present was a doll with painted arms, legs, and head attached to a soft cloth body. I named her Shirley, after my favorite farm lady, and kissed her cold, brown-painted hair. She smelled like a drugstore. Then Mom brought my stocking, which Santa had filled with a bag of peanuts in the shell and an orange.

Lotus had had chicken pox, so she was allowed to visit me later in the day. She asked what Santa Claus had brought me, and when I told her, she gave me a funny look. "Gol," she said, "you really must have been bad."

"I was not."

"Well, he sure didn't bring you much. Did you write to him?"

I nodded, thinking of the squiggly lines I'd put in my stocking. I had more to say than I could express in the few words I was able to print, and I was sure that Santa would be able to read the kind of writing I'd been practicing for as long as I could hold a pencil. Realizing that he couldn't upset me so greatly that I scratched my pox. Mom was two rooms away, but she seemed to know, and she yelled at me to stop it or I'd have scars.

"What did you ask him for?" Lotus said.

"A doll, but he knew Mom was getting me one." That was it. If Mom and Santa were in cahoots, maybe my writing was O.K. after all. Even so, the seed of doubt had been planted.

Out of some kind of delicacy, Lotus had left her Christmas doll in the other room with her coat—or so I thought until she returned with a big Shirley Temple doll with real hair and held it out of my reach, saying, "I didn't want her to get the chicken pox, but I guess she won't."

Covetousness swamped my soul until the presence of my own Shirley reminded me of something Mom had said, "You look like you, and that's better."

After Lotus was gone, I gave a lot of thought to the subject of writing. Jess never answered me from that place in Clarinda. If neither he nor Santa Claus could read my messages, I'd have to learn to write the way Miss Sheriff did on the blackboard.

7

W H E N   W E   M O V E D into the house on Tenth Street, I was surprised and happy to see some of the furniture from the farm again. I thought all of it had been carried off to the sound of the auctioneer's strange chant, but Mom said friends and neighbors had been storing it until we needed it again.

My new room had sloping walls that joined above my bed like steepled hands. Its windows, like all the others in the house, were covered with Bon Ami to preserve our privacy until Mom could do something about curtains.

When nobody was around, I snapped the light switches on and off, staring at the miracle of immediate illumination and enjoying the exploding afterimages. I wanted to tell somebody about the wonder of it all, but I knew the other kids would laugh at me. They took electric lights for granted. Aunt Kam listened, though. She even played a game with me. I'd signal by flipping the light switch, and she'd answer from across the street. Marianne thought that was dumb, and she said it was bad enough when we lived at Grandma's house, but to have us this much closer was impossible.

I still could walk to school in no time at all, and one noon on my way home to lunch I went out of my way to stop at Grandma's house. From the way the rooms felt the minute I walked in, I knew she wasn't there. Some force that beamed from her was missing. I found her in the back yard lying beside the rain barrel. Her eyes were open, but she didn't look at me, and she wouldn't or couldn't get up. I ran to the neighbors for help.

Grandma had had a stroke, and she seemed to come out of it completely, but Mom and Aunt Kamille went on fussing about it. After dinner one Sunday, the grownups pushed the dirty plates to the center of the table, put their elbows on the cloth, and decided that Grandma would come to live with Mom and me. Uncle Karl and Aunt Kamille would fix up her house and move into it because they didn't need as much room now that Jack Russell was married and gone.

I hadn't thought about Jack Russell for a long time. He had a wife named Velie and a little baby they called "the man-child." Nobody talked about him much, but when they did, they sighed a lot. I thought Velie was fat and not a bit pretty and that it was dumb of Jack Russell to go off with her when I would have loved him forever. Furthermore, the man-child had eyes like Barney Google's.

3 7

Grandma didn't want to leave her house, but they all talked at once until she threw up her hands and said she'd do it just to get some peace.

Two clerks from Uncle Karl's hardware store helped her move, and then workmen came to tear her house apart and put it back together again. Aunt Kam was down there every day telling them what to do, but Grandma refused to look. She didn't want to hear about it either, but we got a full report every Sunday afternoon when Uncle Karl took us for a drive in the country.

"The kitchen is half the size it was, Mama," Aunt Kam said. "I'm using the front part for a living room."

"Where's the dining room?" Grandma asked.

"People don't have them now."

"How can a Dane live without a dining room?"

"Will you close your window, Karl?" Mom said. "I feel a draft on my neck."

With all the windows closed, the inside of the car was blue-gray with cigarette smoke. Uncle Karl lit one after another as he listened to the baseball game on the radio.

"The Norgaard place sure looks run-down," Aunt Kam shouted above the noise of the radio. "Wasn't she one of the Rasmussen girls?"

"No," Mom said, "she was a Matthiesen from Cuppy's Grove."

"You're both wrong," Grandma said. "She was a Jensen, a cousin of Torvald Jensen out in Jacksonville."

Uncle Karl drove fast, wanting to get the ride over in a hurry, but even if he was out of cigarettes, Aunt Kam ran him all over Shelby County before she'd let him take us home. I was carsick in the back seat, trying to sneak the window open just a crack for some air, but Mom always felt the draft and made me shut it.

The radio blared: "Did you hear that swat, folks? Must have split the hide right off the ball! Corsiglia slides—he's home!"

"Wish *I* was," I whispered.

Then the news came on—something about Highly Molasses and Italian soldiers.

"Such a brave, little man," Aunt Kam said.

"The Lion of Judah," said Grandma.

I thought of lions wallowing in molasses and felt sicker than ever. When we got home, I was barely able to manage the obligatory "thanks for the nice ride." I had to lie down for half an hour before the white line around my mouth disappeared.

Aunt Kam was really proud of the changes she had made in Grandma's house. Cream-colored paint covered the old dark blue exterior. The long porch and the back-yard pump were gone forever, and, of course, there were faucets and electric lights. Grandma was in no hurry to behold these wonders.

"You'll have to see it *sometime,* Mama," Aunt Kam said.

Grandma sighed. "Not until you're living in it. When that happens, my memories will move out, and I'll have a different feeling about it."

"Oh, Mama, you know it's for the best, and it's not like having strangers there. We're family. Why do you keep on fussing about it?"

"Peter was there with me."

"He hasn't been since 1893."

"Oh, yes, he has, and that's where he is now—wondering where I've gone."

"You can't hang onto the dead, Mama."

Mom put her arm around Grandma's shoulders. "What do you know about it, Kam? I understand what she's saying."

"Well," said Aunt Kam, "we're moving in next week, and that will be that."

They did, and as soon as they were settled, Grandma went there for supper. She walked back to our house before it was dark, and all she had to say was, "Kamille has things nice."

The new people who moved into Aunt Kam's old house on Tenth Street were the Shenks. They had a girl my age named Wyonne and an older boy whose name was Max. Wyonne quickly became Mary Lois Engle's best friend, which killed any chance of a true bond between us, but I was willing to pretend because of Max. I hadn't been so smitten by anyone since my preschool obsession with Jack Russell.

The Shenks made Max practice the violin half an hour a day. He put in part of that time on the sidewalk in front of their house, dancing up and down to the terrible cat-yowls that were supposed to be music. I sat on our front steps across the street and admired him.

One day I saw him on his steps ringed by a mysterious assortment of small boxes. I approached, madly curious, and he knew I was coming, but pretended not to notice. His fingers moved busily in the boxes. When I was close enough to see what he was doing, I gasped and kicked the boxes out of his reach. Some of the box elder bugs got away, but the ones he had maimed spun and struggled in agony. I expected him to hit me for kicking the boxes, but Max ignored me, bent on capturing the escaping bugs.

"That's mean!"

"No, it isn't. I'm going to be a doctor, and I have to see how much these insects can get along without." He picked up a bug and removed one of its wings.

"Don't!" I screamed. "Doctors are supposed to make people well, but you like hurting things."

"Do I?" His eyes glittered as he flicked the red-edged wing at me.

Wyonne yelled from an upstairs window for me to come in, but I couldn't just yet. Max was reaching for a box elder bug that almost had made it to the safety of the grass. I kicked his hand. This time, my expectations were met. Max twisted my arm behind my back until the fingers were above my shoulder. I screamed, Max fled, and Mrs. Shenk ran onto the front porch, saying, "What on earth is going on?"

3 9

My original feeling for Max overwhelmed the revelation of his cruelty. I wouldn't tell on him. I didn't even rub my wrenched shoulder as I told her I'd come to play with Wyonne.

"Well, that's a funny way to announce it."

My arm and shoulder hurt all the time we were making dolls with hollyhocks and toothpicks, but I cherished the pain because Max had caused it. When we went upstairs to Wyonne's room to play with the Jane Arden paper dolls she'd cut from a whole year of funny papers, I peeked into Max's room as if it were a shrine. The fact that it once had been Jack Russell's room strengthened the illusion. I seized the opportunity to snatch a relic—a balled-up sock just inside the door. The elastic waistband of my underpants would secure it out of sight, and I'd have a way of touching Max by proxy whenever I wished. I even persuaded myself that the sock didn't smell bad because washing it would ruin everything.

Wyonne pushed past me to bulge Max's window screen with her forehead. "Look, the iceman's at the Kepharts'."

"You go first," I said, hoping to smooth the bulge at my waist when her back was turned. The door slammed behind us as we ran to the Kepharts' driveway to claim the dirty bits of ice that fell to the tarpaulin when the tongs chewed into the block. They tasted like dead leaves. The iceman chipped some bigger pieces for us and told us to get back or he'd drop the block on our bare feet.

Going barefoot in the morning was one thing, but toward noon the hot sidewalks and the bubbles of tar in the streets could inflict real pain. All over the neighborhood window shades were being pulled to keep the heat out. When Wyonne's mother called her for lunch, I went home to dream of Max. Reaching for the precious green and orange striped sock, I felt a terrible sense of loss. I braved the hot cement to look for it at the Kepharts', but it wasn't there. I could hear what was going on next door, however. Mrs. Shenk was scolding Max.

"When will you ever learn to pick up after yourself? I found your sock in the front hall."

"Well, *I* didn't—"

"No excuses, just put it in the hamper."

The first time doctors hurt me, I remembered Max and the box elder bugs. It happened in the winter of the maroon snowsuit, and ever after that color reminded me of pain. At first it was a small earache—sharp, little stabs that came and went—but then it was demons pounding inside my head; a terrible pressure that made me scream, "I want to die!"

Mom and Grandma talked about how awful it was that Dr. Gus had stopped practicing. He would know what to do. They weren't so sure about Dr. Petersen, whose fingers were all red and scaly from getting in the way when he gave radium treatments. Besides, they hated to call him in the middle of the night.

The next thing I knew, Uncle Karl was there with his new Chevy. I was in my pink flannel pajamas, but Mom didn't make me dress or even put on a coat. She just wrapped a blanket around me, and Uncle Karl carried me to the car. Mom held me while he drove "like sixty," and she didn't say a word about how fast he was going, because I was screaming with pain all the way to Council Bluffs.

At Jennie Edmundson Hospital, they put me on a cart for another fast ride down a long, green hall. Mom was running beside the doctor, both of them talking, and I didn't know or care what they were saying.

The real horror began when they clamped a cone over my nose and I had to breathe something worse than gasoline. I struggled like a snake under a hoe, fighting annihilation.

"Count to five, and you'll be gone," somebody said. I counted to ninety-two.

Gone? Not quite. The high bed was surrounded by white curtains. Everything was white: the dress and cap of the woman beside me; the bedspread and the stiff nightgown that had replaced my pink pajamas. The woman held a mirror, and I saw that my head was turbaned with white gauze. Everything looked fuzzy to me, but the pain was gone. The woman said she was surprised I was awake—she'd just told Mom to get some air, but she'd find her.

Mom came with her coat on, bringing the winter with her, and when she touched me, we both got a shock. She kissed me at the edge of the bandage and said, "Thank God!" She sat beside me until she thought I was asleep, but I was just drifting. I knew that Uncle Karl came in and understood that he had watched my operation. After all, he was the family's only man.

"I thought I'd pass out when they drilled into the bone," he said, "and the smell of it!" When Mom gave a little moan, he said, "Sorry, Petra, I shouldn't have said that to you."

"That's all right, Karl, I appreciate what you did. She had one chance in a thousand the doctor said, and we still have her because you got us here in time."

Uncle Karl made a noise as if something were stuck in his throat, and I wondered hazily if he'd caught the choking fits from Aunt Kam. "This is the first time a Jorgen woman has had a good word to say about my driving."

I heard music from far away, someone singing, "The music goes round and round, whoa-o-o-o-o, and it comes out here." Then everything went round and round and all was quiet.

Though I wasn't recovering as I should, I took an interest in what was going on in the ward. Other kids walked in the hall in striped bathrobes. Nurses came on duty with wet hair after a swim in an indoor pool, something I could scarcely imagine. A doctor and a nurse kissed, thinking they were hidden behind my bed screen, but light from the window gave them a distinct silhouette.

Aunt Kam sent me a book about the Dionne quintuplets with lots of pictures, and Mom brought me a new doll with painted blonde curls, but what I really wanted was a Pekinese. I'd seen a picture of one in the *Omaha World Herald,* and that was what I wanted as a reward for staying alive—for beating the ether.

And then the cone descended once more. This time I counted to ninety-seven. Uncle Karl watched my operation again, but he didn't talk about it. All I heard was that I'd had six blood transfusions from a Holy Roller with the same kind of blood as mine. The man came to visit me, and I was desperately disappointed that he didn't roll—not even once. He didn't seem very holy, either. In a way, I didn't mind, because I had mixed feelings about the possible effect of Holy Roller blood flowing through my veins. When I left the hospital in the wan and tentative sunlight of early spring, I was happy enough to roll from the front door to Uncle Karl's Chevy.

8

I T ' S S T R A N G E that you can't remember the exact day when you know you can read. You ease into it, and suddenly you're getting pictures in your head from letters on a page. What you do remember is the teacher who seemed to make it happen.

Miss Clark was a little person who could sit on classroom chairs without hanging over the edges the way most grownups did. She was a brunette in a population of light-haired Danes and Germans, set apart so vividly that I believed dark hair to be a special gift of God.

Soon after I came home from the hospital, Miss Clark came to our house to talk about helping me catch up in my schoolwork. She and Mom liked each other so well that she came back many times to sit at our kitchen table, talking and drinking coffee. Grandma said that was good, because Mom didn't have many friends.

"Doesn't anybody like her?" I said.

"They would if she'd let them. When you lose somebody, you tell yourself you're never going to let anyone come close again. What you don't have can't be taken away. Say, weren't you going to the library?"

I certainly was. My books were due, and I'd rather die than pay a fine.

Grandma ran her finger along the spines of the skinny books with lots of pictures. "Don't you ever read anything but fairy tales?" When I shook my head, she said, "Well, I guess that's natural for a Dane."

"Do you read fairy tales, Grandma?"

"Not anymore, but I've told a few in my time. You'd better get going, or you'll be late for supper."

I saw that she was putting barley into the soup and wished she wouldn't. Those little gray rounds with dark dividing lines felt slimy between my teeth, but she always said that soup without barley just wasn't soup.

As I passed Fentons' candy store, Lotus Hess was coming out, setting the bell ajangle. She carried a bag of what I knew to be her favorite red and black jawbreakers. Just as she offered me one and I was debating the merits of the two colors, Grant Stoll jumped out of the bushes and ran away with the whole sack. Grant was the meanest kid in our class, so it was good-bye, jawbreakers. Lotus took it better than I would have because she got an allowance and could buy more.

"We ought to think of something awful to do to him," I said.

"He'd just pay us back with something worse. Hey, I'll go to the library with you if you'll go to the drugstore after. I have to get some pills for Mom."

I agreed, but I soon knew it was a mistake. It was best to come to the library alone, walk up the stone steps, then take the creaky wooden steps inside, and open the glass doors at the top to stand a minute breathing in the smell of books. After that I'd stand on tiptoe to be sure the returned books were firmly placed on the high desk before rushing to the fairy tale shelves in the children's section. I'd choose a big armload and carry them to the long table that reflected my face in a finish that looked like hardened honey. I always took out as many as I could carry, including a few that were too hard for me. Sometimes Miss Winnie Craig the librarian raised an eyebrow and paused with her rubber stamp in mid-air, but she always brought it down on the card with a sound like a hard kiss.

Lotus behaved differently in the library. She ran straight to the fountain to get a drink of water and didn't even look at the books. She talked to me out loud until Miss Craig said, "Shhhh!" While I was looking through the shelves trying to find something I hadn't read, Lotus kept saying, "Hurry up, will you?" Then she fogged the shine of the tabletop with her breath and wrote her name on it with her forefinger. I was so embarrassed that I grabbed three books just to get her out of there, and I'd read two of them before.

We crossed the street to Norgaard's drugstore, where Lotus ordered two fountain Cokes and told the man in the white coat that she had come for her mother's medicine. He said it would be a few minutes, and it still wasn't ready when we finished our Cokes, so we looked at the Evening in Paris display. The perfume in deep blue bottles conjured up more glamor than we could handle.

"Wonder what it smells like?" Lotus said.

"I don't know. I don't think anybody ever opens one."

The clerk, who was one of the Rasmussen girls, heard us and picked up the blue bottle with a squeeze bulb to give each of us an icy squirt on the wrist. We sniffed ourselves dizzy breathing it in.

"Well?" she said.

"Nice," we said in polite chorus, but as soon as we got out of the store, Lotus started to giggle. "Nice? Better than a hog house, I guess."

I said, "I liked it better before I knew."

That was the way it went with books, too. I'd bring one home with high hopes, expecting it to be the best I'd ever read, but it never was. Someday I'd make my own story just the way I wanted it, but not for a long time. I supposed that the people who made books—whose names were written on them in gold or whatever—were dead, and that was something I didn't want to be for as long as I could hold out against it.

I stopped at Lotus's house for a minute, but when her mother gave her Hail Columbia for taking so long with the medicine, I left in a hurry. Remembering that I should have stopped at Aunt Kam's for the newspaper, I doubled back to get it. We couldn't afford to take the *Omaha*

World Herald, so Aunt Kam saved hers for us. We got the news a day late, and I was the last to know what happened in "Terry and the Pirates."

While I waited for Aunt Kam to find the paper, I stood at the piano and picked out the notes of a song Miss Clark had taught us that day. Aunt Kam started to walk into the room and stopped, fixing me with the look she gave Grandma's house before she started moving the walls around.

"I think I'd better go home," I said uneasily.

"Just a minute, Margaret, I have an idea. How would you like to take piano lessons?" She gave me no time to answer. "Agnes Dever would take you, I'm sure, and you could come here to practice."

A shriek of protest came from Marianne's room. I was amazed at how well Marianne could hear everything that was said in the living room—even with her door shut. My own hearing hadn't been too good since the operations, and Aunt Kam repeated her suggestion.

My first impulse was to say "No, thank you" and run, but then I remembered that Mary Lois Engle played the piano with her unlined, padded hands. What a satisfaction it would be to out-play her.

"O.K., if Mom will let me."

"I'll handle that," Aunt Kam promised, and somehow she did.

Agnes Dever was an old maid who lived in north Harlan, the part of town that some people looked down upon. Since Grandma and Grandpa had come to town when there was scarcely any town at all, it was lucky that they had landed in the better half. It could be poor as dirt, but a south Harlan address was more prized than a mansion in north Harlan. The difference was there the minute you crossed the crucial dividing street, mysterious but unmistakable. Not that the houses were much different—each section had its mixture of small wooden bungalows, white with green trim; big two- and three-story houses with long porches and peaked roofs; enlarged doll houses of dark red brick; tarpaper shacks and railroad cars with curtained windows. It wasn't a matter of being on the wrong side of the tracks, because the railroad ran along the east and south edges of town with farm fields on one side.

The grade schools did look different. My own Laurel School was a block of dark brick with pale stone trim, but Park School in north Harlan was an ogre's castle with turrets and peaks. Its bricks were a raw orange that left fine dust on your fingers when you touched the wall. A big round tube came down from the third floor, and if I hadn't been scared of the north Harlan kids, I would have tried to work my way up the inside and slide down. Jimmy Meakin said he did it, but he slid right into a gang that beat him up because they "didn't want no kid from Laurel hanging around." They were always on the playground—even on Saturdays—and I had to pass them on the way to my piano lesson. My heart thumped against my beginner's book until I was certain that they were ignoring me.

Agnes Dever's house was tan with brown shingles halfway down.

Surrounded by old elms, it was further shaded by a swaybacked porch roof, and Miss Dever must have had a terrible electric bill from all those rose-shaded lamps that burned all day. Her doorbell sounded a melancholy triad. When I heard her coming, I took one last, deep breath of fresh air, knowing the house would smell of mothballs, cats, and bad breath.

Everybody's house smelled different, it seemed. Wash day and baking day offered variations, but the deep, underlying, identifying smell was a constant. Our house smelled like sheets brought in from the line and the *frikadeller* we ate so often. Aunt Kam's house smelled like Lady Esther powder and Lucky Strike cigarettes. The Shenks' house smelled like the dried rose petals from the farm that Mom kept in a china jar, and the Hesses lived in an atmosphere of chocolate and hot radio tubes. If I spent as much time in Miss Dever's house as I did in the others, I supposed I would get used to the smell of it, but once a week was not enough.

Miss Dever wore a high ruffled collar that completely covered her throat. He dark, gray-streaked hair was combed high with curly wisps escaping from the hairpins that fell out on the keyboard when she sat at the piano. She would brush them off to the flowered carpet, saying she would get them later. I doubt that she ever did, because the floor beneath the bench was a mass of shifting metal.

"Andante, Margaret, andante," she said.

With no notion of what was meant, I tried again. The keys were damp, and I mentioned it, hoping I'd found a possible excuse for my lack of andante.

"Oh, dear, yes. Billy Gruber. I can't imagine why his mother sent him when he was that ill. Let's take it again—slowly and with feeling."

I tried very hard because I knew Aunt Kam would be upset if I didn't get a gold star on the lesson. Having taken it upon herself to make a musician of me, she sat beside me for half an hour every day, taking up three-fourths of the piano bench and counting monotonously. How could music be made with somebody droning, "One-and-two-and–"? At least Aunt Kam smelled better than Miss Dever.

Aunt Kam was a lady, she was quick to tell anyone, and yet on a summer day she'd pick up her skirt and fan her thighs with it, saying, "Whooo, but it's hot!" It surprised Grandma the first time she did it, and Aunt Kam explained she had been reading a book about "unhealthy inhibitions." I couldn't imagine Miss Dever whooshing up *her* skirt, because she looked as if she had stepped out of one of the brownish pictures in oval frames on her own wall.

I played my scales doggedly until Miss Dever said, "That's fine, dear, you're coming along very well." She searched through the jumble on top of the Gulbrandson for a gold star, touched it to her tongue, and pounded it to my lesson page. I untied two quarters from the corner of my handkerchief and traded them for the lesson and a treat—a Nabisco cooky that had been around long enough to smell like mothballs.

The bright sunshine made me blink like a mole as I walked along holding my book open to dry the spit on the star. I was of two minds about the cooky. It was store bought and therefore a novelty, but it was almost too petrified to chew. The solution was to offer it to a friendly dog that sniffed and declined it, so I forced myself to eat it. Waste not, want not.

Aunt Kam was delighted with my star. She said she had known Miss Dever for a long, long time. "Agnes was an absolutely beautiful girl—a real artist, too. She could have gone anywhere—risen to any heights."

"Why didn't she?"

"When Carlyle Fraser gave her the mitten, it just took the heart out of her."

I'd heard that expression before, but it was unclear to me. Always sensitive to puzzlement, Aunt Kam explained that Carlyle Fraser had forsaken Agnes Dever for someone else.

"Was the new one prettier?"

"Heavens, no! I told you that Agnes was a beauty, but that wasn't enough. Carlyle just couldn't bring himself to marry a girl from north Harlan. The other one lived south of the Square."

"Miss Dever should have put her house on a whole bunch of roller skates and pushed it south."

"Poor Agnes—climbing on the bus three days a week to give lessons in all those one-horse towns—she ought to have had a man to take care of her. I feel sorry for women who have to work because they don't have husbands."

"*We* don't have a man, and Mom doesn't have to work."

"The day might come when she does, Margaret, but we won't worry about that now. Let's get to work and earn another star."

I worried. I couldn't imagine my mother being anywhere but home. Would she have to go off on the bus like Miss Dever? Aunt Kam cleared her throat meaningfully, and I applied myself to the keyboard.

"Must you?" Marianne called from her pink and green bedroom. "How can I study with that kid torturing the piano?"

"Now, Marianne," Aunt Kam said, "we won't be at it for very long. Surely you wouldn't want to discourage a future concert artist."

"Ha!" said Marianne, "That's the laugh of the century!"

9

I W A S A M A Z E D to learn that health was not free. My long hospital stay, the medicines, the ether, and the doctors had been so expensive that Mom decided she'd have to look for a job. She had been a teacher and a secretary, but she said that was a long time ago and things were done differently now. Besides, nobody in our town needed a teacher or a secretary. They had plenty of both.

The boxy black Ford had been sold, so she walked uptown to look for work. After a long time, she came home and sat down very slowly. Grandma didn't say anything. She poured two cups of coffee and sat down on the other side of the kitchen table.

Mom spread her fingers wide and pushed them through her hair, a thing she did when she was at the end of her rope. "Well, Mama, the only thing I could get was candling eggs at the produce."

"It's honest work."

"I know, but it's not quite like getting dressed up every day to type letters and briefs—or even starting the wood stove in a country school. It's a comedown, and Kamille will die of shame."

"She shouldn't. I ironed other people's clothes to feed my children, and she was one of them. Petra, I grew up in a home where I lacked nothing, and my husband was a good provider, but when things changed, I did what I had to."

"I know, Mama, and nobody ever thought less of you for it. I'll be all right when I get used to the idea."

Mom started her job the very next morning, leaving for the produce before I went to school. I was shocked to see her dressed in Daddy's pants and shirt. A few women in town were wearing slacks, wide-legged navy blue things, but Daddy's Sunday pants didn't look like that on Mom. Her hips strained the seams, but the waist puckered like the neck of a drawstring bag when she belted it tight. The thought of her walking all the way from Tenth Street to a block north of the Square made me cringe. She couldn't help but run into somebody we knew, and what Mary Lois Engle would have to say about her appearance was too awful to contemplate. She put her coat on, and that helped a little but not enough. I was too mortified to kiss her good-bye.

As soon as we were alone, Grandma spoke to me fiercely. "Margaret, your mother is my baby, and when you hurt her feelings, it makes me mad. Why are you being so pesky?"

I left for school immediately, cutting across lawns all the way. I was early. Miss Clark, who was now last year's teacher but still Mom's friend, told me I couldn't come inside yet and asked me to tell Mom she planned to come to our house after school. I told her Mom wouldn't be there because she had to work.

"Oh? Doing what?"

"I don't know," I said sullenly.

For three days Mom put on Daddy's clothes and walked to the produce. When she came home, she undressed on the back porch and hung the clothes outside in case any chicken mites were hiding in them.

"I suppose the neighbors will think we have a man over here," she said.

That's when I told her how I felt about her walking around in those clothes.

"Oh, Margaret, I'm so sorry! I hadn't even thought about *you* being embarrassed—only Kam. I've been careful not to walk past her house." She gave me a quick hug and went into the kitchen to ask Grandma if Aunt Kam had said anything.

"No, and she'd better not."

Mom wore a dress when she left for work the next day. She carried the pants and shirt in a grocery sack and said she'd change in the toilet at the produce. After a paycheck or two, she bought a few new clothes that enabled her to walk to work and home looking like any married lady making a trip to the A & P to pick up something for supper. Seeing her in a blue-gray swagger suit relieved me enormously, but my joy was incomplete because I felt I'd failed some sort of a test with Grandma in this situation.

When Aunt Kam told us that Geraldine was coming home to be married, Mom bought a cardinal red hat and matching gloves to go with the swagger suit. I thought the outfit made her look every bit as good as Mrs. Engle and Mrs. Shenk and better than Mrs. Hess, who looked like a pigeon no matter what she wore.

Geraldine was the older sister of Marianne and Jack Russell, and she *was* old—almost thirty. I'd never seen her because she'd been away for a long time playing in an all-girl orchestra. I couldn't wait to meet her.

When news of the wedding appeared in the *Harlan Tribune,* I became important because I was the cousin of a person who was *somebody.* People stopped me on the street to ask questions about Geraldine.

"They say she looks just like Harlow. Is that so?"

"I guess," I said, not knowing Harlow from a hole in the ground.

"What does your aunt think about having a theater owner in the family?"

I shrugged. There were some things that you didn't tell. After Geraldine called from Chicago about getting married, Aunt Kam went to bed for two days and didn't eat a thing but poached eggs. Central must have listened in and told, because the next day the *Tribune* called with all kinds of questions. I was there when Aunt Kam answered the phone.

"I'm sorry, Arlene, but you've been misinformed."

Donald Duck sounds came from the phone. I wouldn't have known about Donald Duck if Miss Dever hadn't given me a dime for the movies when I told her I'd never seen one. She hurried through my lesson so I could get to the Harlan Theater in time to see Shirley Temple in *Heidi*. She said she'd call Mom and explain where I was. She did, but I still got scolded for "taking things from people" and making myself "beholden." I figure that Heidi, Grandfather, the goats, and the Donald Duck cartoon were worth it.

As the quacks from the telephone went on, Aunt Kam's eyes were yellowing, and I knew there was trouble ahead for Arlene, the lady who wrote the stories about people who "motored" to visit somebody and told all about brides' dresses.

"If you print one word of that, I'll cancel my subscription!" Aunt Kam said.

The story came out on Thursday, and Aunt Kam said they had it all wrong. She *did* cancel her subscription.

"Just look at that!" she said, throwing the paper on our kitchen table and stabbing the headline with her finger. It said Fay Day to Wed Theater Owner.

I couldn't see what that had to do with Geraldine until Mom explained that Fay Day was her professional name. Even then I wasn't sure and asked why she had two names.

"Because she doesn't want to cheapen her own," Aunt Kam said.

Mom added, "And because 'Geraldine Jensen' is no good for a marquee." She could see that I was about to ask what a marquee was and put a finger to her lips. Aunt Kam was too upset to put up with my quest for knowledge just then.

I started to read the story, and I had just come to the part about the Casa Roma Theater when Aunt Kam grabbed the paper and cut out the piece with Grandma's sewing scissors.

"Shouldn't cut paper with those," Mom said.

"Oh, bother! Who can worry about a cutting edge at a time like this? I'm just glad that Else didn't live to see it."

"What makes you think she'd mind?" Mom said with a faraway look. "Else never got the man *she* wanted, and she'd probably be glad that Geraldine is having better luck."

"I'm not convinced that it's love," Aunt Kam said. "She's probably just tired of working."

Mom said, "Geraldine is old enough to know her own mind—has been since she was ten. I hope this Vito Scarpelli knows that he'll have his hands full with her."

Aunt Kam groaned. "Scarpelli! When I think of all the nice, Danish farm boys who wanted her—but no, she'd have none of them."

Mom laughed. "Can you see Geraldine as a farm wife?"

"They weren't *all* farmers. Some of the boys who were interested in her went into business—like Karl."

Geraldine came home on the train with all kinds of suitcases and boxes. She wore a black, skinny-looking dress and a long piece of silvery fur that gave off waves of perfume. Her hair was white as the fluff from a milkweed pod, and the thin arches of her eyebrows made her look surprised.

The station was crowded with people who claimed to be meeting somebody, but Geraldine was the only person who got off the train.

"Nosey parkers!" Aunt Kam said with a sniff, but her eyes were bright green with joy, and she had to fight back a smile at all the attention Geraldine was getting.

Our family never did much kissing, so I was surprised when Geraldine kissed everybody right and left. Uncle Karl turned red, Grandma gave Geraldine a quick pat on the back, and Marianne stood there with her mouth slightly open. The kiss I got was soft—like the touch of a butterfly's wing.

"Is this one yours, Aunt Pete? I'm going to have one just like her."

"Not with any black-haired Italian, you're not," Aunt Kam muttered, and for some reason Geraldine thought that was funny.

We all piled into the Chevy, holding hatboxes and small cases on our laps. Geraldine's perfume filled the car with a sweetness that had a sinful edge. We wouldn't have needed the car except for the suitcases, and we were at Aunt Kam's house in no time. Geraldine said nice things about the remodeling, but she looked sad as she went from room to room.

"Somehow I always thought this house would stay the same—the way it was when I was a kid."

"Nothing stays the same," Grandma said.

Geraldine was to share Marianne's room, and I was allowed to come in and watch the unpacking. Marianne held a shiny silver dress up to her body and went on about how "gorgeous" it was.

"Want it?" Geraldine said. "You can have that and more, though God knows what you'll do with them in this town."

Marianne's eyes shone as dresses with spangles and fringes flew from the cases into her arms. "Boy, wait until Wayne sees me in these!"

"Hold the phone, kid," Geraldine said. "You can't run around this town in stage clothes. Furthermore, it isn't smart to lay it all out for your boyfriend. Cover up what you've got and let him guess."

"I'll bet you didn't get Vito that way."

"Never mind how I got Vito, but I'll tell you this much—it wasn't by making myself as available as pretzels in a bar."

"Are you really crazy about him?"

"Sure. I'm also crazy about the idea of giving my violin to the Salvation Army."

"You mean you aren't going to play anymore? After all those lessons and everything? Aunt Kam will have a stroke."

"I'll write her a check for every nickel she saved out of the grocery money for the lessons. How's that?"

"It's not just the money—she thinks she discovered your talent."

"Let's not tell her that she made a mistake," Geraldine said. "I got by on guts and drive and flashy looks, but I've had enough training to know what's missing. What about you, kiddo, do you have talent?"

Marianne's chin shot up. "Yes, but Aunt Kam is too busy making Margaret practice to notice."

Geraldine grinned. "Jealous?"

Marianne tossed her head. "Of course not. Why should I be?"

"Because she has a mother *and* Aunt Kam, but don't let it get you down, Marianneski."

"Don't call me that, I hate it!"

Then they talked about my dead Aunt Else's second husband, Sandor Cieliski, for awhile. Geraldine said it was a good way for Marianne to get him out of her system. He never had any money because he bet on horses, and he was mean to Aunt Else, but Geraldine said he always was nice to her.

"Not to me," Marianne said, "never to me. Every time he called me 'Marianneski,' I wanted to kill him!"

"Hey, not in front of the kid," Geraldine said.

I hadn't said a word, and I'd even breathed shallowly, hoping to go unnoticed long enough to learn something. Pride made me leave the room before I was asked to go.

1 0

S E V E R A L   D A Y S after Geraldine came, Vito Scarpelli arrived in Harlan, astounding everybody but me and maybe Grandma. I didn't know what an Italian was supposed to look like, and Grandma had seen more kinds of people than the rest of us had. You had to know either nothing or a lot to take Vito Scarpelli for what he was, I guess.

When Geraldine rushed into the arms of the tall, light-haired man who got off the train, Aunt Kam gasped. "Well, I never!" Mom was surprised too, but Grandma just smiled.

Vito wore a dark suit like a preacher and a diamond ring on his right hand. He called Geraldine "Gero" and always had a hand on her shoulder, her waist, or her arm. He was polite to Aunt Kam and Uncle Karl and Mom, more than polite to Grandma, and flirty with Marianne, but he kept me at arm's length as if he thought I might have sticky hands. I heard him tell Geraldine that he didn't know much about kids.

She laughed and said, "I thought Italians produced them in bunches."

"Maybe that's why I keep away from 'em."

When I exasperated Grandma, she'd say, "I hope you have a dozen children," making it sound like some awful prediction in a fairy tale. Vito sounded like somebody trying to ward off an evil spell.

He came on a Monday, and the wedding was to be on Saturday. I went out of my way to stop at Aunt Kam's house before school to keep current on the plans. It was a point of pride to have a new nugget of information for anyone who inquired. Usually Vito and Geraldine were still asleep when I came, but on Thursday they were up and sitting at the kitchen table.

Vito yawned. "God, what an hour to be conscious!"

Geraldine was wearing full makeup, but sleep had made her face puffy as a rising loaf of white bread. When Aunt Kam set a bowl of oatmeal in front of her, she wrinkled her nose.

"Just coffee, please—black as night, hot as hell, and sweet as love."

"I taught her that one," Vito said with a laugh. He looked at his watch, admiring the sun rays dancing in its wide gold band. "What time does that license place open?"

"Eight-thirty, and we'll have to hurry, because we're supposed to see the preacher at nine."

"Do you need a dog license?" I asked.

Vito laughed hugely. I hadn't meant to be funny, I just thought I might help by telling him how the Shenks saved money. They told the man at the courthouse that their dog Milly was fixed, even though she really wasn't.

Aunt Kam looked cross. "They're talking about a piece of paper that gives them permission to get married—a marriage license. Now get going, or you'll be late for school."

I wasn't even close to being late. In fact, my elaborate explanation of marriage licenses made me the belle of the playground until Buster Weir said, "You don't know what you're talking about."

"I do, too! You have to have a paper that says you can get married. It's like a dog license, only different."

"You can do anything you want without any paper," Buster insisted, giving me a shove.

I couldn't understand why he was so angry, and it would be years before I would know that Buster's mother habitually did anything she pleased without a paper of permission.

As soon as school was out, I ran back to Aunt Kam's house and found Vito sitting on the front steps smoking gloomily. The windows were open, and I could hear loud voices—Aunt Kam's and Geraldine's.

"What are they mad about?"

Vito exhaled a shaft of smoke, flicked his Lucky Strike into the spirea bushes, and lit another cigarette before he answered me. "The old lady just found out I'm a fish eater."

"You won't get any around here. They don't have it at the A & P."

Vito shook his head in disgust. "Haven't you ever heard Catholics called fish eaters? What I'm trying to say is that I'm Catholic—not that I pay much attention to that stuff."

"The Shenks are Catholic. Wyonne and Max have to go to catechism every Saturday morning at St. Michaels. Do you have to do that?"

"Used to," he said with an odd smile, "and a fat lot of good it did me!"

"Wyonne says you have to learn all that so you won't go to hell."

"That's a lot of crap," Vito said, tired of me.

I opened the front door soundlessly and tiptoed inside just as Geraldine said, "Of all the narrow-minded, hick attitudes! I expected better from you."

"Do you want Rome to run your life?" Aunt Kam asked. "Do you want to be a broken-down brood mare in a few years? I think Reverend Hansen is absolutely right—'be not unequally yoked with—' "

"The word is *unbelievers,* and it doesn't apply to Vito. He's a believer in his own way."

I couldn't see from the entry hall, but I supposed that Aunt Kam was at the window, because she said, "Shh. We'll have to talk about this later. Here comes Marianne."

"So what? She might as well know what she's up against in this family. After all, Wayne Andrews doesn't have a drop of Danish blood,

5 4

and he's an Episcopalian to boot. When are you going to put on your sheets and go after him?''

I ducked into the coat closet to avoid Marianne. She passed close enough for me to smell the cherry Coke on her breath.

"What's new?" she said. "Did the Fashion call about my dress for the wedding?''

"You won't need it," Geraldine said. "Reverend Hansen won't marry us because Vito's Catholic, and Father Burke won't because I'm not. That leaves the Justice of the Peace, and we're not waltzing into Eldon Frahm's office in full wedding regalia. I went to school with that cluck, and never in my wildest imaginings did I —"

She broke off, laughing until I thought she'd break something inside, and then she began to cry like a kid with skinned knees. Marianne cried, too, because she couldn't wear lavender satin and carry purple asters.

"Stop it!" Aunt Kam said. "You are Jorgen women."

"And what's that supposed to mean?" Geraldine bawled.

"Jorgen women accept whatever fortune brings with dignity. We are strong, and we do not quail at the slings and arrows of outrageous fortune.''

"It's outrageous, all right," Geraldine said. She blew her nose and laughed. "Marianne, call Fern's Fashion and cancel that dress. Tell her we'll be in to choose something in street length instead."

"You can't take yours back—she said so."

"That's O.K. I'll put it away for one of the dozens of kids who are going to make me into a broken-down old brood mare. And we might as well do this Friday instead of Saturday. Why wait?"

I escaped without discovery, saw that Vito had disappeared, and went home to talk things over with Grandma. She was busy cleaning the garden for the winter, so I thought I'd try the Shenks. They ought to understand all this, being Catholic themselves.

Mrs. Shenk let me in, but she wasn't glad to see me. She was washing Wyonne's hairs. Yes, hairs. To Wyonne and her mother, hairs were "them"— the enemy. She told me to sit and wait.

"Ouch!" Wyonne shrieked. "You're pulling them. Now you've got soap in my eyes.''

"Shut up! I've got to get them clean."

Wyonne wouldn't be allowed to go outside with wet hair, so I resigned myself to a session with the Jane Arden paper dolls. Meanwhile, I stared at the things fish eaters hung on their walls: crucifixes and hearts dripping blood from punctures made by thorns.

Max came home, ignoring me completely. From where I sat, I could see into the kitchen. Watching him slice a banana onto a peanut butter sandwich, I wondered if Rome ran his life. Maybe it was just as well that I no longer loved Max. When he got out his violin and mixed its terrible sounds with Wyonne's towel-muffled shrieks, I went home.

5 5

Aunt Kam got to the back door before I did and caught Mom in her underwear on the screened porch.

"Petra, for the love of heaven! What if a salesman should come along?"

"He probably wouldn't be too thrilled."

When Aunt Kam had told the whole story and gone home to make supper, Mom said, "Well, Mama, what do you think of that?"

"It's Geraldine's life. If she wants the spice of difference, she'll have to take the heartburn that goes with it."

They wouldn't let me go to the wedding because it was during school, but as soon as the last bell rang, I ran to Aunt Kam's as fast as I could. Uncle Karl was sitting in the Chevy with the motor running, and Vito was standing beside the open door on the passenger side, waiting for Geraldine. She hugged Aunt Kam and Marianne, crushing the wedding flowers pinned to her suit. They all looked nice, but not as nice as they would have if Vito hadn't turned out to be a fish eater.

"You'll have to come and see *us,* Aunt Kam, because I'm never coming back here."

"Oh, don't say that!"

"Come on, Gero," Vito said, tossing his cigarette into the gutter.

Red leaves from the curbside maple drifted to the roof of the Chevy and the bumpy, brick street. A perfect specimen caught in my sweater, and I handed it to Geraldine.

She tucked the leaf into the center of her corsage and said, "Margaret, baby, grow up fast and get out of this town." Then she blew kisses, tossed the long tail of her fur over her shoulder, and climbed into the car.

As the Chevy leaped forward, Aunt Kam raised her hand in farewell and Marianne bit her knuckles.

"You'd better turn away before they're out of sight, or it will be bad luck," I reminded them.

"Huh!" said Aunt Kam. "I don't see how it could get worse. The nerve of that Eldon Frahm!"

"What did he do?"

"The minute we came in, he started picking at Vito about Mussolini. I was afraid there would be a fist fight right on the spot. Justice of the Peace, my foot! Eldon Frahm ought to be impeached."

I imagined Eldon Frahm's head reduced in size and wedged among the canned peaches in a Mason jar.

"Button your sweater, Margaret. It's getting chilly, and I don't know what your poor mother will do if you get sick again."

I buttoned the sweater, remembering what Mom had said to me on that fitfully sunny spring day when I left the hospital. "We'll have to be very careful with you from now on. You're not like other people."

Was that true? The hair shaved from my head for the first operation had grown back, and I'd even had a permanent. Beulah Pedersen fried my hair into frizzles with the dangling snakes of a monstrous machine. I'd been faithful about rubbing cocoa butter into the neck scar from the second operation, but I wasn't sure that worked. The broad welt was still there. Cocoa butter certainly had done nothing for my doll Shirley when her face cracked after I carried her to the cemetery to visit Daddy and the rest of the family on a cold, snowy day.

Lots of things didn't work. The Little Orphan Annie decoder I sent for with an Ovaltine label didn't, one of the lamps in the front room didn't, and neither did a kitchen cupboard door. Mom could fix the door when she had time, because she had learned to use tools in college, but she couldn't fix everything. Could anyone?

My Sunday school teacher said God could fix everything, but I was pretty sure He wouldn't have time to bother with my Orphan Annie decoder. Maybe he could take care of the lamp, though. Electricity seemed like something He'd be good at.

Thinking about things like that takes time. Sometimes you have to stop and lean against a tree to do it. Grandma was standing on the front porch watching for me, still wearing the black silk dress with the white ruching at the neck she had put on for the wedding.

"Where have you been? I was worried."

"You don't have to worry about me," I said. "I'm not like other people."

"Maybe that's why I do," she said.

M O M   S O M E T I M E S   V I S I T E D with the neighbors south of us on Tenth Street, an elderly Danish woman who shared her small house with an unmarried daughter who had a speech defect, but the neighbors to the north never were home. Their name was Edelstein, and they ran a grocery store just off the Square.

Their daughters Rivka and Esther were younger than I was. After school, they went to the store. One parent or the other (never both) brought them home for supper and took them back uptown until closing time at nine. If you didn't see them coming or going, it was hard to know if the Edelsteins were at home. The window shades always were pulled to the sill.

When I was asked to take care of the girls for an evening, I was wildly excited. This was my first chance for gainful employment, and I would be allowed to enter the mysterious house next door. However, Mom thought I was too young for the responsibility.

"Now, Petra," Grandma said, "we're right here in case Margaret needs us," and that settled it.

Even the doorbell at the Edelsteins' front entrance seemed exotic. It chimed in a melancholy minor that was nothing like Aunt Kam's major-key bell or our own hair-raising rasp that could be heard in the basement. Mrs. Edelstein opened the door narrowly and told me to come in. Like her husband, she was small and dark, and so were Rivka and Esther. They were sitting on a dark, shiny couch regarding me solemnly.

"We're gong out of town," Mrs. Edelstein said. "So if you have a problem, God forbid, you'll call your own mother, right? And if you want something to nosh, there's fruit."

Mr Edelstein was impatient. He snatched a fur cape from a chair back and shook it until his wife backed into it. Both of them were dressed up. Without their white aprons, they looked like strangers.

Mrs. Edelstein lingered, looking around the room as if she'd forgotten something. "She's too young, Sol," she said, and I knew she meant me.

"Come on, Hannah, what's the worst that can happen?"

"Don't ask!"

When they were gone, I sat on a brown satin chair opposite the girls and smiled at them. They did not smile back. I wished they weren't there so I could drink in the feeling of the room—the rich, shadowy atmosphere created by metal lamps with dark shades that confined the light to round pools; the deep greens and browns of heavy, expensive-looking fabrics; a smell of perfume and leather. However, I had been hired to take care of Rivka and Esther, and while I didn't know quite how to proceed, I meant to give it my best shot.

"I'll bet it seems funny not to be at the store," I ventured.

"The store is closed," said Rivka.

"But it never closes this early."

"It's New Year's," said Esther.

"It is not," I said. "New Year's comes in January."

"Ours doesn't," Rivka said, sliding off the sofa. "I want some matzos."

Esther followed her to the kitchen, and so did I. Rivka offered me some flat, tasteless things that came from a box with strange lettering. The pears were better—golden with practically no brown marks—and Rivka proudly told me that her papa knew more about fruit than anybody.

The light in the kitchen was brighter, allowing me to appreciate the coloring of my charges. Their skin had the richness of the black-walnut meats Grandma dug from the shell with a quick twist of her silver pick. Hating my own tilted nose, I admired the downturn of theirs, and their big dark eyes and deep brown hair seemed especially beautiful to me.

We listened to the radio for awhile, and then I told them some fairy tales. When it was time for them to go to bed, I said I'd listen to their prayers. They shook their heads.

"I guess you don't go to Sunday school either, do you?"

"No, but we go to temple in Omaha on Yom Kippur."

"What's that?"

"The Day of Atonement. You say you're sorry for all the bad things you did for a whole year."

"That must take a long time," I said, thinking of Grandma's warning about never letting the sun go down without telling God you were sorry for the wrongs of the day. Sometimes *that* took a long time, but if you did it, Jesus had fixed things so that everything was O.K. between you and God. "Say, do you know about Jesus?"

"We're not supposed to talk about him," Rivka said.

My Sunday school teacher said that everybody ought to know about Jesus, but I couldn't very well tell them if they weren't supposed to talk about Him. Rivka and Esther went to sleep promptly, and that worried me. My own bedtime prayer included the line, "If I should die before I wake, I pray the Lord my soul to take." They hadn't asked for that protection, so I did it for them.

Returning to the dim, opulent living room, I raised the window shade a crack to look at the reassuring lights of home. The only familiar piece of reading material was the *Saturday Evening Post,* but I soon tossed it aside in favor of soaking up the feeling of the house. There was comfort, but not the kind of comfort I knew. One had to be careful because nothing was washable here. The furnishings were expensive and beautiful in their own way, but there was a sadness and the weight of years upon them. Heavy feelings were woven into the draperies and imprisoned in the deep-toned wall coverings—alien feelings—and yet I felt at home. My kinship with this place surprised me. The Edelsteins were not as different as I had expected them to be. When the parents came home and gave me a fifty-cent piece, I walked around the block to think it over.

I had a new friend, Monica Reilly, whose family had moved into a big house two blocks north of us. Monica's father was the doctor who had come to town to help Dr. Petersen when the radium burns made him too sick to take care of all his patients. Monica's mother was vague but pleasant. Her hair always was a mess—probably because she was busy with six kids, five of them younger than Monica. You never had to ring the doorbell at the Reillys', and nobody cared how much noise you made. Their furniture had been nice once, but the kids had wrecked it.

Monica was thin as a stick and full of ideas for having fun. Her only drawback was being Catholic and having to go to catechism on Saturday mornings. I waited for her outside of St. Michael's because we were making a time capsule—a Karo syrup can filled with both newspaper stories and our own life stories that we wrote on tablet paper.

"Let me read yours," Monica said.

"O.K. if I can read yours."

We exchanged, read, and looked at each other silently. Finally she said, "Well, what's the matter?"

"You didn't say much, and what you *did* say could be about any old girl."

"Yeah? At least I didn't make up a bunch of stuff about a grandma crossing the ocean on a big ship and a cousin being famous."

"It's true! Grandma did, and if you'd moved here sooner, you'd know about my cousin Geral—Fay Day. She played the violin before she married a fish—" I stopped, stricken.

"I know what you were going to say." Monica's tone was ominous. "And if you don't like us, why do you hang around with me and Wyonne? Why don't you do stuff with the kids from that dumb church *you* go to?"

"It's *not* a dumb church!" I said stoutly. It was none of *her* business why I didn't choose my friends from it, but the fact was—they never did anything at all. Every human pleasure was sinful. Lotus, a Methodist, had a slightly broader view of life, but even she failed to rise to the reckless joy of the Reillys, who, it seemed, could do anything that pleased them and wipe out the consequences in the confessional.

"I'll tell you what," Monica said, suddenly conciliatory. "You write my life and I'll write yours."

That project was sidetracked as we sorted our clippings. One of them was headlined Errol Flynn Accused of Rape.

"What's rape?" I asked.

"I don't know. Let's ask Mom."

We found Mrs. Reilly in the basement laundry room trying to sort underwear into six piles. When Monica put the question to her, she paused and brushed the flyaway strands of hair from her eyes. With a deep sigh she said, "Oh, Monnie, ask me again in ten years."

At my house, Grandma was kneading bread dough in a huge, brown crockery bowl that weighed a ton. She gave each of us a snippet of dough. I ate mine with relish, but Monica grimaced at the raw, yeasty taste.

"What does rape mean, Grandma?"

She plopped the big wad of dough down hard before she spoke. Just when I thought she hadn't heard me, she said, "That's something you don't need to know just now. Why do you ask?"

"We read about Errol Flynn."

"Whoever *he* may be."

We told her that he was in the movies—Robin Hood or some guy in fancy clothes swinging from the light fixture with a sword in his hand. "Hmph!" she said.

Who *would* tell us what the word meant? We couldn't wait until Mom came home from the produce, so we went to the library and looked in the big dictionary: "The act or instance of robbing and despoiling; violent seizure; the act of carrying a person away by force."

Monica said, "So what? He does stuff like that in the movies all the time."

"There's more," I told her, stumbling over the pronounciation of "illicit sexual intercourse without the consent of the woman."

She shrugged. "I don't know what that means. Shall we put him in our time capsule or not?"

"Sure. Whatever it is, it happened."

We had no time to fix our life stories because the crew fixing a sidewalk on Baldwin Street had their job nearly finished. If we wanted wet cement, it was now or never. Monica made the approach, holding out a paper plate, and they gave her a gob of it. We packed the syrup can, took turns at standing on the lid to be sure it was tight, and plastered the rim with the cement. We couldn't bury it until the cement was dry, but we dug the hole for it in the bank of dirt at the far end of the Reillys' back yard.

The actual ceremony was a week later, and it was an enormously satisfying experience.

"Do you know what this feels like?" I said.

Monica considered. "It's what I wish somebody would do for me. I wish I hadn't buried it so I'd have the fun of finding it."

"I think it's like writing a book. Maybe we'll both be dead before somebody finds our time capsule, and it won't matter because they'll know what we were like."

"But if we're dead, we won't *care* what they know."

"I will. When I get books from the library, I think about the people who wrote them being dead—but not really—because I make them alive when I read. I think they know."

"Then when you shut the book they're dead again?"

"I guess so."

We soon forgot about immortality and rape and found our excitement in hitching a ride on a county-road maintenance rig to the farm home of one of Mom's few friends, Ethel. They had gone to school together.

Monica had been a city kid, and I was eager to show her the pigs, the cattle, and even the green-furred watering tank, but at the rate we were going on the slow-moving grader, the afternoon would be gone when we arrived. Somehow I'd thought we'd be back before anyone missed us, but this now seemed unlikely.

Monica wasn't missed. It's easy to come and go as you please in a family of six kids, but I was the object of a widespread search that ended when Ethel saw us and telephoned Mom. I had scarcely had time to show Monica anything when Uncle Karl's Chevy screeched into the lane. Mom jumped out while the car was still moving, and then Uncle Karl got out looking mad as thunder. They headed straight for the house, and something told me we'd better lie low until Uncle Karl cooled down. It takes a lot to get a Dane angry, but when it happens, watch out!

I grabbed Monica's arm and dragged her to a row of rhubarb plants along the garden fence, showing her how to bellyflop and wriggle under the broad umbrellas of the leaves.

When Mom, Uncle Karl, and Ethel came out yelling our names, we stayed so still that our heartbeats sounded like hammer blows. Once Uncle Karl came so close that I could see the scuff mark on the toe of one black shoe. I held my breath until my lungs nearly burst.

"Where are those kids, Petra? I have to get back to the store."

"I'm sorry, Karl, I shouldn't have asked you to bring me, but I didn't know where else to turn."

Their voices grew fainter, and finally the door slammed, indicating they had gone into the house. I told Monica that she could wait in the car while I went in to face the music. Affecting happy innocence, I greeted Ethel and thanked her for letting me drop in with my friend. With great surprise, I noticed the presence of my mother and my uncle.

"Margaret!" Mom hugged me, then shook me.

"You ought to have a real licking for this," Uncle Karl said.

Without further speech, we joined Monica in the car and started home. After a few miles, Uncle Karl said, "You'd better tell that kid never to hook rides with strangers. Anything could happen—murder, rape—"

Monica and I exchanged glances. There was that word again.

"Oh, Karl, please!" Mom said. "I don't even like to *think* of what might have happened. You're right, though. I'll find a way to impress it on her mind."

She did. I was not permitted to leave my own house and yard except to go to school and church for three months. I missed going to the Reillys' terribly, and when I saw Monica at school, I asked what her punishment was.

"Nothing. When I told my mom, she said, 'That's nice, dear.' Of course she was kind of busy when I told her."

"Busy doing what?"

"Grabbing something for Brian to throw up in. He does it all the time."

1 2

W H E N M O M S O L D the Tenth Street house and bought a bigger one with an upstairs apartment at the corner of Ninth and Willow, she said it felt good to be back on the street where she was born.

The vine-covered front porch stretched along both streets, meeting in a Greek-temple peak. During the growing season, the front rooms were submerged in green gloom, but the dining room and kitchen were bright with many south windows. Grandma's potted plants did well on the long window seat in the dining room.

The former owners were the Farleys, who had been rich until bad investments and long illnesses ate up their money. They decided to give up the struggle with Iowa winters and go west to die in a gentler climate.

I came to know the Farleys by the books they left behind in cases with glass doors that lifted and slid back on tracks. Winston Churchill and Sax Rohmer novels shared a shelf with treatises on hydrotherapy, phrenology, and vegetarianism. A set of *Beacon Lights of History* was bound in dark green, and the covers of the 1883 encyclopedia volumes were soft calf leather. Age-scorched flyleaves were inscribed "To my dear husband, Charles, from Lavinia, Christmas, 1902" or "To the incomparable Lavinia from her greatest admirer, Charles, May 6, 1907" or simply "Boots from Carrie, October 14, 1912." It amazed me to consider that the ancient Farleys had been young once, celebrating special occasions with gifts of books. Nobody ever gave *me* a book. I was expected to use the library.

Too old and sick to care about possessions, the Farleys left many of their things behind: a black leather couch with carved lion heads, mouths frozen open in a silent roar, on the arm rests; a long library table with Ionic snails for feet; a black lacquered bedroom set with a triple-mirrored dressing table and matching chairs and benches with caned seats; a storage bench in the front hall; painted plates and silver fruit knives. Their things resisted belonging to us, and Mom put them in the front rooms, which we seldom used.

The kitchen, dining room, and back bedrooms were Langelund territory and were filled with familiar furniture from the farm and Grandma's house. That was where we lived. In the winter, we "pulled our horns in" even farther, as Grandma put it, because the kitchen stove was our only source of heat. On the rare occasions when Mom tried to fire the furnace, blue smoke belched from the registers. She soon gave up on it.

6 4

Feeling the need to lay claim to the Farley portion, I wrote a note: "This house belongs to the Langelunds," and the date. By pushing one of the sliding doors between the front rooms deep inside its track, I could reach a ledge gritty with plaster and deposit the notice.

Soon we had tenants in the upstairs apartment: Miss Clara Benton, an unmarried teacher; Mrs. Henrietta Benton, her widowed mother; and Scipio, an orange tomcat. We could hear footsteps above our heads and the sound of rushing water, but we never heard their voices. Mom didn't want them to hear us, either, and I was shushed so often that I spent more time in the houses of friends than I ever had.

Lotus Hess had bought a bottle of green nail polish that she let me try. I reasoned that if I went home before I was called, set the table, and kept my hands out of sight, the grass-colored nails might survive to be shown off at school the next day.

Mom was just coming home from the produce as I crossed the street. We waved, and I started to run, thinking I'd open the door for her. But she wasn't going to the door. She was in the alley striking a match and holding it to the sack she used to carry her work clothes. It took three matches before the brown paper blazed.

Grandma came out the back door wiping her hands on her apron and said, "What are you doing? Those things have more wear left in them, don't they?"

"I quit!"

"Kamille will be glad to hear it," Grandma said.

So was I. I wanted to rush up and ask questions, but decided I'd learn more if I didn't. I lurked behind the grape arbor.

"How did you come to do that?" Grandma asked.

"I couldn't stand working with trash one more minute. Maude Gear was going on about some truck driver taking her to the Chicken Hut and what he said and what she said and how when he took her home, she didn't have the heart to make him leave, and how she—"

Grandma spotted me behind the grapevines and said, "Little pitchers have big ears."

Mom nodded and poked the burning clothes with a stick. The charred wool smelled awful. "Usually I can shut my mind to that kind of talk, but today I was listening and seeing it all. When I realized what I was doing, my hands just let go of the eggs. Bill Lundstrom yelled at me, and that was it. I told him I wouldn't be back."

Grandma ran her fingers over the gold earpieces of her glasses the way she did when she was thinking hard. "I could do ironing again."

"You won't have to. We have the rent from the Bentons, and besides, I have another job."

My joy faded. Just when I was starting to savor the feeling of having Mom around when I went to school and when I came home, the possibility was snatched away.

Grandma asked what kind of a job it was, and Mom said, "They're

6 5

going to train me to run the switchboard at the Farmers' Mutual Phone Office. I guess I can learn to push and pull plugs as well as the next person."

I knew very little about town telephones because we didn't have one, but the one that hung on the wall at the farm lifted the hair on your head when it rang. After Mom had been at the telephone office for a few days, two men came to put one like it in our dining room as part of her pay. Now we wouldn't have to go to Aunt Kam's to use the phone in an emergency. Our ring was two shorts and a long. I rang Central just to hear Mom say "Number, please" and hung up right away. Our ring sounded immediately.

"Margaret," Mom said, "you must not play with the phone. Never use it unless you have something important to say."

I couldn't figure out how she knew it was me, but I didn't touch the phone for a long time after that. Why should I? The town had two phone systems, and nobody I knew had ours. Stores and businesses had both to call town people and farmers, but we couldn't even call Aunt Kam. When I heard our ring and Grandma told me to answer, I always said, "Hi, Mom." Who else could it be?

The day a man's voice asked for Mrs. Langelund, I was so surprised that I dropped the earpiece. By the time I had caught the thing in its wide swing, Mom had cut in. Central always stayed on the line long enough to be sure the connection was made.

"This is Mrs. Langelund," she said. "You may hang up, Margaret."

I disobeyed and heard him say, "This is Dr. Evan Lewis."

That scared me. If Mom got sick, what would we do? She didn't *seem* sick.

"The chiropractor?" she asked.

"Yes, ma'am. Considering that I've only been here a month, I'm surprised that you recognize my name."

"It's a small town."

I had heard her tell Grandma that since going to work at the phone office, she'd learned more about her hometown than she'd picked up in all the years before. Centrals knew everything, but they weren't allowed to tell.

"I'm told that you have quite a collection of books," Dr. Lewis said. "Things I might be interested in. I thought we might make some kind of a deal."

"I don't really know what's in the bookcases—they came with the house—but you and Mrs. Lewis can come and look them over if you like."

He said he wished they could, but Mrs. Lewis had passed on just before Thanksgiving two years before. He finally couldn't stand staying in the town where they'd been happy so he had found a new place.

Mom said she was sorry she mentioned something that made him feel bad and that he could come about seven. After he hung up, she said, "You're still there, aren't you, Margaret?"

"Uh-huh," I confessed, amazed that she knew.

6 6

She didn't scold. She just told me to have Grandma air the front rooms and I was to dust. Because we didn't use those rooms, they seldom needed cleaning. I was leery of dusting the open mouths of the lions on the couch. What if they should clamp shut on my hand? I flicked the tail of the dust cloth through them in a hurry. Dusting the snail feet of the library table, I mourned the green fingernails that Mom wouldn't allow. We had no nail polish remover, so she had made me go back to the Hesses and take it off. She might have let me keep them if Grandma hadn't said I looked like Nebuchadnezzar, some old king in the Bible who ate grass like a cow. Grandma talked about Nebuchadnezzar a lot, and when I asked her why he had to eat grass, she said it was to teach him who was boss.

"Who is?"

"God. The sooner you figure it out, the better."

Our front door had two bells, and when Dr. Lewis rang ours, Miss Benton came down, certain that it was meant for her.Nobody ever rang *our* bell. Our company knew us well enough to walk in the back door without knocking. Mom and Miss Benton nearly collided in the front hall, and then Miss Benton lingered to find out who was there. She stared at Dr. Lewis with her bugged-out eyes, and the golf ball in her neck shifted when she swallowed. That golf ball was a goiter, Mom said—a suitably ugly name for an ugly object.

"Well," said Miss Benton, "I didn't know that chiropractors made house calls."

"They don't," he said. "How long have you had that exophthalmic condition?"

Miss Benton didn't answer. She just ran up the stairs panting like a dog while Dr. Lewis shook his head. He was carrying a strange-looking floor lamp, and I wondered how he knew he'd need it in the dim Farley parlor.

"I thought I might trade you this thermo-lamp for some books," he said.

I could see that Mom didn't care for the lamp, but she opened the glass doors of the bookcases. When she saw that the light from the peach-colored bulbs in the chandelier was too dim to read titles by, she went to get a flashlight.

When she was gone, Dr. Lewis noticed my scar and said, "Under the knife so young? Some adjustments for you can be part of the deal."

Wary of him, I retreated behind the colonnades. He looked like a monkey because of the close-curled brown hair that grew low on his neck and on the backs of his hands. He chose an armload of books, told Mom how to use the lamp, and said, "Bring that girl to the office Friday after school. I think I can do something for her, and that can be part of the trade."

Mom didn't say yes or no, but after Dr. Lewis had gone, Grandma said that cracking necks was a lot of *pyat* (a Danish word meaning foolishness).

"It won't hurt to try it," Mom said. She decided to get the night

6 7

telephone operator Lottie Andersen to work for her while she took me to Dr. Lewis's office on Friday. He did whatever he did to people in his house on Farnam Street.

Friday seemed to rush toward me. I was so filled with dread that I couldn't concentrate in school. When Miss Graham scolded me for the second time and asked if I felt sick, I said I certainly did, but I didn't think it was anything catching.

On the terrible day, Mom wore her swagger suit and looked so nice that I would have felt proud to walk with her if I hadn't been too paralyzed to feel anything. We entered the waiting room, a sun porch with slatted green blinds that smelled of dust and mildew, and the paralysis turned to panic.

Two old men, a woman with thin-plucked eyebrows and a bright red mouth, and Mrs. Andrews, the mother of Marianne's boyfriend Wayne, were sitting there on tan enameled kitchen chairs. Mrs. Andrews got red in the face when she saw us.

"I've been doctoring for years with my back," she explained, "and it hasn't helped a bit, so I thought I might as well *try* this."

"You'll be glad you did," said the woman with the thin eyebrows. "The chiro can fix you up in nothing flat. He's a real wonder—especially for female troubles."

Glancing at the old men, Mrs. Andrews got even redder.

Dr. Lewis appeared in the doorway in a white smock buttoned down the back. "I'm ready for you now, Mr. Eastergaard."

The old man gave no sign that he heard, and when Dr. Lewis spoke louder, he tried to rise but fell back, tilting his chair on two legs. Dr. Lewis hoisted him up and helped him into the other room.

Almost immediately, the doctor was back, beckoning to Mrs. Andrews.

"What happened to Mr. Eastergaard?" I whispered to Mom. "He never came back."

"He probably left by another door."

When Mrs. Andrews, the second old man, and the woman with thin eyebrows vanished in the same way, I was sure that Dr. Lewis had broken their necks and tossed them into another room. When office hours were over, he'd call the undertaker to come and get them. The only thing I couldn't figure out was why they didn't fight and scream when he grabbed their necks.

"Mom, I want to go home."

"Don't be silly, Margaret. Dr. Lewis won't hurt you. He's just going to line up your spine so you'll feel better."

"I feel good now." I skipped around the porch with false vivacity to prove it and nearly crashed into a woman on a pair of crutches trying to enter.

Mom told me to hold the door for the lady, which I did, hoping to make a run for it as soon as she was out of my way. Mom seemed to read my mind. She had me by the arm when Dr. Lewis called my name.

The inner office had bedroomy wallpaper patterned with tiny flowers that seemed, like underwear, not meant to be seen by everyone. A padded table with a hole in it stood in the center of the floor, a small desk and chair were in one corner, and the rest of the space was taken by a tangle of lamps like the one Dr. Lewis had traded for books. A big framed diploma from the Palmer School of Chiropractic in Davenport, Iowa, hung on the wall. The year on it was 1932.

Dr. Lewis held out a hairy hand to me, saying, "Scramble up on the table and do a bellyflop."

I refused until Mom spoke my name warningly. Those lowered eyelids meant there would be no living with her if I continued to resist. When Dr. Lewis tried to help by promising me an all-day sucker when we were finished, I scorned the bribe but seized the implication of survival. I climbed on the table, breathing shallowly to minimize the odor of sweaty leather. It was not pleasant like the smell of horse harness, but nastily human.

Dr. Lewis's fingers played my spine like a piano keyboard, and that wasn't so bad, but when I turned my head and saw his big, flexed hands hovering above my neck, I screamed.

"Margaret!" Mom said sharply.

"Her nerves will be better after we've taken care of this subluxation," Dr. Lewis said, turning my face back to the tissue-paper-covered leather.

The chopping blow or whatever it was came so fast that I wasn't sure it happened. I found myself leaving by another door, just as Mom had said, a red sucker in my hand.

"Your color is better already," she said.

"At least he didn't use ether."

We walked over to the A & P to buy some coffee. When the clerk put the beans into the grinder, I inhaled the aroma with the ecstatically heightened senses of the survivor. Even when it was put into the red Four O'clock bag, the coffee smelled wonderful—better than it tasted, Mom said.

Mr. Hulsebus, the manager of the telephone company, was coming out of Levendahl's drugstore as we passed. He always rubbed the side of his stomach where he was ruptured, whatever that meant.

"Petra," he said, looking puzzled. "Who's on the board?"

"I traded with Lottie because I had to take Margaret to the doctor."

He looked relieved, and it seemed like a good time to ask him if it would be all right for me to stay all night with Mom at the telephone office when she paid Lottie back.

"Can't see why anybody would get a kick out of that," he said, "but I don't care as long as you don't keep your mother from tending to business. Don't tell the world about it, though."

"Really, Frank," Mom said, "it's not necessary."

"Oh, please, Mom!" I glowed and dazzled, demonstrating what I hoped she would interpret as chiropractically induced health. From the

6 9

reflection I glimpsed in Levendahl's plate glass window, it seemed that she ought to be impressed.

"Won't hurt her to lose a little sleep once in a blue moon," Frank Hulscbus said, departing with the upraised index finger gesture known as the Shelby County Salute.

Mom still looked skeptical, and I decided that men were easier to convince than women. However, she did promise that I could come along on the night she owed Lottie.

T H E *Weekly Reader* was full of Hitler, but he didn't seem real to me until the spring day when I came home to find Grandma kneading bread dough furiously and muttering in Danish.

"*Slange! Svin!*"

That sounded bad, but I didn't know how bad until she translated and explained. Hitler was a snake and a pig because he had taken Denmark. Filthy German boots were tramping through Ausig, the town where she grew up. Disgusting Germans were everywhere in Copenhagen, gaping at the Little Mermaid and looking for fun they didn't deserve in Tivoli.

After Mom got home from the telephone office, Aunt Kam came over, and the three of them called Hitler more names while they drank six cups of coffee apiece.

Finally Mom said, "Isn't it sort of shameful that the Danes didn't even try to fight?"

Grandma snorted. "If they had, they'd all be dead. They have no mountains to hide in like the Norwegians, and there's no place to run like we have here. They stayed alive to give Hitler more trouble in the long run. He'll learn there's nothing meaner than a Dane with a grudge, and they'll never get caught at what they do to prove it."

"How can that be?" Aunt Kam said. "Say what you will about the Germans, but they aren't stupid. Think of all their composers, poets, and philosophers."

Grandma stared into the deepening twilight as she explained, "When you live in a small country, you learn to stab with a smile. Then who can believe you've done it?"

"I could never do that," Mom said.

"No, and that's because you're my most American child." Grandma pushed her cup aside and went to her room, returning with a folded square of red silk creased sharply by years of storage. She wiped the table with the flat of her hand and opened the square to reveal a white cross. "The *Dannebrog*," she said, "the flag from heaven. Now where's that silk American flag Lauritz brought home from France, Petra?"

Mom found it in a box of old pictures, and Grandma ironed both flags through a dish towel. She strung them on a thread across the kitchen window, the Dannebrog on the right and the Stars and Stripes on the left. Mom said the American flag had to be on the right, and Grandma said, "It is—when you're outside looking in. We have the right to be Danes in our own house."

Aunt Kam always saved the *Omaha World Herald* for us, and we read the news a day late. Grandma said that probably would work out fine until the day after the world ended. "Bad news travels too fast anyhow."

Every now and then I would see a small story about the German advance and try to imagine what war would be like. I saw people running in the night, afraid and shivering in clothes too thin for the weather. I hurried to the closet to test the strength and thickness of the material in old dresses and coats Mom and Grandma no longer wore, deciding what to grab in a hurry if Hitler came and we had to run away. The best thing was Grandma's old coat of Hudson seal. It was bald in spots, but that didn't matter. Other choices were a long woollen cape Mom had worn when she was seventeen and a fringed shawl as big as a blanket—heavy stuff we could wear by day and sleep under at night.

I filled a cardboard box with canned fruit and vegetables from the cellar shelves and hid it under the corn cobs in the shed at the end of the garage. I was the one who always fetched the cobs to start the kitchen stove, so there was small chance of anyone else discovering my cache. We had so many pale blue Mason jars of peaches, pears, apples, beans, and beets in the cellar that no one would miss the ones I took. I really hated canned beets, but I included a few jars because they were supposed to be good for people.

Rationing didn't affect us much because we had no car and were accustomed to austerity. Even if the furnace had worked, Mom probably would have closed all rooms but the kitchen to save money. The kitchen stove burned hard coal for cooking, and the comfort of its heat was a bonus.

We were used to seeing our breath in unheated bedrooms. Thick bathrobes and hot flatirons wrapped in dish towels to warm the icy sheets made bedtime bearable. The trick was to remember that the iron was there and avoid a long stretch that could stub a toe.

In the morning we ached from the contortion of curling up in a ball against the cold and from the weight of many quilts. Our bedding was quite different from the bright, fluffy blankets I saw in the warm bedrooms in the homes of my friends. Our quilts were made by hand from pieces of Grandpa Jorgen's old suits, irregular chunks of velvet, and parts of warm dresses Grandma had worn in Denmark when she was young. The pieces were lashed together with stitches that looked like bird tracks in the snow, and somebody had embroidered 1893 on one of them. When a quilt started to show wear, Grandma put a new cover on it. Some had as many as four layers. She made our pillows, too, stuffing striped ticking with goose and chicken feathers. Our bedspreads were pieced quilts—the Butterfly, the Double Wedding Ring, and plain patchwork. Embarrassed that we couldn't afford the shiny jacquards and fluffy chenilles sold at the Golden Rule, I barred my friends from our sleeping quarters.

Each night just before sundown I walked three blocks to Jens Jacobsen's dairy barn with two empty Karo syrup cans to get our milk.

Jens's barn and pasture were in town, and the neighbors complained about the smell, but I loved it because it reminded me of Daddy and the farm. I had to work harder to remember Daddy now and was grateful for any help I could get.

Jens's bald wife, Carrie, fascinated me. Sometimes she forgot to put on her fringe of false hair when she came to the door, and the interesting bumps of her skull gleamed in the porch light. She looked like the pictures in the phrenology book the Farleys had left behind.

I wasn't sure whether Carrie caught me staring or felt the cool evening air on her head, but she covered her pate with both hands and said, "Nuh, suh! There I go—scaring children again."

"I'm not scared," I said, telling her about the *Omaha World Herald* picture of French girls with their heads shaved.

She laughed. "French girls, huh? I'll have to tell Jens I'm right in style." She motioned for me to come in out of the cold. Locating her monk's cap of dull, reddish hair on top of the refrigerator, she clapped it on crooked and exchanged my empty syrup cans for two that were full. I untied two nickels from the corner of my handkerchief and dropped them into her apron pocket.

On the way out I turned to say, "When I was in the hospital, they shaved part of my head, but the hair grew back. Maybe yours will, too."

Carrie lifted one of my long braids and let it drop on my back. It felt like the swat of a friendly dog's tail. She sighed and said, "Sure it will—when the sun rises in the west."

I didn't get home for half an hour because I put the milk buckets down and climbed a tree to watch the sun set in a bank of purple, gold, and deep rose streaks. I pretended that the sun was rising and Carrie's hair was growing like the speeded-up film of sprouting beans that Miss Graham showed in school. According to the paper, the French girls lost their hair because they "consorted with Germans," whatever that meant. Was it possible that Carrie had done the same and that Germans were here, hiding among us? I jumped out of the tree and ran home to ask Mom, but I couldn't because Aunt Kam was there.

Eyes bright green with excitement, she said, "Margaret, how would you like to play an instrument?"

I shrugged, rubbing the grooves the syrup can bails had dug in my palms. I wasn't sure what she meant.

"I just found out that it doesn't cost anything. The school band man will teach you for nothing, and they even have an instrument you can use. What about a flute? That's a nice, feminine thing to play. Of course I hate to take you away from Agnes Dever, but you really haven't made great strides on the piano, and this way you can practice at home."

"By yourself," Mom added, and that cinched it. No more "one-and-two-and-" from Aunt Kam. No more slobbery stars or mothball cookies from Miss Dever.

The next day Mom sent a note, and I was excused from class to go to the school's music room, where Mr. Wenzel gave me a metal wand of cold silver and showed me how to hold it and how to shape my lips. He had been leaning against the blackboard, unwittingly chalking his coat with half-erased staffs and notes. When he told me to blow, I inhaled a cloud of chalk dust and forced it into the mouthpiece until I swayed dizzily and saw his lips move soundlessly.

His voice seemed to come from far away when he told me I had the wrong mouth for the flute. "Here, suck on this reed, and we'll try a clarinet."

The reed tasted like something you shouldn't put in your mouth, but when Mr. Wenzel put it on the instrument, it did make a squeak. What a clarinet that was—gilded with clanking keys. The school had bought it when a dance band broke up, and it was the only gold clarinet for miles around, Mr. Wenzel guessed. Not real gold, but it certainly looked like it he said. He also told me that the first reed was a present, but that I'd have to buy the next one from the Weavers, who had a dark little music shop separated from their living quarters by a curtain of beads. I had gone there once to pick up a piano book for Marianne and was not eager to return because Mrs. Weaver looked like a witch. I'd have to make that first reed last forever.

Anyone who could play a simple scale was thrown into the high school band immediately. The lowest chairs in every section were occupied by grade school players terrified of committing a gross and humiliating error. But it was a different kind of ignorance that humiliated me on Monday, December 8, 1941. Pearl Harbor Sunday didn't happen for me until Monday.

Elise Bartelsen, who sat next to me, said, "What do you think about those dirty Japs?"

I shrugged, not knowing what she was talking about, and followed Mr. Wenzel's downbeat for "Finlandia." I could almost manage that one and prayed that he wouldn't do "Country Gardens" next.

After a few bars, he cut us off with an angry baton tattoo. "Concentrate, people, concentrate! We all know there's a war on, but as far as this band is concerned, it's business as usual."

"War?" I whispered to Elise.

"Where have you been, down a well?"

I reddened and let her enlighten me in snatches throughout the rehearsal. Aunt Kam and Uncle Karl surely would have told us, but they had arrived home very late after a weekend at Marianne's college. The big radio the Farleys had left in the house stood in the cold dining room, and while we usually wrapped ourselves in blankets to listen to Jack Benny on Sunday nights, we had forgotten to turn him on until it was too late and had given up on radio programming for the evening. We probably were the only people in the entire country who didn't know.

By lunchtime, Germany and Italy had declared war on the United States, and I had had so little time to absorb the first shock of the Axis assault that I was reeling. I rushed home to check my hidden supply of canned goods and take another inventory of the closet.

Grandma sighed. "At least we have no men to give up, but think of the folks who do!"

Wayne Andrews was one of the first to volunteer for the Navy. Marianne came home from college, hoping to marry him before he reported for duty, but both families insisted that they wait. They yielded to the pressure reluctantly and exchanged presumably passionate letters daily. During Christmas vacation Wayne's letters came to Marianne at home, and because she was hired as extra holiday help at the Golden Rule and couldn't open them the moment they arrived, she asked me to bring them to her at the store.

I couldn't see Aunt Kam's mailbox from the warm part of our house, so I put on my coat and stood in the Farley parlor until the mailman came. With a paring knife and a small jar of paste in my pocket, I could lock myself in the bathroom in the library's basement to open, read, and reseal the letters from the Great Lakes Naval Training Station before delivering them to Marianne at the Golden Rule.

Expecting grand passion and exalted phrases from a fighting man to his love, I was disappointed by Wayne's dull reports of his daily routine. Half the time he didn't even tell Marianne he loved her. I was madly curious about what she said to him, but I knew I would never find out. She wrote to him at night and mailed the letters on her way to work.

Once when I got the paste on the envelope flap slightly lumpy, she said, "The censors must be reading these. Imagine them using plain old library paste!" Before she went back to school, she gave me a necklace of hers that looked like tiny bits of hard candy in return for my delivery service. I'd always admired that necklace, but I couldn't wear it without a pang of guilt. I wished I'd never read Wayne's stupid letters.

When the *Harlan Tribune* ran a story about lonely servicemen who wanted pen pals, I spent the better part of a Saturday morning composing a passionate, encouraging letter to one Private Timothy Gaither at an APO address. Perhaps Private Gaither was killed in action before he received the letter signed "Your Secret Love." That was the only reason I could think of for his failure to reply. It was just as well, I supposed, because the meager supply of coins I had stashed in a metal paper-towel dispenser the Farleys had left behind wouldn't buy much stationery, and even *I* knew that fatal women didn't write letters on lined tablet paper.

1 4

M Y L O N G P U N I S H M E N T for running away on the county maintenance vehicle had put me out of favor with the Edelsteins, blighting my budding career as a baby-sitter. I considered telling Mrs. Edelstein that I was older and more responsible now, but I didn't have the nerve. It seemed easier to solicit business among those who hadn't witnessed my disgrace on Tenth Street.

The Arps down the block on Ninth Street had three kids, and Mrs. Arp liked to play golf. I rang their bell, but even after Mrs. Arp opened the door, I had trouble getting her attention. She was carrying Tyler, the baby, and he was pulling on a lamp cord. As she steadied the lamp, he yanked the plug from the socket and beamed at the prospect of an electrified pacifier.

I stated my business as Mrs. Arp deprived Tyler of the cord. He bawled.

"What do you charge?" she shouted.

"What do you pay?" I shouted back.

"Ten cents an hour."

"That's what I charge."

She thrust Tyler into my arms, and he was so surprised that he stopped screaming. It seemed that I was to be put to work immediately. After telling me that Jimmy was outside somewhere and Marilyn was upstairs, Mrs. Arp touched up her lipstick and left.

With Tyler balanced on my hip like an animated bag of flour, I rounded up Jimmy and Marilyn and told them I was in charge. They took the news with a certain degree of belligerence.

"O.K.," I said, "just go back to whatever you were doing, then. I'm going to tell Tyler a story."

"He's too little for stories," Marilyn said scornfully.

I ignored her and began, "Once upon a time there was a big, fat genie who lived in a bottle as big as the water tower. In fact, it *was* the water tower, and everytime somebody turned on the faucet—"

"What?" Jimmy pressed. "What happened when they turned on the faucet?"

"The genie made himself all skinny and slithered out into the sink."

"That's silly," Marilyn said, but I noticed that she wasn't going back upstairs. She sat on the carpet, cross-legged.

Making up the story line by line, I kept the Arp kids quiet for two hours and earned twenty cents. I should have paused to change Tyler's diaper, but I didn't know how, and besides, that would have broken the spell.

Mrs. Arp seemed pleased with my services and asked for my phone number. When I told her we had the other phone, she sighed and said she'd send one of the kids up with a note when she wanted me.

When I told Wyonne about my new job, she said she felt sorry for me. She'd taken care of the Arp kids once, and they tore the house apart. She never went back.

"You just have to know how to handle them," I said loftily.

Mrs. Arp went out a lot—enough to make the dimes jangle loudly in the paper-towel dispenser. Jimmy and Marilyn said I was their favorite baby-sitter, and Tyler would have said the same if he could talk. All I had to do was make up stories, the scarier the better. I adapted Arabian Nights tales, throwing in a few extra beheadings and boilings in oil. Little did I know that I was giving the Arp kids screaming nighmares. I found out the day I walked past their house and saw a high school girl chasing Jimmy around the yard, grabbing him and prying a book of matches from his fist. Marilyn was sitting in the grass near the sidewalk dumping the contents of a silver salt shaker on an anthill. I asked her who the girl was.

"June. She's a dumb baby-sitter, and I hate her!"

"Why didn't your mother call me?"

"The stories. I told her we *like* to be scared, but she called June anyhow!"

"How did she know about the stories?"

"I told her the one about the princess they threw in the hole with the snakes. I couldn't remember all of it, and Mom said that was a good thing. Tell it again, Margaret, please!"

I was touched by her interest but determined never to give away anything I could sell. I sighed and went home to count my dimes, wishing I had collected more before the roof fell in.

It was summer, however, and I found a newspaper ad for a hired girl on a farm west of town. Because Grandma lived with us and did so much of the housework, I wasn't skilled, but I called the number, and when Mrs. Beekman came to town for groceries, she stopped at our house. I think she figured I had to be all right if I was related to Grandma, and besides, she said hired girls were hard to find with everybody off somewhere doing war work. She told me to pack my things, and she'd pick me up when she had finished her shopping. I wouldn't even get to say good-bye to Mom—except by telephone.

The next morning I got up before daylight to help with breakfast, and the long day was filled with cleaning and kitchen jobs like shelling peas and peeling potatoes. The peas I could manage, but the potatoes were miniaturized by my knife. The worst job of all was washing the separator, which had a rancid, metallic smell.

Mrs. Beekman kept me busy every minute of the day except for the half hour after the noon meal. At that time she retired to an upstairs room to rest while her husband and the hired man stretched out on the grass for a quick nap. Janis, the Beekmans' four-year-old daughter, was supposed to nap, too, but she often sneaked downstairs to disturb my free time. A massive upright piano decorated with carved leaves and with one piece of sheet music on the rack stood in the stale-smelling parlor. I took great pleasure in picking out "My Heart At Thy Sweet Voice" on the yellowed keys.

"Listen to my fond wooing," I sang softly, and then I felt it—moisture on my upper arm. Janis stood behind me grinning, saliva trickling from her lower lip. The first time she spit on me to get my attention, I couldn't believe it had happened. The second time, I told her it was a disgusting thing to do. The third time, I grabbed her and wiped my arm on her dress.

"I'll tell Mama!"

"If you do, she'll know you're not napping. Just go away and leave me alone."

"I don't have to. This is *my* house."

"Then *I'll* go." I stalked out of the parlor, skirted the sleeping men, and headed for the watering tank near the barn. Mossy scum floated at the edges of the water, and I rubbed a gob of it between my fingers, thinking it was both delicious and disgusting. It hinted at things I knew nothing about. "My heart at thy sweet voice unfolds like a flower—"

I didn't see Janis, but I felt her, and when I wheeled to glare at her, I saw that she was carrying a cooky—a big, sweet wheel studded with fat raisins. Though we had just finished a meal, I lusted for that cooky. My hunger was constant, and Mrs. Beekman's pointed remark, "You eat like a thrasher," humiliated me, but it didn't stop me from taking second and third helpings of everything. I never had been unduly interested in food, and this new ravenous appetite puzzled and disturbed me.

Determined as I was not to utter them, the words escaped from my mouth. "Give me a bite, Janis."

"No!" She thrust the cooky behind her back and ran to the other side of the tank.

I caught her easily, breaking the crisp cooky from her fingers. As Janis screamed for her mother, I ran to an alfalfa field, cleared two strands of barbed wire, and devoured what I had stolen. Then I stood there taking deep, frantic breaths. Even with the sky wide above me, I felt suffocated. The summer was heavy on my body, and I longed for cold weather, when the trees would drop the leaves that kept me from breathing, when the blue inverted bowl would lift and give me air.

Mrs. Beekman shrieked at me from the porch, "Come here this minute!"

My impulse was to run the other way, but I walked toward her doggedly, ashamed that my guts were so much stronger than my will that I would stoop to stealing from a child—even an obnoxious child like Janis.

"Get your things. I'm taking you home right now, and it's not just because you're mean to Janis. You eat more than you're worth."

As I put my belongings into an old suitcase of Grandma's, I caught my reflection in the streaked mirror above the dresser. My upper arms were like broomsticks, and the faded cotton dress that had fit me the summer before hung from my shoulders like a sack. Where did all the food go? What was the matter with me? I tore at the neck of the dress, choking in the hot, close room. At least I'd be back in my own bed and away from the smell of cornshucks—away from the dead quiet of country night and the blackness that lay on my face like a wet cloth.

Mom and Grandma were surprised to see me, and Mom raised an eyebrow when Mrs. Beekman complained about my disgraceful appetite.

"I find that hard to believe," Mom said. "From the looks of her, she's been eating table scraps."

"Ha!" said Mrs. Beekman. "If I don't watch her, she'll eat the whole meal before it gets to the table."

"Thank you for bringing Margaret home," Grandma said, and Mrs. Beekman knew she had been dismissed.

As soon as she was gone, Mom phoned Dr. Petersen and begged him to see me right away. I asked her why I couldn't go to Dr. Reilly, and she said that Dr. Petersen knew my history. I decided not to remind her that Dr. Petersen hadn't been so smart when I went to him with my earache.

The one good thing about Dr. Petersen was his subscription to the *Saturday Evening Post,* which I read in the waiting room. It was a few months old, but I was accustomed to being behind the times. Had I not felt hungry and stifled, I would have been fairly content. We didn't have to wait long, because most of Dr. Petersen's patients had switched to Dr. Reilly, and we weren't in the examining room long either.

Probing my neck with his red, scaly hands, Dr. Petersen said, "We'll keep an eye on her for awhile."

"What's wrong with her?" Mom pressed.

"She's too young for what I think it is. Let's wait and see."

"The last time you said that, we nearly lost her."

Now, Mrs. Langelund, don't get all excited. Whatever she's got, it's nothing you die from."

On the way home we stopped at Aunt Kam's because she wanted me to try on some clothes of Marianne's that could be made to fit me. I hated to stand still while Mom and Aunt Kam pinned, measured, and argued, but I did it, slipping so deeply into reverie that they had to shout "Turn!" Several times before I responded.

"She has a waistline like Scarlet O'Hara," Aunt Kam said. "You really ought to see that movie, Petra, it's fantastic."

"Movies take time and money, and I don't have much of either."

I wasn't crazy about Marianne's clothes. She had gone through a sophisticated phase, only to discover that Wayne preferred the girl-next-door look, and the black, slinky dresses she was discarding were even more unsuitable for me.

7 9

"We'll have to put a handkerchief across the bosom of this one," Aunt Kam said, pulling a black silk jersey dress over my head. "I don't know why I ever let her buy it."

"Maybe Margaret can wear a blouse under it," Mom said. "It's beautiful material."

It was plain awful, and if Mom ever made me wear it anywhere, I'd double back and change before anyone saw me. With a pointed hat and a broomstick, I'd be ready for Halloween.

As it turned out, I did have to wear that dress once. Mr. Wenzel ordered us to "put on something dark and plain" for a district music contest. The lace insert Grandma had sewn into the neckline choked me, and I ripped it out, displaying an expanse of winter-white skin that moved the judge to write on my rating sheet: "This girl should be spanked." But in spite of his inattention to my musicianship, he gave me a first rating.

I continued to eat like a thrasher, look like a skeleton, and gasp in the cold air that failed to bring me the expected relief. Dr. Petersen still wanted to wait and see.

In the alley behind our house was an old cistern the Farleys had been filling with trash for years, and I managed to slide the heavy, metal cover aside to thrust the black silk jersey dress into its odorous depths. I told Mom I'd lost the dress.

"One doesn't lose a dress," she said. "Particularly when one doesn't travel."

"Maybe one would like to," Grandma said, giving me a look that came as close to a wink of complicity as she ever got. "Never mind, Petra, it was all wrong for her."

"But it was such good material."

"Too slippery for quilts," Grandma said, and that was the end of it.

1 5

D E S P E R A T E for gainful employment, I tried picking strawberries, but the continual squatting and rising was too much for the muscles at the backs of my thighs. After a single day in the big patch on the Hoover place at the south edge of town, I resigned.

Mom sometimes said she had "a dark brown feeling," and I knew what she meant as I washed dried mud and strawberry juice from my hands at the whining pump and reviewed the remarks of the other pickers.

"Old Langelund just sits in the row like a toad."

"Naw, she crawls."

My harvest was meager, and I think Mrs. Hoover was relieved when I told her I wouldn't be back. At least she wasn't unkind when she gave me a handful of cool silver.

"Something wrong with you, honey?"

I shook my head, fighting tears. Something *was* wrong. I had to pull myself up a flight of stairs with sheer arm power, and I wouldn't be upright now if Mrs. Hoover hadn't given me a hand at the end of the row. It was humiliating.

The worst part was going home to confess that I'd quit. I could just hear Mom saying, "We're not quitters," and I had to be the exception to the rule. Why couldn't I be like Wyonne? She shinnied up the rope in gym as naturally as she breathed and took the school steps three at a time.

Mom didn't scold. I would have felt better if she had.

"The library is open tonight," she said. "Why don't you walk up there with me?"

Looking at books improved my spirits. I was feeling almost cheerful when I picked Cornelia Otis Skinner's *Our Hearts Were Young and Gay* to take home. Time melted so fast in the library that I supposed I was keeping Mom waiting, but I was the one who had to wait. She was busy in the reference section until Miss Winnie Craig flicked the lights to signal closing.

Clearly she didn't want to tell me what she was looking up, and since my dark brown feeling had returned, we walked home in a tense silence of avoidance. Grandma had a pitcher of lemonade waiting for us. She had saved the squeezed lemon cups for me to turn inside out and nibble. Usually I sprinkled them with sugar, but tonight I took them straight in penance for being a quitter.

When the hybrid seed company advertised for corn detasselers, I figured that anyone who could walk could do the job. I signed on, hoping to make up for my disgraceful showing in the strawberry patch. Talking Lotus into joining me wasn't easy. With her allowance, she didn't need the money, but I pointed out that she was too old to make plaster plaques in the park, she didn't like to read, and she was sick of visiting her married sisters on the farm. It would be something to do.

The crew was to meet on the courthouse lawn at 6:15 A.M., so I set the Big Ben alarm for 5:00 A.M. Mom and Grandma got up, too. They stoked me with hot oatmeal and toast and fixed *frikadeller* sandwiches for my lunch. I wanted to wear my good slacks, but Mom said I'd ruin them and made me put on a pair that was nearly worn out and one of her old blouses. She told me I'd have to wear a jacket, too, and worried that I didn't have a cap with a sun visor.

"After all, Margaret, you're not going to a party."

Viewing my triple image in the Farley bedroom mirror, I died a little. This was as bad as Mom's egg candling outfit.

Lotus met me at the O'Neills' corner, and she didn't look much better. She gave me a sour look and said, "I don't know why I ever let you talk me into this."

Slumber parties had taught me that Lotus was not at her best in the early morning, so I didn't try to make conversation as we walked toward the Square. I had that simmering feeling of being on the brink of an adventure that heightens the senses. Everything registered—a dewdrop caught in a cobweb, the Mentholatum tingle of morning air that smelled like bleached sheets, the way our long shadows did a left face as we turned north.

We were early but not the first to assemble at the foot of the Civil War statue, a doleful soldier in a billed cap and a long coat holding a gun and staring at his boots. I was amazed to see Mary Lois Engle there, but I wasn't surprised that she was dressed as I'd wanted to be—in good slacks, freshly-polished saddle shoes, and a crisp plaid blouse. She was straight out of an Andy Hardy movie. Some of the guys were horsing around, punching each other on the arms while the rest of us made nervous small talk. Nobody seemed to be in charge until a flatbed truck with no sides pulled up and stopped. The driver jumped out and told us to sign his clipboard.

Jerking her thumb at the truck, Lotus said, "Are we going to ride on that?"

"Yeah," the driver said, "climb on."

The truck bed was high—too high for me. Lotus scrambled up and tried to pull me, but my muscles just wouldn't cooperate. I was ready to give up and go home when a husky guy grabbed me and pitched me aboard. I recognized him as Muscles McGowan, a one-time Park School kid now doubly scorned because he rode a motorcycle.

"Thanks," I said, grateful in spite of the fact that he'd landed me on my lunch sack and squashed my sandwiches.

He grinned, clenched his fist to make a Popeye muscle and tossed another girl onto the truck. She didn't need help and she slugged him.

When the truck lurched into motion, we clutched anybody close to us and screamed, expecting to be thrown off and under the wheels. I managed to back up against the cab, and the ride got easier when we had passed a stretch of old brick street. Mary Lois was giggling with Muscles and some of his friends, tossing her head when her hair blew across her face, and fingering the gold heart locket around her neck. She made a great mystery of the picture in that locket, but I happened to know it was her mother. I looked while she was taking a shower after gym, but I didn't tell anybody. The knowledge was simply a secret shield against the inferiority she made me feel so often. I also knew that she didn't shower after gym. She fooled the teacher by undressing and turning the water on, but she was plastered to a dry side of the stall the whole time.

Somebody started "There's a Hole in the Bottom of the Sea" and we all joined in, bellowing add-on verses. I sang as loudly as anyone, but I couldn't lose myself in the group. I seemed to float beside or above the truck viewing an animated painting—happy workers on the way to their labors.

The truck stopped with a jolt, and we had to get down to business. It was well past the Fourth of July, when the oldtimers said the corn was supposed to be knee-high, but I hadn't expected stalks above my head. When the rows were assigned, I entered a tunnel of greenish light so hot and steamy that it made me gasp. Moving among the long leaves that funneled collected dew all over my body, I reached and tugged. My shoes became huge mudballs. Those long leaves also slashed like knives, forcing me to protect my face with a forearm. Struggling for a reach-pull rhythm, I heard my own heart's rocking thud. I'd never felt more alone.

"Lotus?" No answer.

"Mary Lois?" Nothing.

"Who's yellin'?"

That was Muscles McGowan's voice, and it came from up ahead. I'd have to work faster.

After what seemed like two days of slogging and pulling, the overseer blew a whistle for lunch break. We rushed to the truck for our lunch sacks. The truck bed provided the only shade in sight. Lotus rolled under it in a hurry and saved me a spot.

My sandwiches were squashed and the cookies were crushed. Only the apple was in its original condition, the way Mom packed it that morning. Wrapped in newspaper and stored in the cellar since the fall harvest, it looked like an old woman's face. It would taste O.K., but nobody I knew kept apples like that. Embarrassed, I shoved the apple into my pocket to eat later in the privacy of my own steamy row. The postponement cost me something, because I'd scarcely taken the edge off my appetite with the rubble of two double sandwiches and the crumbs of a dozen sugar cookies.

Mary Lois pulled the crusts off the white-bread of her sandwich and began to swing her arm to throw them away. I caught her wrist and heard myself begging for them. I didn't mean to ask, I didn't want to ask, and I couldn't believe that I was doing it, but the voice was mine. She dropped the crusts in my hand with a look that took me back to the day when I colored my tree trunks black, but I didn't care. Something fierce and demanding inside me had to be fed, and no humiliation was sufficient to deny that need. When I finished Mary Lois's crusts, I scavenged other leftovers until the whistle sent us back to our green tunnels.

Soon after lunch the overseer swore at me for working the wrong row. Fortunately, I hadn't gone far when the mistake was discovered, but now I had the nervous feeling that he was watching me every minute from some unseen vantage point.

I tried to distract myself by reviewing *Blood and Sand,* the Tyrone Power movie I'd seen at least six times. That funny little bullfighter's hat with the ears didn't do much for Tyrone, but he was gorgeous in the scene where Rita Hayworth wore a bright red bra under a sheer white blouse.

Even Tyrone Power couldn't blot out my misery. Tiny slashes from the corn leaves smarted like paper cuts. The sun that burned away the morning dew replaced it with sweat. Exhausted by the reaching and pulling, I longed to drop where I was and sleep, but only a hog would lie down in that muddy row, so I kept moving. I was hungry again, too. I reminded myself that Mary Lois Engle was suffering just as much, punishing her perfect, unlined hands in another row. If she could do it, I could.

The quitting whistle was a cadenza from the Angel Gabriel. Muscles McGowan scarcely had the strength to hoist me onto the truck, and when we were dumped at the courthouse more dead than alive, the driver told us to report at the same hour the next day.

"I'm not about to," Lotus said flatly.

I wished I could say the same, but after the strawberry picking, it was impossible. At least I'd made it through the day.

A violent thunderstorm in the night cut the next day's working hours in half. When I presented myself at 6:15 A.M., I was told to come back at 1:00 P.M. I went home and slept like the dead until Grandma woke me for a big lunch.

Half a day might be bearable, I decided. I missed Lotus, but Mary Lois was back, this time in an old pair of slacks and a faded top. She told me she was earning money for a new dress for her piano recital and asked what brought me back. I didn't really answer her, because I didn't want to talk about quitting at the strawberry patch, and I didn't want to tell her that having some money would make me feel safe. That was what money did, I thought, but I couldn't be sure because I'd never had much of it.

The humid afternoon was horrible. We struggled to breathe the

8 4

heavy, steaming air, feeling like stewing chickens in a lidded pot. Sunlight through the corn made us green all over, and the knife-edged leaves hatched our arms with cuts.

The overseer caught me shielding my face with one arm and hauled me out of the row, yelling, "How the hell can you see the tassels with your eyes covered up?"

"I can see over my arm."

"In a pig's eye, you can! I'll pay you for a day and a half at quittin' time, and that's all for you."

Stunned, I stumbled back into the row and looked for the place where I had been interrupted. It was hard to see anything through a salty wash of tears and harder still to believe I'd been fired. The shame of it was beyond bearing.

Somehow I finished the day and got as far away from Mary Lois as possible on the way home. After hoisting me up, Muscles McGowan hunkered down beside me, smelling like a thousand gym lockers and picking at the burrs on his socks.

"Jeez, what a job!" he said. "It almost makes you hope you'll die before tomorrow."

"Yeah," I said, hoping he wouldn't notice my swollen eyes. Crying beautifully was reserved for the movies. Muscles gave me a stick of Juicy Fruit gum, and I decided he was pretty decent for a north Harlan guy. He had blackheads and wide-apart front teeth, but he was strong, and he was in high school.

When we got to the courthouse (the driver wouldn't stop and let anybody off, even if he passed their house), Muscles helped me down and unchained his motorcycle from the flagpole to ride away. I wondered if he'd miss me when I didn't show up the next day. The thought triggered the return of my shame, and I swore I'd never allow myself to be fired by anyone from any job for any reason ever again.

Dragging myself home, I dumped my filthy outer garments on the back porch floor. Grandma put a fresh cinnamon roll into my dirty hand, and Mom turned on the bathtub faucets, dumping Dreft into the water to make bubbles.

"Margaret," Mom said, "I don't want you to go back to the field tomorrow. I think it's hard on your health."

"O.K.," I said meekly, despising my cowardice but rationalizing that I was sparing her feelings thereby. Swallowing the last delicious bite of the warm roll, I sank into the bubbles and thought about Muscles McGowan. Win a few, lose a few.

But I lost it all that day. Muscles must have been pretty tired after his afternoon in the cornfield. Later that night he lost control of his motorcycle and rammed into the railroad overpass south of town. Mom was puzzled about my crying over someone I didn't even know, and that made me cry all the harder, remembering exactly how it felt when Muscles grabbed me just above the knees and pitched me onto the truck.

"Jeez, what a job! It almost makes you hope you'll die before tomorrow."

I had nightmares for awhile, and that's probably why Mom let me go to the Iowa State Fair with the high school band. We didn't have to wear our uniforms—white duck pants, worn navy twill jackets with gold braid, and gas-station-attendant caps—and Mom offered to make me a new skirt for the trip in her effort to distract me from my mysterious woes. Usually I disliked homemade clothes, but the brilliant aqua print of the skirt was so glorious that it made me feel like Jeanne Crain warbling "It's a Grand Night for Singing."

Some of the band parents drove us to Des Moines in their cars, and after we had finished our pavillion performance and locked up our instruments, we were free to enjoy the fair. Nearly everyone headed for the thrill rides and cotton candy of the midway, but I was lured by the stock barns where I could commune with velvety cattle that had crimped hair, hogs bigger and better than Blue Boy in the *State Fair* movie, and horses that gleamed as if they'd been oiled. The ash-fine dust of the barn floors seeped into my sandals and between my toes as I spoke to the animals. I told a gigantic Chester White hog that I would have been a 4-H girl if Daddy had lived, and then we enjoyed such a long, companionable silence that I nearly missed my ride home.

It was very late when we came over the rise east of town and saw Harlan below us, a tiara on dark velvet. The effect was almost entirely due to streetlights, as all decent citizens were asleep in dark houses.

I thought I was being utterly quiet when I let myself in the back door, but Mom heard me and asked if I brought my clarinet home safely. I had.

"Good. Hurry to bed."

Reviewing the sights and sounds of the day took some time—I did a silent-movie version of my Jeanne Crain act for the bathroom mirror while brushing my teeth, and I decided I needed a quick bath. The windowshade was only half-drawn, but it didn't matter at such a late hour. When I had dried myself, I turned toward the window to reach for my pajamas and froze, transfixed by a segment of khaki-clad torso visible below the shade. The scream was an afterthought, a convention demanded by books and movies.

The sound got instant results. The khaki vanished, Mom rushed into the bathroom, and Grandma would have been there just as soon if she hadn't paused to grab the metal handle used for lifting stove lids as she ran through the kitchen.

"A man was standing there."

Grandma gripped the metal handle tighter and headed for the back door.

"Don't go out there, Mama," Mom said, "he might be dangerous."

"I'll show *him* who's dangerous!"

Grandma disappeared into the night, Mom went after her, and the only thing for me to do was to put on my pajamas and follow. We circled the house and checked the alley, discovering nothing but a barking dog.

"Pesky Peeping Tom!" Grandma said.

I was reviewing my scream, thinking how loud and impressive it had been. I'd never done it before, because Aunt Kam always said "Jorgen women don't scream." Maybe they should, I thought. It was most satisfactory.

It never occurred to any of us to call the sheriff, and we went to bed unafraid, but it was some time before I could encounter a man wearing khaki pants without wondering how much of me he'd seen before.

1 6

I NEVER SAW Grandma so happy as she was on the day when the mailman brought a letter from Uncle Stig saying that he was coming for a visit. At least that's what we *thought* it said. His handwriting was worse than a little kid's with the lines kiting upward to the top right corner of the page.

"My boy, my boy," she said softly, smoothing the folds of the single sheet and putting it between the pages of her Danish Bible. Anything kept in that Bible was precious—a blue silk marker commemorating the dedication of the Shelby County Courthouse in 1893, olive green four-leaf clovers pressed flat and brittle, and this rare letter.

I'd never seen Uncle Stig, but Mom had some snapshots of him in his soldier uniform. He had traveled with a carnival and worked as a cowboy in the west, and when I asked Mom if he looked like Gary Cooper in his cowboy outfit, she said, "No, he looks more like me."

He had just been divorced from his wife, Betty, and Mom and Aunt Kam were having a big discussion about whether they should mention her name to him.

"We've never had a divorce in our family," Aunt Kam said, "so how are we supposed to know how to handle it? I think it's best just to pretend it never happened."

"I know Stig better than you do," Mom said. "We were closer in age. I'd like to know how he feels and what this has done to him. I never was crazy about Betty, but we can't pretend she never existed. Even if she did trick Stig into marrying her, they had some happy times, and we can't just wipe her out."

"*I* can," Aunt Kam said with a sniff. She was good at sniffs because she had what she called "a patrician nose," as straight and strong as if it had been carved by an expert whittler.

"How did she trick him?" I asked, not because I didn't know, but because I wanted to hear it straight out instead of eavesdropping on the story of Betty putting a pillow under her dress and telling Uncle Stig she was going to have a baby.

"Never you mind," Aunt Kam said. "Let the dead past bury its dead."

"Just be good to Stig," Grandma pleaded, and that was surprising, because she never asked for anything.

"You always babied him too much, Mama," Aunt Kam said.

"He's my only son."

"Why did they get divorced?" I asked.

Three pairs of eyes turned on me, and I expected to be ordered from the room as I sometimes was when they became aware of my presence. This time there was silence.

Finally Aunt Kam said, "Might as well tell her."

Mom sighed. "They blamed each other for not having children."

"A judgment for what she did, I'd call it!" Aunt Kam said.

"That's for God to know and us to guess," Grandma said.

I wasn't sure that having children was such a great blessing. They might turn out like Janis Beekman. Aunt Kam never had babies of her own, and Uncle Karl never would divorce *her*. All in all, I thought childlessness was a flimsy excuse, and I said as much.

"There's something else, too," Mom said. "Betty started to drink too much, and they couldn't live together."

"You always talk about Uncle Stig drinking—why should he care if Betty does?"

Grandma looked pained and Aunt Kam cleared her throat loudly, indicating that I was getting too big for my britches.

"A woman can't take booze the way a man can," Mom said. "Not that it's right for *anybody*."

I knew nothing at all about booze, but I did notice that Uncle Stig smelled pretty strong when he came in on the train. He ran toward Grandma and lifted her right off the ground, hugging her while her neat, black oxfords dangled like a doll's shoes.

"*Lille* Mama!"

"*Nuh, suh,* Stig!" she scolded, flailing to be put down.

He laughed and set her on her feet, kissing her hard on the mouth. He kissed Mom on the mouth, too, but Aunt Kam turned her cheek to his lips. While he was talking to Grandma, she pulled Mom aside and whispered, "Don't lick your lips, and be sure to scrub the minute you get home. He's probably got all kinds of nasty diseases."

When Uncle Stig finally noticed me, he said, "Who is this young race horse?"

"You know very well it's Margaret, Stig," Mom said, "and you were the first to know she was coming, remember?"

"His big smile faded. "Yeah, and I thought I'd have the same kind of news for you before you could say 'Jack Robinson,' but it didn't work out that way." Then the light came back to his eyes, and I felt his hard calluses as he took my hand to pull me close for a big hug. Uncle Karl wasn't the hugging kind, so this was a new experience for me. I liked it. He let me go to pick up his suitcase, throwing his free arm around Mom's shoulders as we walked out of the station.

"Well, Pete, you and I have fallen on rocky places."

"We're getting along, Stig, and you will too—in time."

"Sure, sure. I figured it might help to crawl home like a hound dog that tangled with a barbed wire fence. I'll lay around and lick myself for awhile, and then I'll be good as new."

Uncle Stig stayed with us because he wanted to be near Grandma, and besides, Aunt Kam didn't want his germs in her house. Mom put him in the front bedroom with the Farleys' black furniture, and he called it "a bloomin' funeral parlor."

She said he wouldn't know the difference when he was asleep and told him to wash up because supper was nearly ready. I hoped she wouldn't ask me to set the table, because I wanted to hang around Uncle Stig and study him. She seemed to understand that.

He wasn't as tall as Gary Cooper, and he was a lot heavier. His hair, brilliantined to a muddy blond, had stained the band of the wide-brimmed hat he threw on the bed. I snatched it up to prevent bad luck and decided that Uncle Stig looked sort of neglected—like an empty house.

Mom called us to the kitchen, where he pulled out a chair and beckoned to me to perch on his knee. "Tell your fortune, young lady?"

"All right," I said, remembering Mom's story of how my dead Aunt Else hated that. I might hate it too, but I had to be polite to company.

He turned my palm up and spat into it with stinging precision. The saliva felt cool, and yet it burned with an intimacy that bewildered me. The broad forefinger rotating to spread the moisture revolted and fascinated me at the same time.

"There's a bar across the lifeline way down here."

"That would be the mastoid," Mom said, expertly flipping the fried potatoes in an unbroken round.

"Here's another one farther up."

"Oh, no!"

"That's enough, Stig," Grandma warned. "Telling fortunes is the devil's business."

"Don't get excited, Mama, I'll stick to the good stuff. This girl has a star in her palm. That means—"

Grandma seemed to know what that meant and didn't think it should be encouraged, so Uncle Stig dropped it. He lifted a stove burner and rubbed some soot into my hand to make the lines stand out.

"Let's see, now. Aha! Pete, you're going to have to beat the young bucks off with a club."

"Don't give her ideas."

Grandma narrowed her eyes and said, "She *was* born on Midsummer's Eve."

"What does that mean?" I asked, and nobody would answer.

"That's enough, Stig," Grandma said.

"Just one more thing—" he spoke to me now. "You've got a little room inside of you that's padlocked. Don't let anybody jimmy the lock. Wait for the guy with the key. Now jump up and wash your hands."

We had *frikadeller* for supper, and Uncle Stig made a big fuss over it. We had it all the time, but I guess he didn't. Having a man at the table was nice. Mom and Grandma kept his plate full, and he praised everything put in front of him. He said he didn't have room for dessert, but Mom had made a burnt-sugar cake, so he made room. Then he lit a long cigar, the crowning mannish touch. I hoped he would tell stories about the carnival and being a cowboy, but he soon pushed away from the table.

"Guess I'll see what's going on around the Square."

Grandma looked worried, but she didn't say anything.

Mom said, "I don't think any of your old friends are around anymore."

He sighed. "*Ya, suh*! Harvey Wimer went out in the Argonne, Storm Johnson is serving time at Ft. Madison, and I've lost track of Elmer Kautz. Are you sure Elmer isn't hanging around here somewhere?"

"If he were, I'd be the last to know," Mom said. "I'll never forget the first time he brought you home drunk."

"Good, old Elmer. It wasn't that he had a better head for booze than I did—it made him sick, so he pretty much left it alone."

"Too bad it didn't make *you* sick," Grandma said.

"Come on, Mama, I'm a big boy now. Say, Pete, is Green Apple Mary still in town? She must be old as God."

"The wages of sin is the county home. That poor old thing wanders in her mind. She doesn't know anybody—not even her daughter."

"Old Mary's got a daughter? Does she follow her mama's trade?"

"Not for money."

Grandma said, "Haven't you had enough woman trouble for awhile, Stig?"

"They're no trouble when they don't belong to you. Good night, ladies."

As soon as the door closed after him, Mom made a disinfectant solution to scrub the toilet set, wiping all the doorknobs with it for good measure. She separated his dishes and silverware in an enamel basin and poured the rest of the stuff over them.

"Ask me before you go to the toilet, Margaret, and keep your hands away from your mouth."

"Why?"

"Better safe than sorry. I thought Kamille was being silly until I realized that he hasn't changed a bit."

Grandma got up from the table heavily, which told me that she felt bad. She wasn't a heavy woman, but some of her moods weighed a ton. "At least he's not in jail," she said.

Uncle Stig must have stayed out most of the night, because he still was asleep when Aunt Kam came to see him around noon. Sent to check on him, I opened the sliding doors just wide enough to see his clothes puddled beside the bed and sniff the same strong smell that came out of Herman's Tap on a hot summer night.

Aunt Kam was disgusted. She said, "I don't know why he has to come back here and disgrace us."

Grandma told her she shouldn't speak ill of her own blood. I knew he was getting up, because I could hear him knocking into the black furniture. I hoped he'd come out of there before I had to go back to school. He did, cussing his way to the kitchen and collapsing on a straight chair.

"Coffee, the dying man said!" He groaned and held his head.

"Stig, I wish you'd remember that we have to live in this town," Aunt Kam said. "Everything you do reflects on us."

"Don't worry. Mum's the word for that little lady in the trailer court."

"The trailer court!" Aunt Kam shrieked. "Those people are trash. Stig, how *could* you?"

"Almost couldn't—drank too much."

"And how can you talk that way in front of your own mother and a mere child? Margaret, you'd better go into the other room."

I went reluctantly, but not before I heard him say, "Kam, you give me a big fat pain in the ass. You make me want to go out and piss in the street."

That's when Grandma slapped him, the back door slammed after Aunt Kam, and he said, "Oh, God, what makes me do it?"

I peeked around the door frame and saw Uncle Stig sitting on the floor in front of Grandma's chair with his head in her lap. She stroked his hair for a moment, then pushed him away gently, and went to the stove to fry eggs.

When she went into the pantry to get something, he picked up the pancake turner to lift an egg from the skillet and eat it in a single bite. Mom had told me why he did that. When he traveled with the carnival, the dishes were too dirty to eat from. Seeing me lurking at the door, he motioned, and I came to sit beside him. He fed me a bite of toast as if I were a baby bird and started to tell about the time he rescued a lady stuck to a varnished toilet seat.

"That was when I was selling Fuller brushes, and she'd been there for two days, honest to God."

"Why didn't she get up before it dried?"

"Couldn't. It was fast-drying varnish that gripped like a bulldog."

Privately, I thought she was stupid to sit down in the first place, but Uncle Stig was waiting for me to ask how he saved the day, so I did.

"Found a pancake turner—just like this one—in the kitchen and pried her loose. Of course it smarted a little, but she was grateful—real grateful."

"I'd be so embarrassed that I'd die."

"Well, she was older than you, and we got to be real good friends."

"That's not really a true story, is it?"

"What do you think?"

I shook my head, blushing.

"You're right, honey. I was just trying to give you a little something that's missing in this henhouse. There's two kinds of people in this world—men and women—and you won't know scat about the kind you ain't if somebody doesn't teach you. Isn't that right?''

I nodded, thinking how much I had to learn about men. Wyonne and Monica had fathers and brothers, and Lotus at least had brothers, but I'd have to learn as much as I could from Uncle Stig while he was here. I followed him outside to the grape arbor and watched him light a cigar. Just when I was thinking about skipping school to stay with him all afternoon, he told me I'd better get going. I had to run all the way to beat the last bell.

When I got home, Uncle Stig wasn't around, and that gave me a chance to ask Grandma if he was a fair example of what a man ought to be.

"He would have been if Peter had lived to bring him up right, but for one reason or another, we're a clan of widows.''

"Not Aunt Kam.''

"No, and sometimes I feel sorry for Karl—saddled with all of us.''

Uncle Karl was sensible, dependable, and tired from being the only man among the Jorgen women. He was about the same age as Uncle Stig, but he seemed a lot older, and he didn't light up any room he entered the way Uncle Stig did.

A car stopped outside. Grandma brightened at the sound of whistling that turned to song. "I'm an old cow hand—''

Uncle Stig offered to go uptown for the makings if Grandma would stir up a batch of ale. She told him it would take awhile for the stuff to work and wondered if he'd be around that long.

"Sure," he said, "that's worth waiting for.''

The kitchen was filled with a raw, living smell as Grandma mashed ground malt in water, boiled the mixture with hops, cooled it, and threw in brewer's yeast. The brown cloudy liquid was poured into stone crocks, covered with china plates, and weighted with flatirons.

Mom walked in on the brewing and laughed. "I hope the preacher doesn't come to call just now.''

Flushed and happy, Grandma said, "I haven't done this since Peter was alive.''

"I remember," Uncle Stig said. "Papa gave me a sip, and you raised Cain. Tell you what—just to get my taste buds in shape, I'll go on the wagon until this batch is ready.''

I asked if I could have some, and Mom said I was too young. As it turned out, no one drank that ale. Uncle Stig couldn't wait for it to sit in the crocks as long as Grandma thought it should. He poured the ale into Mason jars with tight lids that exploded during the night, bringing down part of the kitchen ceiling. Uncle Stig took one look at the mess, tossed some bills on the table to pay for new plaster, and went back to Denver.

Grandma sighed and said, "God has a way of pulling at your sleeve when you're doing the wrong thing.''

"It wasn't God," Mom said, "it was Stig. He always *did* have to have what he wanted the minute he wanted it.''

"Now, now, he did wait a *few* days.''

9 3

Aunt Kam entirely disapproved of drinking and found the whole business disgusting. Uncle Karl was inclined to be amused, but one look from his wife took care of that.

"Well," he said, "Stig's gone, and it's back to business as usual."

He sounded sorry that his vacation from being the only man in the family was over. I was sorry, too. Whatever else he was, Uncle Stig was a male presence, and I could see how one could acquire a taste for having a man around the house. Scipio the tomcat didn't really count, and besides, the Benton ladies didn't want him to associate with me. Every time I found him in the bushes and tried to play with him, they called him inside.

Uncle Stig's visit did put a man under our roof, at least temporarily. However, the plasterer who came to restore the kitchen ceiling was a stolid Danish-American who never said a word and had no distinctive smell or flavor.

"For what he charged, I should have done it myself," Mom said, and we all knew that she could have done it.

Men weren't really necessary, I decided, but the right kind of man might be an interesting luxury.

1 7

LOTTIE ANDERSEN had such a meager social life that she didn't ask Mom to pay back the time owed her until I'd nearly forgotten my yearning to spend a night in the telephone office. Working nights and sleeping days made friendships impossible for Lottie, but she did have one living relative, a female cousin in Underwood.

"Guess I'll just climb on the bus at the Saylor Hotel and go down there for a night and a day," she said. "After all, blood is thicker than water."

Leaving home past my bedtime was a thrill. Mom knew exactly how long it took her to walk to the telephone office, but she always allowed an extra fifteen minutes "in case of emergency," so we didn't have to hurry. I had brushed my teeth at home, I was carrying my pajamas in a brown paper bag, and I had promised to go to sleep the minute we got there.

The night was warm and soft. New leaves on the trees showed their tender green in pools of light from the corner street lamps. More light shone from the basement and first floor windows of the high school, and we could hear music. Mom said it must be prom night.

"Can we go in and look? Just for a minute?"

"I guess so, but we can't stay long."

The halls were filled with laughing girls in long dresses and boys with slicked-down hair whose jackets seemed to stand away from their bodies the way new clothes sometimes did. Feeling out of place, I backed against the wall near a blank-eyed white statue in a niche, hugging my bag of pajamas to my chest.

Mom led the way to the balcony above the gymnasium, and I was surprised that she knew her way around the building. Below us was enchantment. Rosy light played on trellises twined with paper sweet peas. Couples danced bouncily to the music of a five-piece band and a brassy-voiced woman in a lavender satin dress that caught and radiated a pink spotlight. The scent of flowers, Brilliantine, and the stuff kids put on their pimples rose to the balcony in waves. Enthralled, I leaned over the rail for a better view, and my paper bag fell from my hand. It struck a dancing couple. They froze in momentary shock, then looked upward, laughing. I was paralyzed with embarrassment. When the boy bounded up the stairs to ask if I'd lost something, I looked the other way.

"It's mine," Mom said. "Thank you."

I fled and she followed. Even the blank-eyed statue seemed to scorn

9 5

my clumsiness, but it could have been worse. What if the pajamas I had worn for two nights had spilled out on the dance floor?

Thinking Lottie had left for Underwood, Mom was surprised to find her at the switchboard. Lottie explained that her bus didn't leave until eleven, and she had decided to work a few hours to get in on a little of the prom night excitement. She was a mountain of a woman, and when she slid off the high stool, she left the leather seat as warm as newly baked bread. She handed the headset to Mom and lumbered toward the back room to roll out the folding bed.

"Just put clean sheets on yesterday, so I didn't change them, all right?"

Mom couldn't answer because lights were winking all over the board. The corded plugs criss-crossed like red and green spaghetti as she repeated, "Number, please?" When there was a brief let-up, she asked Lottie, "Do people always talk so much this late at night?"

"It's the prom. Everybody with kids that age gets on the line to say how grand they looked and where they're going afterwards—all that. Pretty soon things will quiet down—until the taverns close."

"What happens then?"

"Barney Baker at the Evergreen Inn and Hank Kent at the Chicken Hut start calling the next of kin to lug the drunks home. Well, guess I'd better run."

The very thought of Lottie running made me want to giggle. People were pretty careless with words, I decided, and I wasted a lot of time visualizing what they actually said and missing what they really meant.

After I put on my pajamas in the toilet that smelled like Sweetheart soap, I climbed into the bed that smelled like Lottie. She had kidney trouble. Mom took off her shoes and lay down beside me, but she had to get up right away. The switchboard buzzed like a bumblebee. She tilted the shade of a small lamp to keep the light out of my eyes and told me to go to sleep.

I couldn't—not with the buzzing, the clicking of plugs, and the bright shafts of streetlight spearing through the cracks of the venetian blinds. When I did doze and dream of dancing in a yellow dress perfumed by Evening in Paris that smelled the way I wanted it to instead of the way it did, I was wakened by Mom's alarmed voice.

"Dr. Reilly, please hurry! The trooper says it's bad. The boy is still alive, but the girl—the girl was decapitated." The voice of Monica's father buzzed on the line, and Mom said, "Half a mile north of Avoca."

"What's decap—decap—whatever you said?"

"Oh, Margaret, there's been a terrible accident." She made another connection, and before she closed the key and got off the line, a woman screamed, "No! My God, no!" Lights blinked, the board buzzed, and Mom just sat there with her eyes closed tight.

"Mom? Aren't you going to answer?"

"I was praying for Lucille. I worked with her at the produce—it's Lucille's daughter, Janine. Number, please?"

I knew who Janine was. She worked at the dimestore on Saturdays, but she wouldn't tomorrow, because she was dead. Vivian Corley came to mind. When she died, I thought she was old, but now I knew she hadn't been. Why did God bother to create some people if He didn't plan to get more use out of them?

Could anyone really figure out why God did what He did? I'd gone to Sunday school and church for as long as I could remember, first in the country at Merrill's Grove Baptist Church where Mom kept me quiet with oyster crackers. Church came before Sunday school, and kids of all ages were expected to sit through the service without creating a disturbance. When we moved to town, it was the other way around. Mom tied a penny into the corner of my handkerchief and sent me to Bethel Baptist alone. She came later for church. The first time I went to Sunday school in town, I sang "Jesus Wants Me For A Sun Bean" with some puzzlement. A green bean? A baked bean? No, a sun bean.

The big, red brick church was younger than I was, and its swirled plaster and pale woodwork showed little promise of growing old and holy. The colored glass windows had no pattern—no lily petals to count during an endless sermon.

Baptists went to church from morning until night on Sundays. When I was old enough to attend Baptist Young People's Union meetings, I was sent. The hour conflicted with the Jack Benny program, but that cut no ice with Mom. I hated going to BYPU, I told her, because it was nothing but people who couldn't read getting up and trying to read something. Monica was more than half-right when she called it "your dumb church." After BYPU I had to stay for the evening sermon, slumping in the pew to contemplate the lighted likeness of a girlish Jesus with one hand on his heart and the other pointing skyward. A funeral home had given the church this picture that made Jesus seem like a person you've often seen but never met.

Occasionally Mom asked me if I'd given any thought to making a decision for Christ, and while I didn't dare to say no, I couldn't very well say yes. Every week our Sunday school teacher gave us a chance to take care of this matter, but for some reason, I was holding back.

The kids who went to our church didn't exist for me outside of it. I pretended not to know them at school, and that was fine with them. They were offended by the Tangee lipstick I applied after I left the house. Orange in the tube, it turned virulent pink on the lips. Jeannette Johnson from my Sunday school class said it was "worldly" and told me I looked like "the whore of Babylon," which she pronounced with an audible w.

"The Bible doesn't say you can't wear lipstick," I said in self-defense.

"Timothy 2:9," Jeannette said in her Sunday sing-song. " 'In like manner that women adorn themselves in modest apparel with shamefastness and sobriety; not with braided hair, and gold or pearls or costly raiment.' "

"Where's the 'not with lipstick'?"

"You have to read between the lines," she said with a tone that implied that she could and I couldn't.

Changing the subject seemed to be my best course, so I asked her if she'd seen the poster about the Harmony Gospel Singers on the church bulletin board. I told her I was going to ask Mom if we could sign up to have one of them stay at our house. He could have the Farley bedroom with the black furniture.

"But they're nigrows!" Jeannette said.

"So what? They won't rub off on you like shoe polish."

"My mother says God doesn't want the races mixed. They should stay off somewhere by themselves."

"Does the Bible say that, too?"

"Probably," Jeannette said, flouncing away from me.

I studied the poster again the next Sunday and then went outside to see if Mom was coming. It was about time that she did, because a deacon was reaching for the bell rope. Grandma was the lucky one. She got to stay home because she couldn't stand crowds. She felt that she couldn't breathe in a room full of people, which I understood. My own breathing was rapid and panicky, and I fell down frequently. Dr. Petersen still was keeping an eye on me, but he had reached no conclusions.

I saw Mom and ran part of a block to meet her, falling just short of her out-stretched hands. She helped me up and brushed at my torn knees with no concern for her white gloves. Accustomed to the smarting pain and the formation of scab on scab, I ignored the fall and babbled about the Harmony Gospel Singers, pleading with her to invite one of them to our house.

"We're used to sleeping in cold bedrooms, but we hardly can ask someone else to do it."

"Couldn't we start the furnace—just while he's here?"

"We'd all choke to death. You know how it smokes."

She was right. The blue coal smoke that rose from the registers stabbed the lungs, and I knew we couldn't afford to have the furnace fixed. I sadly gave up the idea of claiming a Gospel Singer.

In the end, they all stayed with Reverend Harper because no one else would have them—not even the Saylor Hotel. They sang for five nights, and I was so hopelessly smitten by all four that I couldn't name a favorite. The bass was tall and thin with a narrow mustache and skin the color of coffee with heavy cream. The high tenor was fleshier—dark and lush as a ripe plum. The second tenor and the baritone were brothers; merry look-alikes with skin the shade of our black-walnut sideboard. When they sang "On the Jericho Road" with the tenor part soaring and the low bass throbbing, goose bumps rose on my arms.

At the end of each service, I would hang back, trying to be the last in line to shake hands with them. The Christian brethren unwilling to open their homes to the quartet would at least put out their hands to them, and while they did so, I could feast my eyes on the singers and listen to them say "thank you" over and over again. I thought how wonderful it would be if one of them said my name, but I couldn't figure out how to make that happen.

On the last night, the high tenor took my hand and said, "You been here every night. Good girl!"

"My name—my name is—"

"Yeah? What's your name?"

"Margaret—Margaret Langelund."

He turned to one of the brothers. "Hey, Cedar? This is Margaret. Say hello to little old Margaret."

"Hi, little old Margaret." Cedar brushed his palm against mine and transferred my hand to his brother's with the deftness of a paperhanger smoothing a panel. His palm was paler than the top of his hand, as if it had faded.

"Art, here's Margaret," said the baritone, and the bass claimed my hand.

"I hate to see you go—if only I could go with you!" I said in a rush, imagining how wonderful it would be to hear them every night forever.

Art quickly dropped my hand. "That surely would be nice, but you need to stay here and get your schoolin'."

My face burned at the kindly rejection as I walked away, stiff with embarassment.

"Hoo-ee!" one of them said softly, and I never knew which one it was.

For weeks after the Gospel Singers left, I could visualize them in the place where they had stood to sing. When the organist played "The Old Rugged Cross," I heard "On the Jericho Road." I wanted to write to them and say I hadn't really meant it—about wanting to go away with them—but when I asked Reverend Harper if he had their address, he gave me a funny look and said he didn't.

A few months later, Bobby John Stryker, the evangelist from Omaha, held a week of revival meetings at our church. What the Gospel singers planted, he reaped. Bobby John was young, thin, and intense. Jeannette Johnson's mother declared he was filled with the power of the Lord, fired by the Holy Spirit. His wife, Miriam, was an added asset. She played the piano with flashy zeal, striking the keys from a great height and adding harplike runs to familiar hymns.

Bobby John's voice shifted from pianissimo to double forte as his full lips shaped the words from Jeremiah: "The harvest is past, the summer is ended, and we are not saved." He went on to describe an abysmal eternity of separation from God for those who would not listen to the call of the Saviour. My chest was tight, my face was hot, and I struggled for breath. I was impaled by the gaze of the painted Jesus, no longer girlish. He summoned me. I resisted, clinging to the arm of the pew. The sound of Marie Torkelsen pulling the organ stops was unnaturally loud. I stared at the peach-colored tracery of powder in Mrs. Arentsen's wrinkles, smelled it, and knew that it was Lady Esther. The color of the wine velvet draperies across the baptistry seemed to pulse, and I wondered if wine really looked like that?

When the organ and the piano joined forces for "Just As I Am," Marie Torkelsen played it straight on the organ, and Miriam Stryker added the fancy parts. Bobby John shouted above the music, "Come, give your heart to Him. If you will, come forward and receive Him. No one can decide this for you—not your mother, not your father, not your husband, not your wife, not your child."

I let go of the polished wooden arm and grasped the pew in front of me to pull myself up, but then I wavered, falling back as if dropping a curtsey.

"My friends, almost persuaded is not enough," Bobby John said. "Will you let pride dictate where you will spend eternity?"

I hadn't realized that Bobby John was looking at me, but obviously he had seen me chickening out. I took a deep, dizzying breath and lurched into the aisle. I couldn't have said whether I walked one step or a mile to fall, literally, at the feet of Bobby John Stryker. His hand was warm on my hair as he prayed, "Dear Heavenly Father, we praise Thee for the rebirth of this young soul. In Jesus' Name, Amen." His gray trouser legs moved out of my tear-drenched vision, and the hands that lifted me up belonged to Reverend Harper.

When the service was over, people who never had taken notice of me came to the front of the church to shake my hand. The Johnsons even offered me a ride home, which I accepted gratefully. I was worn out.

Mom had stayed home from the service with a headache, but my news cured her immediately. She laughed and cried and said, "I wish Lauritz were here. I'll never forget the day when he stood up in church and said, 'As for me and my house, we will serve the Lord!' "

Grandma was glad too, but she warned me, "The devil won't take this lying down. He's always after me the hardest right after communion. It makes him mad when it looks like the other side is winning."

"He can't get me now," I said confidently.

Before I went to bed, I sneaked out and threw my free sample tube of Tangee lipstick down the cistern.

I was the only one to show up for church membership instruction on Saturday because the others who had come forward at the revival meetings were just back-sliders who needed to be put right. Reverend Harper asked if I would like to do something for Jesus. Running the church bulletins on the mimeograph machine wasn't exactly what I had in mind, but I reasoned that Jesus would appreciate the sacrificial element of my performing this grubby task when I'd rather be trading movie-star pictures with Monica or reading.

I turned the crank for Jesus, blackening my hands with the sharp-smelling ink that was harder to wash away than sin. The machine was set up in the church kitchen, where I spent a great deal of time at the sink scrubbing with a green bar of Palmolive. To me, the smell of Palmolive soap was the odor of sanctity.

Grandma was right about the devil. During the instruction sessions in Reverend Harper's study, the foul fiend plagued me with the impression that the minister was naked. He sat behind his desk, and as I looked at him, the wood melted and his clothes dissolved. The anatomical detail of the adult male was outside my experience, but I did see an obscene expanse of pink skin. How could this happen to somebody who was saved?

Unaware of my problem, Reverend Harper lectured placidly, "The tree is known by its fruit, Margaret, and that's why your life must conform to your profession of faith."

I slid down in my chair, blinking to dispel his nudity, but to my shame, it persisted. Obviously, I was the kind of tree that should be uprooted and burned.

I was baptized on a cold, winter night in a white summer dress that was too small for me—the only white dress I had. Reverend Harper stood waist-deep in the baptistry with the full sleeves of his robe floating on the water like black lily pads. I climbed down the steps to join him, terrified that the robe would dissolve, leaving him naked in the lukewarm water. He remained robed as I walked through the water, but I didn't want to push my luck, so I fixed my eyes on the painted backdrop of the baptistry: palm trees framing a distant, misty mountain that was an unknown artist's conception of the Jordan River region.

"I baptize thee in the name of the Father and of the Son and of the Holy Ghost!"

A folded white handkerchief with a slightly scorched smell covered my nose and mouth as I went down. Water roared in my ears, beating against the thin wall of my mastoid scar, and I fully expected to drown until wet, black arms raised me up to the news that I was dead to sin.

Beyond the brightly-lit baptistry the church was dark. Disembodied voices sang, "Just as I am, without one plea—but that Thy blood was shed for me—" Reverend Harper handed me a single red rose, a miracle in itself this snowy night. Its single thorn pricked my finger, and I wiped a rusty-red trail on my wet dress as I labored up the steps, begging my unreliable leg muscles not to let me down.

The baptistry opened into my own Sunday school room, where Mom was waiting with a pile of towels. While she rubbed me vigorously, muttering that I'd catch my death of a cold with wet hair on a night like this, I stared into the crimson heart of the rose, testing myself for differences. Chiefly, I was no longer afraid of hell. If I did catch my death of a cold, so what?

Grandma said people never got sick from being baptized—not even when they broke the ice on a river to do it. I guess she was right, because I didn't sneeze even once.

IF I HAD ANY NOTION that baptism would wash me clean once and for all, it soon was dispelled. Every evil impulse I'd ever recognized in myself seemed to be alive and well, proving that souls had to be laundered repeatedly. I envied Wyonne and Monica their Catholic confessional, a clear-cut way of doing the wash that freed them to get dirty all over again with good cheer.

It was Wyonne who told me that Lillian Smith's novel *Strange Fruit* was a dirty book. It must have been, because Miss Winnie Craig wouldn't let anyone our age check it out. We got around that by sneaking it down to the library's basement toilet every night after school until we finished it. Wyonne was a slow reader, so I spent a lot of time staring at the cracked plaster and waiting for her to turn the page. I couldn't find the dirty parts, but Wyonne said I was too dumb to recognize them if I saw them.

"I'll bet you don't even know what makes babies," she said scornfully.

I was torn between lying to save my pride and admitting my ignorance to get the information. Mom didn't talk about things like that, and Grandma certainly didn't. I played for time with a question.

"Who told you all that stuff?"

"Max. He knows everything because he's going to be a doctor. He even tried to show me once, but his thing crumpled and wouldn't go in. He said that was because I was his crummy sister."

Diapering Tyler Arp was my sole exposure to what I presumed she was talking about, but where was it put? I said, "You probably know more about it than I do, so why don't you explain it?"

"Sure!" she said with the joy of the born instructor. "It's like when you go to the gas station."

"We don't go," I reminded her. "We don't have a car anymore."

"Oh, I forgot." She rummaged in the purse I envied (Mom said pockets would do until I was older) and brought out a lipstick—Revlon's Cherries in the Snow—that put my late, lamented Tangee in the shade. She whipped off the cap, replacing it with a thrust as she said, "This goes into that."

"I see," I said, but I didn't see.

Not long after that, Wyonne went to a movie with Bruce Thompson, a high school kid, and Mom said I shouldn't spend so much time with her because she was "precocious." The dictionary said that meant early ripening. The morning after her big date, Wyonne didn't have much to say about Bruce Thompson, but she said the movie knocked her out.

"When Paul Henried lit two cigarettes and gave one to Bette Davis, I thought I'd die. It was the way he looked at her."

Mom didn't care how much time I spent with Lotus Hess, and when the two of us spent her fabulous allowance at the drugstore soda fountain, Lotus got fatter, but I got thinner. When we weren't holding down a booth at Levendahls, Norgaards, or Pextons, we holed up in Lotus's frilly bedroom with its skirted orange-crate dressing table to try the free cosmetic samples we sent for with magazine coupons: Italian Balm, Ponds face cream, tiny lipsticks, and small pots of deodorant.

Tiring of that, we worked on our movie-star scrapbooks. I collected Hedy Lamarr, and she collected Lana Turner. I didn't value blondes because I was one and the town was full of them, but Lotus had brown hair and thought Lana was divine. My scrapbook was the best one around, because I could trade one Lana Turner, Rita Hayworth, or Betty Grable for several shots of the black-haired beauty from Vienna. What I really wanted and knew I'd never have was a still of Hedy's famous nude swimming scene in *Ecstasy*. Movie magazines might write about it, but they'd never print the picture, I was sure.

Hedy's real name was Hedwig Eva Maria Keisler, and she was said to love the simple life. She preferred it to dining on solid gold in the company of ambassadors and heads of state, according to writers of articles like "The Other Side of a Legend" and "Hedy Lamarr—Every Wife's Phantom Rival."

Hedy herself wrote "Don't Copy a Movie Star," a piece that upset me by thwarting my intention: "True copying cannot be done from the outside. The exterior, of course, is the least significant element of a person. The real person lies inside. What a person is—not what he looks like—is called 'character,' and this is impossible to duplicate. Why? Because character is the result of experience. And no two persons live the same life in the same way."

I read this and sighed, returning to the evidence of Hedy's exterior in my scrapbook. In *Tortilla Flat* she wore braids and a sultry look. Wearing a fur-edged parka and mittens sprinkled with fake snow or walking her Great Dane in full-cut slacks, she was wholesome. On the opposite page she danced in the strapless bra and long, slit skirt she wore in *White Cargo,* and Lotus had given me several spangled *Ziegfeld Girl* photos because Lana Turner was in that one, too.

My friends frequently saw their idols in motion on the Harlan Theater's screen, but the only Hedy Lamarr film that ever played there was *Boom Town.* I saw it four times, concentrating on Hedy to the total exclusion of Clark Gable and Spencer Tracy.

Our church disapproved of movies. The theater gave a ticket discount to ministers and their families, but Reverend Harper scorned it, not wanting to lead his flock astray. Even *Snow White and The Seven Dwarfs* was a "worldly, corrupting influence" to be avoided at all costs. Card playing and dancing were just as bad, if not worse.

The only card game we played at home was Old Maid, and Mom said that wasn't the kind of cards Reverend Harper meant. Whatever he *did* mean, I cared nothing about cards, but I did want to learn to dance. I'd been corrupted by the glamorous image of Ginger Rogers and Fred Astaire gliding elegantly around a polished floor in some movie, plus a few minutes of watching a high school prom from the gymnasium balcony.

Jackie Bartelsen promised she'd teach me. I had moved up in the clarinet section to sit beside this popular ninth-grader who wore tight sweaters and bright lipstick. Her clarinet reed looked as if it had been dipped in blood. Jackie was generous with her superior knowledge of clothes, cosmetics, and boys, sharing it with such enthusiasm that Mr. Wenzel broke several batons pounding on his stand to get her attention. She apologized with such charm that he simply sighed and gave the downbeat for "In a Persian Market" or "Knightsbridge" without further comment—and without a baton. When he stopped the band so he could woodshed a few bars with the trumpet section, Jackie invited me to her house after school for my first dance lesson.

She had a record player in her room, but she said we'd have to take it to the kitchen to get away from rugs. When she opened her closet to find some records, I saw a shelf of folded sweaters that looked like layers of cotton candy in pink, blue, lavender, yellow, pale green, and white. I had a half as many, and they were in dark, practical colors like navy and hunter green.

Jackie put "Elmer's Tune" on the phonograph and told me where to put my hands, saying, "I'll be the boy."

No one in the world could be less boyish, I thought, but I would try to believe it. When she explained the footwork, I had to confess that I didn't know right from left until I visualized my third grade classroom—left to the windows, right to the blackboard.

"Oh, my gosh," she said, "you don't have time to mess around with that when a guy asks you to dance. Wear an ankle bracelet."

Eventually I caught on to the simple step-slide pattern, but then Jackie accused me of trying to lead and advised me to "just go limp." I could see that she was getting impatient with me.

"That music is a little fast, Jackie."

"Just count the way you do in band."

When I had stepped on her new saddle shoes as long as she could bear, she changed the record. The slower tempo of Frank Sinatra's "All The Things You Are" made it possible to move and think at the same time. I considered the Sinatra sound, wondering why it made some girls scream and swoon. I asked Jackie if she would do that if she heard him in person.

"Yeah, I probably would. Wouldn't you?"

"No."

She tried to twirl me around, but I wasn't ready for that, and we fell against the kitchen table.

"That's your trouble, Margaret, you won't let yourself go. If you want to be a good dancer, you've got to loosen up—swoon a little for Frankie."

I was afraid to take her advice. Loosening up might release something inside me that never could be coaxed back into its cage.

The dancing lesson ended when Mrs. Bartelsen came home from Ladies' Aid and told Jackie to get her phonograph out of the kitchen because it was time to start supper.

Little as I had learned, I had the occasion to use it when Lotus's brother George came home on leave with his Merchant Marine buddy Roger Wilcox. They went to the Chicken Hut or the Evergeen Inn at night (much to the distress of Mrs. Hess) and slept most of the day, coming to life about the time that school was out. Lotus and I played ping-pong doubles with them on the dining-room table, and when we beat them, Roger asked me to dance to a Frank Sinatra record. If I had any inclination to lead, this huge, black-haired Merchant Marine overwhelmed it.

"What's with you?" he said. "Most gals get real pliable when Frankie sings."

My rigidity was sheer nerves. I tried to hide it with what I hoped was Hedy Lamarr's Viennese world-weariness, saying, "I'm not like most gals. Character is impossible to duplicate."

Roger laughed. "You're a funny little bird," he said, circling my arm with thumb and pointer. "All bones."

I had hoped he wouldn't notice that, and I was almost relieved when George lifted the arm of the record player to stop the music.

"Hey, Rog," George said, "put the baby back in her buggy and let's find some action somewhere."

I ran out of the room, out of the house, and Roger called after me, "Hey, Peg, don't go away mad."

Peg? Nobody ever called me that. Roger and Peg. Peg and Roger. I touched the arm his fingers had circled. Lotus came onto the porch and picked at the silver-lace vine on the trellis. I was not glad of her company.

"I should have told you before," she said.

"Told me what?"

"Roger has a wife, but they're mad at each other and might get a divorce. Her name is Lillian, and George says Roger's so crazy about her that he can't see straight, but he's mad because she went out with somebody else while he was at sea."

"How could she do that to him?"

"He wasn't there, and the other guy was."

"I'll make it up to him."

"Who do you think you are—Hedy Lamarr?"

That smarted, because for a moment I *had* been "every wife's phantom rival."

The next afternoon Mrs. Hess ran to keep the back door from slamming when Lotus and I came in after school. She said the boys were in bad shape. Mrs. Hess was built like a pouter pigeon with her rounding shelf of bosom, narrow hips, and skinny legs that bowed to her feet like a slingshot. She wore old-lady dresses with a brooch at the neck. Although she never tried to be a pal to her kids, she was easy-going about their behavior, saying they'd get some sense eventually; the older ones had proved it. Once we were inside, she went back to beating raw eggs with tomato juice and worcestershire sauce. When the thick mess was ready, she told us to take it up to them.

Roger was sprawled on the bed in shorts and an undershirt. He made a halfhearted attempt to pull the sheet over his black hairiness.

"Where's George?" Lotus asked.

"Getting rid of what he shouldn't have swallowed in the first place."

Lotus took one of the glasses from the tray and went down the hall to pound on the bathroom door, leaving me alone with Roger. I held out the glass, and he motioned for me to come closer. He put his lips to the rim without taking the glass from my hand.

I was wearing my best dress, a rose wool jersey of Marianne's that bunched around my bony hips and made me look fatter. The jersey danced over my heart as I tilted the glass for him.

"Roger—"

"Yeah, Peg?"

"Don't think that nobody loves you—" The rest came out in a rush. "Because I do!" Having sailed out farther than I could row back, I was terrified. What if he laughed—or swore at me—or threw me out bodily?

Suddenly the glass was gone from my hand, and as I breathed the smell of stale liquor and doctored tomato juice, I thought, "This is my first kiss—I'll think about how it feels later," but it was over before I could grasp much to remember. There was warmth and nearness and my own determination to ignore all that was unlovely about someone I loved.

"That's for good-bye." Roger said, "I'm just a beat-up salt, but I've got better sense than to mess up a nice kid like you."

"I'm *not* a kid!"

He groaned. "Please don't give me a hard time. I'm not up to it."

That's when Mrs. Hess yelled up the stairs, "Margaret, your mother wants you home right now."

With a despairing look at Roger, I fled. I didn't like to leave things the way they were between us, but since Mom *never* called me home from the Hesses, I knew the summons was serious.

The sight of her throwing her clothes and mine into suitcases dumbfounded me. We never went anywhere, and besides, it was fall. I had to go to school.

"I know what's the matter with you now," she said. "I figured it out from some books I borrowed from Dr. Lewis, and Dr. Petersen says I may be right."

"Do I have something awful?"

"A goiter."

"But I don't have a big lump in my neck like Miss Benton."

"Sometimes they grow inward. You've got all the symptoms—the eyes, the weight loss, and all that falling down—so I'm taking you to the Mayo Clinic right now. They're the best."

I went outside and spoke tragically into the twilight, "Oh, Roger, just when I'd found you!" It was a line worthy of Hedy Lamarr.

U N C L E K A R L couldn't leave the store long enough to drive us to Rochester, Minnesota, and we soon discovered that people without cars who wanted to engage in north-south travel weren't much better off than users of the Underground Railroad. Getting there was possible, however.

I'd never had a train ride and was enchanted by the lurching coach with wicker seats and steam puffing from cracks in the floor. The car was filled with servicemen who were sleepy, bored, or lost in their own private reveries. Mom warned me not to look them in the eye, and the only good way to avoid that was to gaze at my own reflection in the dirty window. I drooped my lids for a Hedy Lamarr effect, wishing that Roger could see me as the mysterious traveler. I imagined myself en route to some marvelous city where I would step out of the shadows, wearing a cloud of furs, into a pool of light under a lamp post to meet a soldier waiting for me.

The bus from Mankato was less alluring, offering no new experience, but imposing the pervasive odor of sour baby formula.

We took a boardinghouse room with a Mrs. Schickel, who wore size thirteen shoes, evicted deadbeats bodily, and pounded fiercely on the bathroom door when someone stayed there too long. She gave us breakfast and dinner, monitoring the helpings as the dishes were passed. The sight of Mrs. Schickel at the head of the table quelled even my unreasonable appetite, until I could get back to our room and the big box of soda crackers Mom bought for me.

The sun seemed to rise in the south in Rochester, making the days unnatural from beginning to end. We spent hours and days in the cathedrallike waiting room of the Mayo Clinic, watching sweaters grow from the knitting needles of sick women. Just when we decided that my records had been lost, we heard the long-awaited "Langelund, Margaret."

In due course, Mom's diagnosis was confirmed and surgery was scheduled. I avoided thinking about my operation, but the inexorable fact of it lay like a cold stone deep in my stomach. I might die, I thought, and if I did, I would miss most of life's experiences.

That's why I took the single cigarette from a crumpled pack I found in the boardinghouse living room and hid it until I could pick up a book of matches in a restaurant near the clinic.

My big chance came when Mrs. Schickel was out shopping and Mom was deep in conversation with some of the other boarders in the living room. I locked myself in the bathroom and lit up. The smoke made me dizzy, but not too dizzy to admire the wickedly slanting eyes and the glamorous corruption of smoke-spewing lips reflected in the medicine-cabinet mirror. Avid to be a worldling, I smoked the bent cigarette until it was so short that I felt heat on my fingers. My ears rang, and I swayed as I picked bitter shreds from my tongue. How did the beautiful women in magazine ads manage those steady, sultry looks straight into the camera after puffing a cigarette?

Mom's voice startled me. "Margaret, are you in there? Are you sick or something?"

"I'm O.K. I'll be right out."

I threw the short butt into the toilet and was appalled by the loud hiss that I was sure she could hear through the door.

"I'll be in the room," she said.

So far, so good. I climbed into the bathtub to open the window above it, leaning out to let the cold wind blow the smoke from my hair. Then I saw that my shoes had marked the tub. The scouring powder can was empty, and fear of Mrs. Schickel set me to work with a wad of wet toilet paper and bar soap.

If Mom knew what I had done, she would be both furious and disappointed. The disappointment would be the hardest to bear. Then there was Jesus to consider. Reverend Harper had lectured on the evils of smoking and drinking at BYPU, saying how it grieved the Lord to see a young person defile the body, the temple of the Holy Spirit. I felt rotten—defiled by a Camel—and vowed to reform.

However, the memory of my smoke-wreathed mirror image was seductive, and it wasn't long before I was scrounging forgotten cigarettes. Somehow the last Camel or Chesterfield in a crumpled pack did not qualify as a stolen object. It was more like grain left for the gleaners in the field of Boaz. When the smoking boarders left the house without locking their rooms, I did my gleaning there, and that's how I knew about the soldier's wife. Her picture on the dresser was inscribed with violet ink: "For my beloved husband, Lenny, Eternally, Evelyn."

Sergeant Lenny Chalmers appeared to be a perfect physical specimen: tall and well-muscled with sad, dark eyes. He was going through the clinic for tests and wouldn't say why. Until I saw Evelyn's picture, I had a crush on him, imagining what a comfort I could be to him in the mysterious, tragic illness that was likely to carry him off at any time.

Looking at Evelyn's sweet, trusting, hand-tinted face, I knew that she must have some compelling reason for being absent from Lenny's side in his hour of need. With her brown hair rolled in a sausage bang and a bologna-ring pageboy, peachbloom cheeks, golden-brown eyes, and Tangee natural lips parted to reveal a glint of Pepsodent white, Evelyn was the girl-wife who wouldn't sit under the apple tree with anybody else but Lenny. Who could betray eternal Evelyn?

Lenny could, apparently. One night when I got up to go to the bathroom, I saw a flash of olive drab at the quickly opened door of Sylvia Derwent, the crippled girl who had to be carried anywhere her wheelchair wouldn't go. Lenny did a lot of the carrying and seemed to enjoy it. Mom liked Sylvia and felt sorry for her, saying, "She'd make a wonderful wife for someone if they could overlook her handicap."

The opening door made me think about a story I'd tried to write that simply wouldn't work out. Because I seemed to have a cold perpetually, I tried to create a romantic heroine with a runny nose. Her name was Avonelle, and she looked a lot like Hedy Lamarr—so beautiful that her sniffles didn't matter. Unfortunately, even *I* couldn't believe that.

Sylvia's door closed silently. After I had attended to my urgency, I had a Nancy Drew urge to put my ear to Sylvia's keyhole. Lenny's whispering was breathier than Sylvia's, enabling me to tell them apart.

Sylvia: "I thought you'd never come!"

Lenny: "Lots of movement in the halls tonight."

Sylvia: "Maybe waiting makes it better."

Lenny: "They don't come any better than you, baby."

If the lights had been on, I could have seen through the large skeleton keyhole and learned something, but it was dark, and the whispering gave way to rustling and murmuring that was not too instructive. Nevertheless, I stayed there, shivering and straining my ears until I heard Mrs. Schickel's size thirteens on the stairs. It was her last patrol before midnight, and I made it back to the room without meeting her.

Mom stirred but didn't wake. For a long time I stared into the darkness, reflecting on what was happening in Sylvia's room. It was intriguing, but I was indignant about it for Evelyn's sake.

At breakfast Sylvia was pink and pretty in a ruffled blouse and a dark skirt. She avoided Lenny's eyes, but when he looked the other way, she ate him up with her gaze. When she wheeled from the table, I followed, twisting the bottom of my sloppy-Joe sweater as I tried to figure out what to say. *Something* had to be said. Lenny passed us on his way out of the house with a wave that included both of us. Sylvia's color deepened.

"You like him?" I ventured.

"Oh, very much. Of course, I don't know him very well."

My mouth fell open. "You don't?"

"Well, he's never told me much about himself, but in a place like this everyone is cut off from real life. I suppose there isn't much point in talking about it."

"Does he ever talk about Evelyn?" There. It was out.

"Evelyn?"

Sylvia's eyes were unwary and deep blue like those of a very young baby. They made me regret the moral zeal that had forced me to speak. My heart hammered, and I wanted to run, but I remembered poor, trusting Evelyn and steeled myself.

"Evelyn is Lenny's wife."

Sylvia was so still that it frightened me. The only evidence that she had heard was the moist welling of those deep-blue eyes.

"Will you please ask one of the men to help me upstairs? I think I'll lie down for awhile."

The only man I could find was Mr. Turner, who had dizzy spells. Fortunately, he was not dizzy at that moment.

I spent an uneasy day at the clinic, scarcely seeing the turbaned Sikhs and robed Africans waiting for treatment or feeling the palpation of my neck and the drawing of blood. I had the feeling that I had broken something that couldn't be repaired. When we got back to the boarding-house, Mr. Turner told Mom that the sergeant had moved out.

"Did they find out what was wrong with him?"

"He didn't say."

Sylvia wheeled herself to the dinner table and toyed with the creamed eggs without speaking to anyone. She was so pale that the veins at her temples looked like blue lace on a white handkerchief. I couldn't bear to look at her and bolted my food to make a quick escape to our room. To my horror, she swerved her wheelchair to block my passage.

"Thank you for telling me," she said evenly. "I guess I knew it was too good to last, but I'm grateful for what I had." Then she backed to let me pass.

The Camel-smoking worldling climbed the stairs heavily, thinking how one corruption had led to another and how a right could be all wrong.

"Sylvia, I'm sorry!" I whispered, but not to her.

The next day we were told that my operation had been scheduled, and I was convinced that I deserved to die under the knife for what I had done to Sylvia. That notion persisted until she left the boardinghouse, and even after that I was afraid.

The surgery performed by Joseph DeJarnette Pemberton, a top specialist, was another medical curiosity. I was uncommonly young for the condition, and the goiter was wrapped intricately around my wind-pipe. Interns and medical students paraded through my room, talking about me as if I weren't there, in terms I couldn't understand.

Fantasy passed the time in my hospital room on the top floor of the Kahler Hotel. I was a sophisticate in a penthouse with closets full of furs, the beloved of Joseph DeJarnette Pemberton, whom I'd never seen. The nurses told me that Pemberton appeared in the operating room after lesser surgeons had opened the throat, plucked out the goiter with great skill, and departed, leaving the closing of the wound to underlings.

When I was well enough, I walked the hospital corridor in the hope of meeting Pemberton. Considering that I had decided to love him, it was important that I should exist in his consciousness as more than a diseased throat. At last one of the aides, who dimly grasped my obsession, jerked her thumb toward the nurses' station and whispered, "That's him."

The Joseph DeJarnette Pemberton of my imagining was tall, dark, and soulful—a little like Tyrone Power—but this man was short and plump with roan hair. His rimless glasses caught the lamp glare, masking his eyes as he spoke in a monotonous voice to an obsequious nurse. The atmosphere of deference was thick in the corridor.

I went back to my hospital bed and cried with disappointment. My efforts to find someone to love seemed doomed. Max was cruel, Roger and Lenny were married, and Joseph DeJarnette Pemberton was impossible.

We stayed in Rochester for several weeks after I left the hospital. During that time my goiter became an exhibit in a medical museum where an armed guard watched over body parts pickled in jars. Standing and looking at something that had been a recent part of me, I felt a strange detachment. It looked like cooked liver.

Mom swallowed hard and turned away. "I can't look at it. It's you."

I moved closer and stared at the thing. Could this have been the cause of my ravenous appetite? Since the operation I hadn't been hungry, much to Mrs. Schickel's satisfaction. Even so, I was gaining weight. My own clothes were too small already, and I was wearing a somber tweed skirt of Mom's. My reflection in the glass case looked like someone else—a not too attractive someone else.

Worried about missing so much school, I asked for permission to sit in on an algebra class in Rochester. That worried me even more. Besides my total incomprehension of the classwork, I suffered from the guarded glances of the students. I felt entombed in my own flesh, unable to move as lightly as the slender girls in swinging pleats whose legs rose like flower stems from thick bobby socks. The gauze bandage on my throat might excuse me now, but how would I face the kids at home? I particularly dreaded my first meeting with Mary Lois Engle, but it wouldn't be that much easier to meet Lotus and Wyonne and Monica, friends of the skinny Margaret.

Mom took me to an indoor ice-skating rink. Her skating ability was famous in the family, but to me it was a myth, and I expected the worst. My spirit felt as heavy as my body as I sat on a bench dourly anticipating a terrific fall for my too-venturesome parent. She glided away from me, and when a man asked her to skate with him, she hesitated, then laughed like a girl and nodded. Her skate blades flashed evenly and expertly as they crossed hands and sped away. I felt old. It was as if we had switched generations.

When we got home, Mom and Aunt Kam collected the family castoffs to create a new wardrobe for the new Margaret. Grandma helped. Their voices rose as they argued about tucks and darts. The treadle sewing machine whined, and the dining-room rug was crawly with bits of thread and snippets of cloth. Standing like a statue for hem markings made me dizzy, and the heavy scent of Aunt Kam's Djer Kiss talcum didn't help.

"Now that you have some meat on your bones, you're starting to look female," she said.

Grandma sighed deeply. "So soon?"

Three Jorgen women looked at me knowingly, conveying the mixed pain and pleasure of something that was beyond my ken.

2 0

I WASN'T THE ONLY ONE who changed during that time in Rochester. When I came back, I discovered that Wyonne Shenk's waist was smaller and her bra size was a proud 36C. Wyonne approved of the fleshier me, which caused me to spend more time with her than I did with Lotus and Monica. Mom didn't approve.

"Why don't you like Wyonne?" I asked. "You used to."

"She's fast, that's why."

My understanding of that term was vague, and it seemed best to skirt it, so I simply said, "She's fun, though."

"So I gather."

Mom let it go at that and didn't discuss Wyonne again until the question of the double date came up. Wyonne knew a sailor from Denison, and he was coming home on leave. He had a friend, also a sailor, who needed a date. I wouldn't consider it at first, and Wyonne thought she persuaded me. Actually, I persuaded myself, thinking how lovely it would feel to be inside one of those cars that circled the Square on Saturday nights, safe from the raucous remarks of cruising young males who pounded on their car doors as they drove.

Wyonne went with me to the telephone office to talk to Mom about it, and that was a mistake. First of all, Mom didn't like to have me bother her at work. And second, the very sight of Wyonne was a spark striking tinder in Mom. Before I'd even explained what we wanted, Mom was tightening her mouth.

"What's the matter, Mrs. Langelund?" Wyonne said. "Don't you trust Margaret?"

"It's not Margaret I don't trust."

"But Duane's father is a preacher—a Baptist preacher."

"That settles it. The answer is no."

"But why?" I yelped.

"Number, please."

When it was time for Mom to come home from work, I positioned myself on the front steps and tried to look tragic. She sighed, put down the bag of groceries from the A & P, and sat on the step beside me.

"This isn't your one and only chance to go out on a date, you know."

"Yes, it is! If I'm going to have a date, it has to be somebody from out of town. The guys here think I'm peculiar because I read and practice clarinet all the time."

"Wyonne will do things she shouldn't, and you'll think you have to do likewise."

"With a preacher's kid?"

"Especially with a preacher's kid. They cut their teeth on *don'ts,* and when they find something their parents are too embarrassed to mention, they have at it."

"But *I* wouldn't, Mom, even if it's something you never told me I couldn't do. Please, don't ruin my life."

She looked at me steadily for a long moment and then said, "You have so much to learn that I suppose you might as well begin. All right, you can go out with this Duane."

My fierce hug knocked over the groceries. I chased a rolling onion with joy before I ran all the way to Wyonne's house to tell her the good news. Max was home from medical school for the weekend, and this was the first time he had seen me since my operation. He whistled.

"It that you, Margaret?" he said.

"It's me."

Max was thin and sallow from long hours of study. I marveled that I'd ever loved him and couldn't resist rewarding his new interest with the news that I was going out with a sailor.

"Fasten your figleaf, the fleet's in," he said nastily.

Fortunately I wasted no more time on Max and got to Wyonne just as she was going to the phone to find another date for Duane.

The week crept toward Saturday like an inchworm. Exhausted by alternating anticipation and dread, I was dressed and waiting an hour ahead of time. Hair washed in rain water and rinsed with vinegar gleamed and bounced. Waves of valley lily scent rose from a wad of cotton thrust into my bra. An apple-green dress of Marianne's had been let out to its limits to span my hips, and I wished I could trim those hips with a meat cleaver. If I kept my coat on most of the time, Duane might not notice their size.

What if he didn't like me? What if he did and wanted to kiss me? Should I wipe off my lipstick first? Members of our family seldom kissed each other on the mouth, and I wasn't sure how it was done. That quick brush with Roger hadn't taught me much. I was practicing on the back of my hand when the phone rang.

"They had a flat tire, and it's a good thing," Wyonne said. "I'm not half ready. Why in heck can't we have the same phone? I had to put my coat on over my slip to call you from the Kepharts'."

The added delay gave me a carsick feeling. I hung up and rubbed my clammy palms, wondering if I should dust them with talcum powder. No, the Cashmere Bouquet would fight with my valley lily cologne. How could Wyonne be so casual—half-dressed five minutes before the appointed hour?

Mom suggested that I read for awhile, and I tried, but I eyed the same paragraph over and over without the slightest knowledge of what it said. Every time a car slowed outside, I tensed and reached for coat and purse. When a horn honked insistently, I sprang to my feet.

"It's them!"

Mom pushed me back into the chair. "Let them come to the door for you."

The horn sounded again. I was frantic. Then Wyonne hurried inside without knocking. Her red dress matched her Revlon mouth exactly.

"What's holding you up?"

"I'd like to meet your friends," Mom said.

I groaned and Wyonne rolled her eyes, but she went out on the porch and yelled at the sailors. They stood for inspection under the porch light, holding their tightly-rolled sailor caps in their hands. They were the same height (not tall), but whereas Gene was slender and lazy-eyed, Duane was rounded and earnest. The uniform made them look like boy dolls, and that's probably why Mom smiled to herself when she told us to have a good time.

Duane put me into the back seat and came around to sit close to the opposite window.

"How about going to Atlantic?" Wyonne said.

"Can't," Gene told her. "I've got just enough gas to get home, and I took that from the old man's tractor. What's on at the show?"

"I've seen it. Let's buy some beer and go out to Rabbit Hollow."

I caught my breath sharply. Brewing beer in the kitchen was one thing, but buying it in wicked, brown bottles in a dark tavern was something else. Also, girls who allowed themselves to be taken to the winding road through Rabbit Hollow were trash. I looked to Duane, the preacher's kid, for rescue.

"I'll have Pabst," he said. "What's yours?"

"The same," I said, hating him. I had imagined this first date as a meeting with someone who would recognize the real self I didn't have the courage to reveal. Duane was no help.

It was warm for October, but I was shivering. I pushed my feet hard against the floor of the car to hide the state I was in, but there was nothing I could do about the tremor in my voice when I questioned Duane about boot camp. He answered in monosyllables.

Gene parked in front of Herman's Tap on the Square and went inside to buy the beer. I was terrified that someone I knew would see me. As Gene was coming out with his bottles, Mary Lois Engle walked past. She was so goggle-eyed at the sight of a sailor that I couldn't resist rolling the window down and calling to her. Suddenly it didn't seem so terrible to be observed outside Herman's Tap.

"Why, Margaret," she said in what she thought was her Kathryn Grayson voice. "I didn't know you dated servicemen. In fact, I didn't know you dated. Aren't you going to introduce your friend?"

I presented Duane, and Mary Lois showed her dimples. She was Corliss Archer now. For the first time in my life, I had something she did not despise.

Wyonne was tired of being ignored. She said, "Slim pickings tonight? It's pretty late to be on foot, isn't it?"

"I just came uptown on an errand for my mother."

"What you're looking for, your mother doesn't need. Let's move it, Gene."

We burned rubber pulling away. I turned to look at Mary Lois through the back window, and the expression on her face more than made up for her taunts about the lines in my hands and my black tree trunks.

At a well-worn turnoff in Rabbit Hollow, we parked under the oak trees. The beer was bitter, and it gave me a pain in my shoulder. Could that be the location of the conscience, I wondered? When Gene and Wyonne left the car to wander into the trees, Duane and I didn't know what to say to each other. The sweating beer bottle numbed my hand, and I wished I were at home listening to "Your Hit Parade." Duane took my bottle and tossed it and his into the underbrush.

"We don't have to pretend now, do we?"

"I didn't know you were."

"I figured you to be like Wyonne, but you're not. I'm not like Gene, either, but being in the Navy teaches you to act like one of those lizards that change color to match whatever they're sitting on. Know what I mean?"

"I think so, but I can't do it. I stay the same color and don't fool anybody."

"That's O.K., you're a nice color."

He touched my hair, and we kissed slowly and tentatively. It was much better than the time with Roger. I shivered with pleasure, which was better than shivering from sheer nervousness.

"Are you cold?"

"Yes and no."

I scrunched down to rest my cheek against the rough serge of his uniform, and when a sudden glare of headlights burst upon us, Duane covered my face with his cap, staring into the lights with the calm confidence of an anonymous out-of-towner. Then we kissed again, and I asked him to tell me what he was like when he was little.

"I worried about sin a lot. Dad's a brimstone preacher."

"Do you still?"

"No, I've got it all doped out. You don't have to earn brownie points to keep out of hell because Christ took care of all that. If you do right, it's because you're grateful, and if you don't, it's not fatal. The bill has been paid."

"That's the best sermon I ever heard," I said, meaning it, but Duane thought I was making fun of him and backed off. I searched for his hand in unspoken apology, bringing him close for another beery kiss.

"Hey," he said, "want some Sen-Sen? I always carry it because of Dad—not that it fools him."

We sucked the tiny, pungent pillows and talked until Wyonne and Gene came out of the woods.

"What have you two been doing?" Wyonne asked archly.

"Getting acquainted," Duane said.

She laughed, picking leaf bits and twigs from Gene's big, square collar. "That's one way of putting it."

Duane and I agreed to write to each other, and we parted with a long, Sen-Sen kiss.

Mom was awake in the dark house. She called to me, asking if I had a nice time, and I smiled to myself, running a finger over my transformed lips.

"Margaret, did you hear me?"

"Yes, I had a nice time. I didn't know what to do or say, but he made it all right."

2 1

WHEN YOU'RE SOMEBODY'S GIRL, you need things like lipstick, nail polish, and a few clothes that haven't belonged to somebody else first. Before I sat down to write my daily letter to Duane, I always tried to make myself look nice. That seemed important. Wyonne thought that was silly, but she was open to my suggestion that the two of us apply for jobs at Fern's Fashion on the Square to earn the money we needed to enhance our appearance.

Fern was a Junoesque woman built like the blank-eyed white statues at the high school. She was of indeterminate age and had a cast in one eye. When she spoke to me, I stepped slightly to one side, trying to meet her crooked gaze. She wanted to talk to me and Wyonne separately, and I was the first to follow her to a curtained back room that served as office, bedroom, and stock room. An unmade cot and a heap of peach-colored underwear on the floor exuded a stale scent as Fern outlined the duties of the job.

"When somebody comes in, don't let them leave without buying something."

"But what if they don't need—"

"I don't make a living off what people need," she snapped. "Your job is to make them want. If they start toward the door, step in front of them and keep suggesting all the way. Understand?"

I nodded, but I cringed at the thought of interfering with anyone to that degree. I wished the room were bigger or less cluttered so I could put more distance between us and avoid the unwashed smell that broke through Fern's strong floral scent.

"And I don't want you standing around when the shop is empty. There's stuff to mark, hats to brush, and windows to dress. O.K., where's your Social Security card?"

"I haven't got one."

"Then go to the Post Office and get one."

"You mean I have the job?"

"I'll give you a try, but if you're no good, I'll know it in a hurry. Send the Shenk kid back."

Stammering my thanks, I backed out of the curtains and beckoned to Wyonne, who had been trying on hats while she waited. She tilted a flower-trimmed cartwheel over one eye, seeing no need for hurry until I motioned more frantically.

"How much will she pay?" she whispered.

"I forgot to ask."

"Stupe!"

"I haven't got all day," said Fern, standing between the parted curtains like a priestess of some strange sect, "and I'll thank you not to maul the merchandise."

While I waited for Wyonne, I watched Mrs. McCreedy put price tags on a pile of lace-trimmed slips. Mrs. McCreedy had worked at the Fashion for years, and she asked if I planned to take the job.

I told her how glad I was to have it and asked, "Do you like working here?"

She glanced toward the back room. The curtains still swayed from Wyonne's passage. "Oh, yes, Fern is a wonderful boss." As she spoke, her marking pencil printed NO! on a paper bag, then SHE LISTENS. She reduced the bag to a tight twist that she put into her own purse fetched from beneath the counter.

Wyonne emerged from the back room with a guarded expression, and we left the shop in a silence that lasted three doors past the A & P. Then Wyonne exploded.

"She's bats! Can you imagine *living* in that crummy little room? She told me we'd have to be quiet Saturday mornings because she'd be asleep back there."

I had an uneasy feeling about the job, but in spite of my misgivings, I was proud to tell Mom I had it.

"You'll get used to Fern," she said. "It's just that you've never met a businesswoman before."

I soon decided that Fern was a bad businesswoman, chiefly because she was a bad buyer. Her taste ran to beaded crepes that no one in town would buy because they were too flashy for church, the dressiest occasion most woman had. Ten years of mistakes crowded the racks until it was nearly impossible to extricate a hanger. When drastic mark-downs failed to move the stock, she shrugged and ordered more of the same. As we unpacked a new shipment, Mrs. McCreedy sighed and said, "She's getting like those crazy brothers near Audubon who locked themselves up with all their garbage for twenty years."

The only time we were safe from Fern's eavesdropping was when she went to the bank, and she usually stayed long enough to allow us some amusement. With Mrs. McCreedy posted near the door as a look-out, Wyonne and I tried on the vilest of the size 44 dresses and laughed ourselves breathless until we heard, "Get 'em off, here she comes!"

The trips to the bank filled Fern with a luminous euphoria that puzzled me until Mrs. McCreedy explained, "It gives her a chance to gawk at Chet Matthias through the bars. She may get him yet."

"How can she?" Wyonne said. "He's married."

"If you want to call that married. His wife has been in Clarinda for six years now, raving crazy."

It soon became apparent that Chet Matthias was missing from his teller's window when Fern went on one of her disastrous buying trips.

"They say he's sick," Mrs. McCreedy said, "but I know better."

Chet Matthias was a spare little man with glasses and graying hair. He was a head shorter than Fern, a fact we didn't know until they started to meet for coffee at Ruby's Cafe and walk around the Square at night with Licorice, Chet's black cocker spaniel. During one of their joint absences, they must have decided to see each other openly.

"He has a key to the back door of the shop," Wyonne said. "Boy, would I like to be a mouse in *his* confessional."

Mrs. McCreedy sniffed. "Huh! He's nothing but a Mason."

"If it's so wrong, why are they so happy?" I said.

"They'll pay in the end," Mrs. McCreedy said darkly. "That's always the way of it."

On a soft, cloudy April afternoon, Wyonne and I came to work after school and were surprised to hear the radio blaring from Fern's back room, giving the details of Franklin Delano Roosevelt's death in Warm Springs, Georgia. It seemed that he had always been my president (this was nearly so), and I felt like a little kid lost in the crowd at a county fair, bewildered and rapidly moving toward terror. Who would run the war?

Someone did, and when the church bells were ringing the joy of victory in Europe, Mom said, "Now Lauritz's brothers and sisters are safe."

I hadn't thought about my Danish relatives being right in the middle of the war because they weren't real to me. I didn't even know how many brothers and sisters my father had—only Uncle Anton, who lived on a farm along Wisconsin Ridge. How strange it seemed to be related to strangers. I asked why the families never wrote to each other, not even before the war, and Grandma said that leaving the Old Country was a lot like dying. It cut family ties with a sharp knife.

"Someday I'll find them," I said, but I could see that Grandma considered it unlikely.

Spring passed and summer set in. Wyonne and I worked full days in the hot, stuffy shop trying to sell ugly cottons trimmed with rick-rack that Fern had bought when we were in kindergarten. Helping a fat farmer's wife into a ghastly lavender print, I prayed that it would fit and look halfway decent. It was Friday. We hadn't sold a thing for two days, and since Fern paid us out of the cash register at midnight Saturday, our prospects were not promising. Mrs. McCreedy was smarter. She demanded a personal check on the Shelby County Bank, where Fern kept a sizeable inheritance.

I struggled to zip the side placket of the lavender dress, but the prewar metal teeth would not meet. A football of flesh protruded stubbornly. Reeling in the scent of the Sweetheart soap emanating from that vast skin surface, I said, "It has good, wide seams."

The woman sighed hugely, and I saw hope die in the vulnerable eyes that moved over her mirrored image. She had hoped for a miracle; an excavation from that mound of flesh. Something in her wanted to soar, but it was grounded by the insufficiency of a lavender print dress, size 46.

"Let me look for something else," I said.

"It's no use. I'll just have to run up something from feed sacks like I always do."

"Oh, please, I'm sure I can find something."

"All right," she said simply, folding her great arms across a bosom of geologic solidity. She paid me the courtesy of indulgence, and her grotesque body took on dignity in its strained slip of rayon knit with shiny stripes. As soon as she walked out the door, Wyonne would laugh at her and call her a hick, but I wouldn't. I couldn't. I knew how it felt to be imprisoned in too much flesh, wearing my mother's clothes.

As I was searching through the large sizes, Mrs. McCreedy put a hand on my shoulder and whispered, "Storm warnings! They've sent Chet Matthias's wife home."

"Is she cured?"

"So they say. We may be sending Fern to Clarinda to take her place."

Moments later, Fern rose from her stale cot and wandered through the front of the shop to the street, hair uncombed, clothes wrinkled. She hadn't said a word to any of us, nor did she speak to anyone else as she crossed to Ruby's Cafe. Chet Matthias was on his way to lunch, but when he saw Fern, he hurried back to the bank.

"The rat!" Wyonne said.

"With Joan home, things are different," Mrs. McCreedy said. "He has to be careful."

Suddenly I remembered my customer waiting patiently in the fitting room. I snatched a green crepe de chine and rushed back to her.

"It smells old," she said, but when it circled her girth with a bit to spare, she smiled. "I'll take it."

I rang up the sale gratefully just as Fern stumbled past. I hoped that the cash register bell would penetrate her numb distress and cheer her.

Chet Matthias used his key one last time to say good-bye, and he was in such a hurry that he forgot to pull it from the lock. When Mrs. Mc-Creedy came to open up Saturday morning, she heard a dog whining in the back and pushed through the curtains to investigate.

I arrived just as she gasped, "Jesus!" and fell back with Licorice pawing at her skirt. "Get Norbert Kline—run! And pull the door shade as you go—we're closed—oh, God!"

"What's wrong?"

"Go! I—I can't—" She bent double, pushing the dog away to grope for the wastebasket. If I had had any notion of being sick myself, I would have to wait.

Sheriff Kline was straining one of the red-plastic counter stools at Ruby's with his weight, coffee cup to his lips, when I pulled at his sleeve.

"Please come, and hurry!"

"Hold your horses, tootsie, you've got no call to spill a man's coffee."

"I'm sorry, but something awful has happened at the Fashion."

Catching the coin he flipped at her, Ruby said, "Lovers' quarrel, huh? It'll be a cold day before I call the law in on my private beeswax."

"Come on, Ruby," Kline joshed, "you know you been out of action since the Armistice."

"Please," I begged, "hurry!"

Once he got started, the sheriff moved his bulk with plenty of speed. The floor of the shop trembled under his feet as he ran to the back room, and I was right behind him, looking under his beefy arm as he pulled the curtains aside.

"Oh, my God," he said softly.

Chet was on the floor in an attitude of prayer clasping Fern's knees, and her upper body was sprawled across the cot, twisted sideways. Blood was everywhere, turning maroon on the floor, on the sheets, on a pile of invoices. Kline pulled a summer-weight blanket from the tangle of bedclothes to cover the motionless figures, and as he turned away, Licorice broke out of Mrs. McCreedy's arms to nose at the merciful covering and whine.

"O.K., Mrs. Matthias," the sheriff said, "let's have it."

I hadn't seen Joan Matthias sitting in a corner wedged between two packing boxes. She was completely still, staring at nothing and clutching a gun so tightly that her knuckles were white. Kline tried to pry her fingers from the gun and couldn't.

"What the hell," he said. "She pumped everything she had into them. That's Fern's old German Luger—had a permit for it, but she didn't have a permit for Chet. Will somebody do something about that damned dog?"

I grabbed Licorice and held him tight to still my own trembling.

Kline tried to pull Mrs. Matthias to her feet, but her body was rigid in a sitting position. "It's like she's turned to stone. Go call Doc Ryan to come and give her a shot or something, will you?"

Wyonne, late as usual, arrived while I was trying to hang onto the dog and talk to Dr. Ryan's nurse at the same time.

"Smells like the cemetery after they shoot off the guns on Decoration Day," Wyonne said. "What's going on?"

As soon as she found out, she started to scream and sob, and Kline yelled, "Everybody out! This is no goddam sideshow! Somebody out there call the undertaker."

Mrs. McCreedy, white but in control, said she would do that if I would deal with Wyonne, who had collapsed just behind the curtain. I put Licorice down and tried to pull Wyonne to her feet, but she shrieked and went limp. All I could do was drag her behind a rack of dresses and wait for the phone to be free so I could call Mrs. Shenk to come for her.

When the men from Rowley's Funeral Parlor came, I had to recapture the dog and keep him from attacking the strangers who were putting his master on a stretcher.

Monica's father arrived next. His first act was to pronounce Fern and

Chet Matthias dead so they could be taken away. Then he tried to do something about Joan Matthias, but he couldn't unfreeze her body, either, and had to ask the sheriff to help him get her to the car.

Just as they were carrying out Mrs. Matthias with the gun still locked in her hand, Mrs. Shenk rushed into the shop and said, "What a terrible thing for young girls to see!" She hadn't seen the worst.

Wyonne couldn't have had a tear left, but she went into another fit of sobbing in her mother's arms. I expected Mrs. Shenk to thank me for calling her, but she looked at me over Wyonne's head and said, "You're a cold one, Margaret."

Cold? I buried my face in Licorice's black coat to hide my resentment. If I had behaved like Wyonne, who would have gone for the sheriff? Who would have called the doctor? Who would have called about Wyonne?

Until that moment, I had been too busy to believe what I had seen. The instant I believed it, I started to shake. Licorice whined and licked my face, reminding me of the sight of his paws on Chet Matthias's dead back. I hadn't had a dog since we left Sofus behind on the farm, and I supposed that I could have Licorice for the asking, but I couldn't take him. Every time I looked at him, I would remember things I simply had to forget. I left him with Mrs. McCreedy and walked home.

Grandma was making bread, and I couldn't imagine how the yeasty, homey smell of it could exist in the same world with the smell of blood and gun powder. One or the other had to be unreal.

"Aren't you supposed to be working?"

I threw myself into her arms and cried hard, not trying to tell her why until the sobs and tears were done. She listened quietly then, and when I asked if she thought all three of them would go to hell, she said, "God is no bookkeeper. He lets us buy our own fate, and it's too bad we aren't as wise as we are free."

"Is that an answer?"

"Yes, though you might not think so right away."

Joan Matthias was sent back to Clarinda, Licorice found a home on a farm, and the contents of Fern's Fashion were sold at auction to a buyer from Omaha. I was amazed at how soon the town forgot the whole thing— or seemed to.

I stood at Fern's grave beside the marble angel south of the mausoleum and thought how sad it was that she and Chet were separated, first by the circumstances of life and then by death. Chet was buried in Boone, the town where he was born. I wanted a love stronger than death, the Song of Solomon kind, and so had Joan Matthias, I supposed. Once you started to think about the feelings of everyone involved in a horrible situation, it was hard to take sides.

2 2

THE DEATHS of Fern and Chet added dimension to my feelings for Duane. I wrote letters to a creature of my own making, a Duane composed of bits and pieces of every book and movie in my experience. My lines on "eternal bonds" and "a love impervious to death" were rather moving, I thought, not that either of us stood in danger of dying.

The town had rung every church bell on V-E Day, and that thankful joy intensified to indiscriminate kissing and snake dancing in the streets on V-J Day. In the aftermath Duane was biding his time until discharge at a naval installation in Hastings, Nebraska, as far from a watery grave as one could get.

He did not answer my letters in kind. When he came home on leave, I scarcely knew what to say to him. We went to Peony Park in Omaha to dance, which we did awkwardly, thanks to our Baptist conditioning. We moved stiffly around the open-air dance floor in an elegaic, end-of-the-season mood that cool September night. The alternative was returning to the table where Wyonne and Gene were having a smouldering quarrel.

"How have you been?" Duane asked, as if we hadn't ridden fifty miles together to reach this bower of romance.

I told him I was O.K., longing to trade his living presence for a letter, thin and blue. He suggested a walk, and we moved into the dark trees. Duane became more real as he grew less visible. We kissed, and it seemed right to say the words I'd written so often on paper.

"I love you, Duane."

"I'm not sure I can take that."

I pulled away as if he had hit me and ran from him. He caught my arm.

"Wait, Margaret, let me tell you why."

"I don't care why. I get the message."

"No, you don't, and I wouldn't bother to explain if I didn't—if—oh, hell, love is a simple thing, but you blow it up into such a big deal that I can't handle it. You're too much!"

"How? Why?"

"Ever focus the sun on paper through a magnifying glass? That's what you do to me—all the love comes from your head, and you're too damned total but not total enough. It drives me nuts!"

"I'm sorry," I said stiffly, wanting to die.

Gene came looking for us in the dark. He said, "Let's cut out—unless you're finally making some headway with the Big Tease."

"Shut up, Gene," Duane said.

Wyonne was sulking in the car, and nobody said a word on the long drive home. The next day Wyonne told me she was afraid to start up where she left off with Gene after what happened to Fern and Chet, but even when she explained, he wasn't a bit nice about it. She was glad she had seen the last of him.

"I'll miss it, though," she said with a sigh. "It takes awhile to stop wanting it, don't you think?"

"I wouldn't know. I'm a Big Tease."

She laughed ruefully. "If I could say that, Father Burke would go a lot easier on me at confession."

When I stopped writing letters to Duane, my life seemed undefined. Was it possible that what I did came alive only in review? Did I exist only when I stepped outside of myself to observe and report?

I hadn't found another job yet, so I read for hours; practiced the clarinet for weekly lessons with Mr. Bardell, the new band man; spent late afternoons in the comforting company of Lotus Hess, who found food more interesting than males. My social life consisted of Monday night city band practice, Wednesday night prayer meeting, and Sunday night BYPU, with an occasional Happy Hour after the evening church service.

I tried out for the class play and got a character role. It was easy to play an acid-tongued spinster in that winter of my discontent, and I wasn't much better in spring. After my usual panic that I would catch the mumps and be unable to play my music contest solo, I got a first rating with no offensive personal remarks from the judge. It didn't mean much, because I'd never had anything less.

Restless and dissatisfied, I was ripe for anything—even Albert Rettig. Albert was twenty-three—too old for BYPU but desperate to belong to something that wasn't sinful. He was serious, righteous, and skilled at carpentry, a trade that pleased him because it had been the work of the Lord.

One summer Sunday night when I was spitting watermelon seeds on the church lawn during a Happy Hour, I became conscious of Albert's tall, stooped figure beside me. His wheat-colored hair was plastered with goo that dimmed its gold, and he regarded me soberly through glasses that had thin, silver rims. Albert never had spoken to me directly before, but now he offered to throw away my rind and drive me home. Not caring one way or the other, I allowed him to dispose of the rind and followed him to his pale blue Plymouth, thinking it would be like riding with a girl. I could say thanks and jump out the minute I got home. That was exactly what I did.

Albert was my undemanding chauffeur for a long time before the night when he headed for Rabbit Hollow. Noting the route and his tense face in the dashboard light, I veered between pity and amusement at his obvious intention. When he stopped the car, cleared his throat, and seized me, I wondered how he dared. I'd never beamed a force of interest—or even awareness—in his direction sufficient to invite this pressure of tight lips on my mouth.

When it was over, he said, "I never kissed a girl before."

"You're kidding," I said politely, though I believed him.

"No, I never did. Are you mad?"

I laughed. "No, just surprised. Shall we try it again?"

My experience with Duane ought to be good for *something*, I thought, and Albert needed instruction. When I finally said I had to get home, he stabbed the key at the ignition five times before he found it.

I knew that I had only myself to blame for getting stuck with Albert. He wooed me with Danish tenacity, paying no attention to my lack of response. He brought me presents: dresser lamps painted with garish flowers and Whitman's Samplers. He came to our house and sat in the parlor while I hid in my bedroom begging Mom to tell him I wasn't home.

"I won't lie," she said. "And the least you can do is come out and get rid of him yourself. He's sitting in there looking like a whipped dog."

"He always looks like that."

I made a languid appearance at the parlor door, leaning heavily on the colonnades as I announced that I was quite unwell and unable to entertain visitors. The lie resulted in Albert's promise to pray for the restoration of my health, but he did leave.

I would have hidden from Albert indefinitely, but how could I resist his offer to teach me to drive? When I ran into a telephone pole and crumpled a pale blue fender, his reaction was a saintly smile and a quiet remark. "You can't expect to be perfect right away."

Albert was sickeningly good, and he wanted to make me good, too. He begged me to stop saying "heavens" because that was as bad as saying "hell," and he could cite Scripture to prove it.

When Albert said he'd build me the best brick house I'd ever seen if I'd marry him, I told him I wasn't good enough for him, beating down his blind insistence that I was.

"You'd better not waste your time with me," I said. "You're not getting any younger, and if you want to get married, you'd better find somebody in a hurry."

"I have. You."

"I'm not out of high school yet, and besides, we don't have anything in common."

"There's church."

"That's not enough. I'm sorry, Albert, but we're just going to have to forget this."

"Jacob got what he wanted in the end, and so will I," Albert said, quoting the verse from Genesis about Jacob serving seven years for Rachel: "And they seemed unto him but a few days for the love he had to her."

"That's an odd verse to know by heart."

126

"I just learned it."

"Albert, leave me alone—please!"

He didn't come around for a few days, and I was at the brink of wary relief when his mother telephoned to invite me to the family cottage at Clear Lake for a weekend. The whole family was going. Dagny Rettig was as stubborn as her son. She brushed aside my stammered excuses and asked to speak to Mom, who came in on the line from the telephone office.

"I guess you heard," Mrs. Rettig said. "How about it?"

Mom, who never admitted to listening on a line, asked for a full explanation. Mrs. Rettig gave it and said, "It would be good for her to get away for a few days. I've noticed how peaked she's been looking in church. It won't cost you a cent, and nobody can say it's not according to Hoyle because me and Chris will be along—not to mention Billy and his intended."

"Mom," I broke in.

"I'm talking to your mother, not to you."

"Dagny," Mom said, "you know that Margaret isn't seriously interested in Albert, don't you? I wouldn't want her to make such a trip under false pretenses."

"Don't you worry about that. What's what today may change by tomorrow if the Lord sees fit to take a hand in it."

They talked on, and I thought longingly of a lake, a real one instead of the blue house roof two streets away that became a lake when I looked at it through pine boughs and squinted hard. The only quantities of water I'd ever seen were rivers: the Nishnabotna (not much wider than a creek) and the muddy, brown Missouri. A large proportion of the population went to Lake Okoboji in the summer and spoke of it as if it belonged to them, but we couldn't afford vacations.

With Billy along, the trip might not be so bad. Albert's younger brother was a black sheep who knew how to have fun. Billy's girlfriend never said much, but she was pleasant. Her name was Lila. If we could leave Albert at home, I'd accept the invitation instantly, I thought. By this time, the inter-mother talk indicated that it was up to me, and the lake outweighed Albert.

At the start of the long drive, I climbed into the front seat with Albert's parents. Dagny offered to change places with Albert, but Billy saved me by reminding her how carsick she got in the back.

As soon as we arrived at the Rettig cottage on the south shore of Clear Lake, Chris Rettig assembled us on the screened porch to give thanks to God for our safe journey. Billy, Lila, and I kept our eyes open to gaze at the water, but Albert and his parents prayed with tightly closed eyes and full attention. Immediately after the amen, Dagny assigned the rooms and started to unpack what looked like enough groceries for a siege.

I was sorry to discover that the room I would share with Lila looked out on a neighboring cottage rather than the lake. I placed a suitcase that had belonged to a grandfather, dead since 1893, next to Lila's baby blue Samsonite and asked her if the Rettigs prayed all the time.

She nodded. "It really got me at first. My folks don't even go to church."

I couldn't think of anything else to say to her, but it didn't matter because we were busy unpacking. Lila stripped completely, exposing her body to the breeze from the window with pagan joy before pulling on a skirted bathing suit that obscured the beautiful lines of hip and thigh.

"Billy hates this suit, but I figured I'd better wear it for Mother Rettig's sake."

"Is that what you call her?"

"That's the way she wants it, but what the heck? It won't be long before we can call her Grandma."

I didn't care what Mother Rettig thought of my bright yellow one-piece. Mom insisted that it be wool to protect me against any possible chill. The precaution was unnecessary, because she never let me go to the new municipal swimming pool unless it was at least ninety degrees in the shade. On this cool but bright day, nobody was consulting the thermometer. I had the delicious feeling of getting by with something.

Lila went to join Billy on the dock, but I stayed in the room until I heard Albert's knuckle tap on the door. We stared at each other for an instant and looked away in an agony of embarrassment. Long days on scaffolding and rooftops had given Albert a farmer's tan. His stooped shoulders had nowhere to hide, and the pinch marks from his glasses were leprous spots in a red-brown face.

"You look just like I thought you would," he said.

"You, too."

As soon as I stepped onto the dock, Billy grabbed my ankle and pulled me into water of unknown depth. I struggled, shockingly affected by his submerged embrace. Why couldn't Albert be more like his brother? Billy released me to climb onto the sun-bleached boards and rub Lila's back in slow-circling motions.

Back on the dock, unable to decide whether Albert had touched me by accident or design, I rolled out of his reach. Why couldn't I be here with someone else? Or alone? Albert's very silence had the force of a yearning that made me want to scream, "Never! Never! Never!" How could I make him understand?

When Billy and Lila swam out to a distant float, I said, "Do you ever read anything at all?"

"The Bible."

"Haven't you noticed that you and I never really talk?"

"We're talking now," he said patiently. "And when we're married, we can talk about things that are happening around us."

"Nothing happens around you."

"What do you want? Whatever it is, I'll—"

"Supper!" Dagny yelled from the porch.

Albert rose dutifully, offering me a helping hand, which I spurned. I was angry with him for bearing my insults without complaint, thus making me feel mean and rotten.

The food grew cold during Chris Rettig's lengthy prayer of blessing, and after the dishes were washed, we had nearly an hour of Bible reading and devotions.

When we were released, I whispered to Lila, "How can you stand it?"

"I just flip a switch in my head. It will be different when Billy and I have our own place." Her eyes softened and her body stirred at the thought.

The lake was pearly in the dying light, and I hoped to enjoy it alone, but Albert was beside me before I reached the dock. Fish jumped from the water and fell back with tiny splashes before a motorboat scared them into the deep. The sound of distant laughter carried over the water. Albert said nothing.

"I'm going to bed," I said abruptly.

Hours later I crept out of the cottage wearing nothing but a towel. My intention was to re-create Hedy Lamarr's nude swim in *Ecstasy*, an act of defiance aimed at the Rettigs in general and at Albert in particular. Satisfied that I had the lake to myself at last, I dropped the towel and eased into the shockingly cold water. Bumping against the slimy pilings beneath the dock wasn't quite *Ecstasy*, but it was the best I could manage. I was ready to climb out when the boards above my head trembled.

"Ought to be bitin' now, maybe."

"You sure it's O.K. to fish here? This is a private dock, ain't it?"

"No sweat. They go to bed with the chickens."

I thought I could find the spot where I had left my towel, but I was afraid the fishermen above me would see my groping hand if I reached for it.

"Hey, those folks left a towel out. I'll drop it on their doorstep when we go back."

I wanted to shout, "Why don't you mind your own business?" but I said nothing. A match flared and hissed as it hit the water. The smell of cigarette smoke came through the cracks in the dock to mingle with the bosky smell of the lake. The dark water was threatening now, and I was cold. What if the Rettigs woke up and found me gone? Panicked by the thought, I pulled myself up to spot the pale blob that was my towel and snatched it.

"What the hell—you see that, Ed?"

"I didn't see nothin'. Shut up, or you'll scare the fish."

"But something raised up over there, and the towel's gone."

"You probably kicked it off when you threw your line."

Weighted down by the sodden towel, I clambered up the shoreline rocks and made a run for the cottage. I didn't want to trail lake water across the porch and into the rooms, so I paused to wring out my clammy sarong. That was when I saw the red eye of a lighted cigarette bobbing toward me. I performed an instant rewrap, holding the towel ends together behind my back.

"Margaret? What are you doing out here?"

"Billy!"

His hand stroked my shoulder and moved down my arm.

"I—I didn't know you smoked," I said idiotically.

"Neither do the folks. That's why I'm out here. What's your excuse?"

"I wanted to do something without Albert—something he'd hate. Oh, Billy, does Albert *ever* do anything wrong?"

"Nope, he leaves that to me."

The cigarette was flicked away and Billy was holding me and kissing me so expertly that I scarcely could concentrate on clutching the towel. I had to break away to preserve more than my modesty. Lying in bed with the taste of Billy's cigarette on my tongue, I listened to Lila's deep breathing and wondered if she dreamed of him. I did, and when Lila winked at me during morning prayers, I felt terrible.

Before we started home, I went down to the dock for one last look at the lake. I could feel a presence behind me, and without turning, I said, "Albert?"

"I've been praying that you'd change your mind about me."

"Sometimes the answer to prayer is no."

We walked to the car, and he got into the front seat with his parents. It was a tight squeeze. Billy grinned at me as he pulled Lila close and settled her cheek against his collar bone. When her eyes were closed in bliss, his other arm went around me. The hand caressed my hip until I sat forward, pretending great interest in a herd of Holsteins.

Dagny Rettig sang, "Count your many blessings, name them one by one—and it will surprise you what the Lord has done!" Albert joined in, and when we parted, he was almost cheerful.

Within a few months, he married one of the Paulsen girls and started to build her the best brick house I'd ever seen. Her name was Leah, I believe. If it wasn't, it should have been.

2 3

MR. WENZEL'S SUCCESSOR, "the new band man," was Brandon Bardell, an easterner who scorned our provincial ways. The scorn was mutual, for the most part. His la-de-da name and suffering-artist mannerisms gave people plenty to talk about. I defended him, pointing out that he did know a wider world than ours.

I took my weekly clarinet lesson at the house the Bardells rented on Baldwin Street, and I came to admire the sparsely furnished living room with its walls white to show off art that looked like nothing recognizable. Bookshelves made from planks and glass bricks held the works of James Joyce and Henry Miller, plus dozens of Penguin pocketbooks. They had stacks of long-playing records, and every time I came, I wondered who Mahler was but didn't dare to ask.

Bardell's wife, Cloris, was an excellent pianist, but they didn't have a piano. She practiced at the school or the Congregational Church. Cloris was tiny and ugly-cute with short, unruly hair the color of straw. Pregnancy distorted her small frame grossly, but she made light of it.

"Just like a gunny sack of basketballs," she said with a laugh, "and do you know that I had no idea what a gunny sack was until I came out here?"

"Get out of here," Bardell said. "I'm supposed to be teaching a lesson."

We worked on the Brahms for awhile, and then Cloris was back, trying to catch her husband's eye from the doorway. That failing, she said, "Bardy—"

"In a minute! Take that cadenza again, please."

I couldn't—not when I heard her gasp and say, "This is ridiculous! It's not time—"

"Mr. Bardell, I think you'd better—"

He looked up from marking my music and saw her holding the door for support, obviously in pain. "Oh, God, are you going to have it?"

"Not it—him. I'm not packed—"

"I can do that," I said. "You go on to the hospital, and I'll bring your things."

Bardell turned his pockets out, dumping the contents on a table to fish his car keys from a pile of change and matchbooks. He half-carried his wife to the car and forgot to turn on its lights until the end of the block. The car squealed around the corner on two wheels. Luckily, the hospital, a remodeled house, was just three blocks away.

Because the Bardell house had no front hall closet, I'd been in the bedroom to leave my coat once a week, but this was my first chance to take a good look at the room. The twin beds with Hollywood headboards were smooth under monk's cloth spreads. The top of the pale wooden dresser was bare and shining, minus the usual wedding picture and perfume bottles. The book on the night table was poetry by Rilke, and the only picture in the room could be viewed while lying in bed. It looked like a tangle of arms and legs, but I couldn't be sure.

Thinking that a baby had been made in this room reminded me of what I was about. I searched for a suitcase in the closet. The only one there would have to do, huge though it happened to be. Bardell's, obviously. I started to open drawers. The first was filled with shorts, undershirts, handkerchiefs monogrammed with a brown B, and a neat line-up of contraceptive packets. Thanks to Wyonne, I knew what they were. The drawer that belonged to Cloris held tailored ivory underthings and nightgowns too austere for a woman in love, but that was no business of mine.

Why think of their intimate relations at all? Bardell was my teacher, not just in music, but also in a manner of living that appealed to me: a clean, uncluttered superiority. Cloris was his partner, contributing to that style without messy emotion. When I came for a lesson, they would be sitting on cushions with the lights low, listening to classical music with sherry glasses in their hands. I longed to be part of that scene, but it wasn't made for three. As soon as I arrived, Bardell turned up the lights, Cloris whisked the glasses away, and it was time to work. Would that ritual continue after they brought the baby home?

I went to the bathroom for Cloris's toothbrush, deciding it must be the yellow one on the left. The red one on the right had a hump of toothpaste near the bristles, and Bardell seemed less likely to rinse thoroughly than Cloris. I took the Ipana toothpaste, hoping Bardell would know enough to use soda or salt in its absence. Cloris wore no makeup, so that was it. I closed the case, then reopened it and tossed in the book of poems.

Although nobody else in town locked their doors, I knew that the Bardells did and flipped the latch before walking to the hospital with my clarinet case in one hand and the suitcase in the other.

A voice from a passing car yelled, "Running away from home?"

Never, I thought. Home was the place where I took the information I'd gathered for interpretation, the place where I found uncritical love to heal all hurts, the place where I belonged without question. Even so, I knew that someday I'd be walking away with a suitcase in my hand. Grandma had done it to marry, Mom had done it to teach country school, and I would have my own reason when the time came. Lotus, Wyonne, and Monica were going to college, but I was pretty sure we couldn't afford that.

It seemed that each generation of Jorgen women left home a little later than the last. What if I had lived in Grandma's time? Would I have married Albert to have the roof of a brick house over my head? Probably not. Grandma always said she married for love, and when I broke with Albert, she said, "That's that, thank goodness! I was sure you had the sense never to say yes until you couldn't say no, but when he kept hanging around, I began to wonder."

The hospital was a big, two-story house on Tenth Street with the kitchen converted to an operating room. Originally, it had stood on the Post Office site, and the move cracked its gray stucco exterior. At the entrance I braced for the smell of ether, remembering my operations. Mrs. Crouch, the head nurse, was famous for her bad disposition. Mom said that was because she'd seen so much suffering. I waited to state my business until she looked up from her paperwork and frowned at me.

"I've brought Mrs. Bardell's things."

"She should have left her husband at home instead of her nightgown. He's in the solarium having cat-fits."

"May I see him?"

"Help yourself." She took the suitcase.

Bardell hung crucified on a window frame, mumbling to himself. As I came in, he tensed and turned expectantly. "Oh, it's you. I thought maybe—"

"It takes awhile, I guess."

"I just hope she's satisfied. It was all her idea. I'm not ready for this— not that *she* is—we don't have one diaper."

It hadn't occurred to me before, but there *wasn't* a crib, a layette, or loot from baby showers in their home.

"Is the red toothbrush yours?"

"Huh? Oh, yeah, I guess. Did you lock the door?"

"I did, but you don't need to." I considered staying awhile to help him pass the time, but I decided he didn't deserve much consideration. Brandon Bardell represented the highest culture I knew, but I was sure the most ignorant tenant farmer in Rabbit Hollow would have welcomed a baby more gladly. What was wrong with him?

Cloris was in labor for sixteen hours, and the baby was a boy. I telephoned my congratulations.

"For what?" Bardell said. "He's a mess. If I had known I couldn't do any better than that, I wouldn't have bothered."

"He'll get better," I said. "New babies never look like much."

Bardell snorted and changed the subject. "You need at least two new pads on that instrument of yours. Why don't we go to Omaha Saturday and have it taken care of?"

When I asked Mom, she said, "You wouldn't think he'd run out of town under the circumstances. Besides, I can't see why you have to go along. Let him take the horn."

I called Bardell again, and he said I should be there to test the instrument.

We left in the morning on Saturday, and not one word was said about Cloris and the baby. Bardell talked to me about the possibility of going to Juilliard and about books, saying that he had loved Thomas Wolfe when he was my age but didn't anymore. He introduced me as his best student to the proprietor of the music store.

We went to the Hotel Fontanelle for lunch, and he treated me as if I'd never seen an elegant menu before. He was right. I hadn't. We had lobster thermidor and white wine that tasted like vinegar.

"Isn't it great to be in a civilized state where you can have wine brought to your table?" he said. Then he narrowed his eyes and stared at me. "That hair—why don't you get a decent cut instead of letting it grow like a crop of alfalfa?"

"I'll think about it," I said, offended by his description of the long, thick, Ann Sheridan look I'd achieved with a rain water wash and a vinegar rinse.

We whiled away the time it would take for the instrument repair by visiting the Joslyn Memorial Museum. Bardell lectured on the composition and style of the paintings, and though I admired his expertise, I wished he would be quiet and let me enjoy the pictures in my own way. By late afternoon, we had collected my clarinet and crossed the bridge over the Missouri River to the Iowa side.

"We might as well stop for dinner—unless you'd like to cook for me when we get home."

"I don't know how to cook. With Mom and Grandma in the kitchen, there's no room for me."

"It's just as well. You won't have to unlearn the meat and potatoes banality of midwestern cuisine."

I swallowed the insult to my town and my kind of people because his tone implied that I was exempt from it, a piece of porcelain on a shelf of common pots. He even invited me to call him Bardy as Cloris did, but I couldn't. He was my teacher.

Instead of angling to the east along the usual route from the cities, Bardell drove straight north along the Missouri. This was new country to me, and I delighted in the broader roll of the land from the river bluffs. We stopped at the Coach and Four, a roadhouse outside the town of Missouri Valley, pausing to look at a spectacular sunset before heading into the icy air-conditioning promised by the neon sign.

A hostess with canary-blonde hair and harsh, black eyebrows guided us through the dimness to a table so small that our knees touched when we sat down. When I turned in my chair to break the contact, Bardell laughed. He made fun of the "English country wench get-up" of an approaching waitress, but he flirted with her as he ordered an old-fashioned and a martini.

"You have to begin somewhere," he said, "and an old-fashioned is loaded with enough wholesome garbage to ease the most Puritan conscience, which, I perceive, you have. Thank God you look older than you are."

I wished he hadn't mentioned God. Reverend Harper's face loomed before me as the waitress slapped down a tiny napkin and a squat glass garnished with an innocent-looking orange slice and bobbing cherries. I remembered Uncle Stig banging into the house after a long session at Jake's Tavern. I thought of Mom and Grandma and Aunt Kamille drinking nothing stronger than coffee and remembered my cousin Geraldine's remark, "Booze is hell on the complexion." Just as I decided to push the drink away, Bardell raised his in a silent toast, and I became Hedy Lamarr. The first sip was awful, but a sizable swallow washed caution away. I drained the glass.

"Hey, easy!" Bardell said. He seemed to undulate as if he were riding an inner tube in the played-out wake of a motorboat. More drinks appeared, a distant jukebox played "All The Things You Are," and steaks appeared from nowhere. I watched Bardell cut his meat, admiring the musicianly movement of his hands and wrists. He commanded me to eat, and when I couldn't, he fed me a few bites from his fork.

Then we were moving into a blast of night heat. Crickets rasped and frogs croaked hypnotically from unseen water. We were in the car, moving, and then the motor was silent and willow branches were reaching in through the open window. I found it hard to believe that I was choking under Bardell's hot, searching mouth.

"You can't know how it's been for me the past few months."

I reached for the door handle.

"What the hell's the matter with you?"

"You're my teacher."

"God, yes, but I thought you'd understand. I thought we had something for each other."

"You're my teacher," I repeated stubbornly. Didn't that say it all?

He jabbed the key into the ignition. "I guess I was stupid as hell to expect more from a hick. If you know what's good for you, you'll keep your mouth shut about this."

The car leaped forward, tearing willow boughs from the tree. Speeding to express his fury, Bardell overdrove his lights, and I was scared. I pushed the lock button and huddled against the door forlornly. After a long dependence on his approval, I felt lost without it. He'd never recommend me for Juilliard now. Tears started and fell unbrushed because I didn't want him to know. He dropped me at our dark house, screeching the car away from the curb without saying good night.

On the kitchen table was a napkin-covered plate and a glass of milk with a note: "Thought you might be hungry." Thinking that the cinnamon rolls might cover the liquor on my breath, I ate them joylessly while the women who made them slept in their good innocence. The thought of Cloris and her yet unnamed son moved me to shove the repaired clarinet under the kitchen couch. I had no idea how I would explain it, but I knew I couldn't touch that instrument for a long time.

Brandon Bardell was released from his contract at Thanksgiving. He had counted too much on the discretion of Kathy Lorimer, the best snare drummer in the band.

The new band man was a horse of a different color. Kenneth Cooper's living room had a matched set of wine-colored overstuffed furniture, a stack of *Saturday Evening Post* magazines, and hand-tinted family portraits on the wall. He loved his wife, Irene, dearly, doted on three kids born a year apart, listened to Glenn Miller records while relaxing with a Dr. Pepper, and never talked about Juilliard. Ken Cooper was referred to as "a man with the right kind of values," but I continued to hope for the combination of such values with some of the qualities I had admired in Bardell.

Though I never told Mom about my day with Bardell, I did mention that Ken Cooper was short on excitement. "Too bad we can't have the best parts of both."

She nodded. "Two probably isn't enough. You'd have to put at least three men together to get the perfect mix."

Grandma laughed. "Who expects perfection in *this* world?"

"*I* do!" I said.

Both of them looked at me with the wise, warm pity that drove me wild. If I expected too much, they expected too little, I thought.

2 4

C H O O S I N G the high school commercial course rather than college prep meant separation from friends I had taken for granted since kindergarten at Laurel School. At first they couldn't believe that I had no hope of college and intended to learn practical skills. Then they pitied me, and I avoided them. I made new friends.

My typing class included the tough, jaunty girls from Park School who wore curlers to class the day of a big dance, chewed gum with their mouths open, and plucked their eyebrows to an arc of perpetual surprise. They were what my family regarded as trash, and I was fascinated by them.

Merrilee Adams was not one of these. Her family had just moved to town, and no one ever would have known that she had borne an illegitimate child and given it up for adoption if she hadn't bragged about it. Once the word was out, Merrilee caused the mothers of sons to tremble, but she kept her tight, enticing little body to herself.

"From now on, I'm taking care of Merrilee," she said, "and to hell with everybody else!"

I'd always gone home for lunch and stayed there as long as possible, but after I met Merrilee, I gulped my food and hurried back to school. Merrilee preferred to bring her lunch. Unless it was raining or snowing, we sat on the steps leading to the northwest door and talked about life. The stone was cold at first, but we sat there long enough to warm it.

"What is it really like?" I asked, meaning the sex act but not wanting to say so.

"Why don't you ask your mother?" Her tilted, greenish eyes gleamed wickedly. "Or would she tell you about the stork?"

"I don't know *what* she'd tell me," I said honestly. I only knew that I couldn't ask her. Jorgen women probably knew more about it than Merrilee did, but it wasn't a thing they talked about. Uncle Stig might have told me, but he was out west somewhere, and Wyonne's long-ago lecture with the lipstick tube was as far as she was willing to go. Besides, Wyonne was college prep now. In any case, I didn't want an anatomy lesson. Understanding the power of it all was what mattered.

Merrilee went to work on a scuff mark on her saddle shoe with a pencil eraser, and neither of us spoke for a long time. Finally she said, "It's nothing to write home about."

I resisted her revelation as I had fought Lotus's insistence that there was no Santa Claus. Hedy Lamarr never would give such a discouraging report. I tried to steer Merrilee into a revision of hers.

"Did you love him?"

"Sure—until I started throwing up in the morning. When the pains started, I knew damned well I didn't, and when those stitches were smarting, I figured I never had."

"Didn't you want to get married?"

"No, that's why I wouldn't tell my folks who it was. I'm going to learn how to make money, and I'm going to have what *I* want instead of getting stuck with a houseful of brats the way my mom did. Would you believe that she wanted to keep my baby and pass it off as hers?"

By this time, I didn't know *what* to believe. "Didn't you hate to give it up?"

She shook her head. "Come home with me after school, and you'll see why."

I jumped at the chance because nobody else ever had been asked. The Adamses lived in a small, yellow house just north of the respectable zone. The minute I got inside, I remembered Grandma's curse, "May you have a dozen children!" Kids were everywhere. All of them had some variation of Merrilee's strawberry blonde hair, and most of them were whining and crying. The boy playing with Lincoln Logs on the drafty floor sniffled, and the slightly older girl who was putting doll clothes on a struggling tiger cat coughed so hard that the cat's ears flattened in the gale. Another boy was pulling the window shade up and down, catching the curtains in its frayed edges. The curtains were dark green printed with big, white orchids, but the wrong side looked like muddy moss. Two other children seemed locked in a death struggle on the cracked linoleum. In the midst of all this, Mrs. Adams concentrated on a story in *True Confessions.* She wore an aqua chenille robe over her clothes for warmth. Merrilee introduced me, and her mother nodded, impatient to return to her story.

Now I knew why Merrilee gave off the sharp scent of kerosene no matter how much Emeraude she dabbed on her pulses. The house was heated by a little kerosene stove like the one we used for summer cooking.

"We can go to my room," she said.

"Take a look at Donny, will you?" Mrs. Adams said. "Don't know what's keeping that ambulance."

I picked my way through the Lincoln Logs to follow Merrilee through two panels of cloth hung from a string. I couldn't imagine how Mrs. Adams could be so casual when she was expecting an ambulance, and I asked Merrilee who needed it.

"Donny—but it's just for something he was born with. His arm's all shriveled up, and they're going to try to do something about it in Iowa City."

She pushed aside a second skimpy curtain, and there sat Donny on what presumably was his parents' bed. He looked dressed up with a red plaid bow tie peeking out of a sweater that was too big for him. The withered arm was hiding in the sweater sleeve.

"All set, Donny?" Merrilee ruffled his hair.

"Yeah, I got all my stuff in here." He patted the brown paper bag beside him. "Merrilee—are they going to cut on me?"

"I don't know, Donny, maybe they'll just stretch your arm." She smoothed his hair, and we left him.

The house was divided into four square rooms: living room, kitchen, and two bedrooms—one with a tiny bathroom partition in the corner. What Merrilee called her room was a dormitory with stacked mattresses that must have covered every inch of the floor at night. She had made a corner her own with hanging what-not shelves for her cosmetics and magazine pictures taped to the walls.

"I change the pictures every month," she said, pointing to the tropical beach scene and the model buried to her high cheekbones in fur. "I pick places where I want to go and things I want to have."

As I admired Merrilee's collection of Revlon nail polish colors and Coty colognes, my mind was on Donny. I knew what it was like to be afraid of an operation. I asked his age, and Merrilee said he was ten. He looked younger than that because of his size. That runt-of-the-litter body had spent its energies fighting a defect rather than growing. He looked older than ten because of the patient, wizened face marked by enduring pain.

"I've had a lot of operations," I told Merrilee. "Maybe I should tell him that it's never as bad as you think it's going to be."

She took a brush from the shelf and attacked her rose-gold hair. "I thought you wanted to talk to *me*."

"Well, I do, but—"

"Donny will be O.K." She pulled the top mattress to the floor and sat on it, motioning for me to join her. "My baby was a girl, and I wanted her to grow up better than me—understand?"

"I guess so, but there's nothing wrong with you."

"That's what *he* said. He acted like I was giving him the greatest thing in the world until he got it."

"Then what?"

"It was nothing. Something he could have without asking. *I* was nothing."

It. Still circling the mystery. What I really wanted to know was something about males. I had grown up with so few of them around me that they seemed to be a strange and different species. I figured I'd either have to find out what to do with them or simply do without them.

"You never say anything about your dad, Merrilee."

"He's off on a construction job."

"I suppose you miss him a lot."

"Are you kidding? As long as he's gone, Mom won't get knocked up. One more kid around here, and I'm leaving."

The ambulance turned out to be a long, blue-gray car with University of Iowa Hospitals written on the side. When the driver came to the door, Mrs. Adams took off her chenille robe, rammed Donny's chicken-wing arm into a jacket sleeve, and told Merrilee, "They're all yours, kiddo."

The rest of the kids struggled for a place at the front window to watch their mother and Donny go down the walk; she with her train case, he with his sack. Then Mrs. Adams turned and came back. The kids brightened and crowded around her, but she plowed through them to pick up her confession magazine and was gone again. At the second parting the younger kids cried peevishly.

"How long will she be gone?" I asked.

"She's been gone too long already."

Merrilee picked up Lincoln Logs, then snatched a roll of toilet paper from a rickety end table and worked her way around the room wiping noses. I asked if I could help.

"Run some water in the bathtub. As long as I'm running this show, things are going to be different around here."

The water bucked and groaned in the pipes before it came out rusty and ice-cold. Merrilee said it never would get warmer, so I heated a pot of it on a kerosene burner. The next problem was catching the kids, an impossibility until Merrilee enticed them with the promise of jasmine bubble bath.

"That many kids will use up the whole bottle."

"Like hell, they will!" she said. "They'll take turns. I suppose that shocks you—using the same bath water?"

As a matter of fact, it didn't. I told her how Mom, the youngest child in her family, was the last to climb into the galvanized wash tub in front of the kitchen stove. Mom laughed about it and said it turned her hair green.

I held the victims while Merrilee did the scrubbing. The tiger cat ran under the bed, terrified by their screams, but when we were finished, Merrilee's siblings were transformed. They sat quietly with old newspaper comic sections while she started supper. I asked what she was planning to fix.

"Cornbread."

"With what?"

"With nothing. That'll fill 'em up."

One thing that stuck in my mind from seventh-grade home economics was the seven daily food requirements, and I worried about the nutrition of the Adams kids, but I kept that concern to myself.

"Delsey," Merrilee yelled, "set the table."

The girl with the bad cough was Delsey. She dealt chipped plates around the sticky oilcloth with bad grace, but she did it. When she dropped one and broke it, I didn't think the loss was serious, but it was. Somebody would have to use a pie tin, and that somebody was Delsey.

One thing we always had plenty of was plates. Mom and Grandma had pooled their china, and there was all the Farley stuff. Surely we could spare some of it for the Adamses, but the proud flash of Merrilee's eyes told me I'd have trouble making the offer.

"Want to eat with us?" she asked.

"I'd better get home. Nobody knows where I am."

"We have a telephone."

"Not the same one we have," I said, thankful for the Farmers' Mutual for the first time in my life.

She saw me to the door, saying, "Now you know."

The next day, I waited for Merrilee on the steps, but she didn't come. The day after that, she was there, but she avoided my eyes, giving me every chance to pretend I didn't see her.

"Hey, Merrilee," I said, "missed you yesterday."

She looked at me warily, gauging my sincerity before she said, "Delsey was home sick. I had to stay with her."

We sat down on the cold, damp steps and talked about being big-city secretaries who wore expensive suits during the day and chiffon with sequins to dance the nights away. We didn't discuss the men who might logically appear in such scenarios. They were too shadowy to matter. That's how it was with Merrilee who knew too much and Margaret who knew too little.

AS SOON AS MY TYPING and shorthand were good enough, I was hired by Gregory Sommer, a lawyer who lived in the town without being part of it. I worked after school and on Saturdays, and while I didn't understand Mr. Sommer, that was no more than I expected.

He didn't own a car, but I did not consider that to be an oddity. We didn't have one either. Sommer walked from his home near the water tower to his office on the east side of the Square, and once in awhile he took the Greyhound bus to Omaha. He carried groceries home, just as we did, and I wondered if he had the same desperate yearning for the offer of a ride that seized me when my arm muscles were ready to give out. It was silly for me to yearn because nobody ever gave me a ride, and I guess it was the same for him. His burdens were heavier than mine, too, because he didn't have a basement filled with home-canned fruits and vegetables like ours: no pale pear halves that looked icy in their blue Mason jars, no warmer-toned apple chunks, no golden peaches with dark red traces of their pit craters, no tomatoes with scattered seeds like tiny eyes, no gray-green beans jackstrawed into their jars, no pickle slices stacked like coins in brine.

How gladly I would have carried cans like his with labels that promised so much in word and image or loaves of gummy, white store bread so magically wrapped. Our food was nameless, robbing our garbage of all distinction.

Mrs. Sommer made out the grocery lists, and I called them in, asking Mr. Clore to have the items sacked and ready for Mr. Sommer when he left the office. Familiarity with Mrs. Sommer's handwriting gave me more information about her than anyone else possessed. No one ever saw her, and her first name was a mystery. Gregory Sommer's rare references to her were formal: "Mrs. Sommer needs a spool of black thread. Will you get some at Farner's?"

Mom said, "Are you sure there *is* a Mrs. Sommer?"

"The handwriting on the lists isn't his, and besides, why would he make up a wife?"

"Stranger things have happened," Grandma said, telling the story of H. Bates, the owner of an early general store in town who was thought to be a man until death revealed her secret.

"Does Mr. Sommer have any clients?" Mom asked. "I never hear about anyone going to him."

"Nobody comes in while I'm there, but I always have a lot of papers to type—'State of Iowa, in and for Shelby County.' I never recognize the names on them."

"That's odd."

I shrugged. "He's nice enough to me."

Sommer did take an interest in me, tossing bits of wisdom just within my reach with a "take it or leave it" expression.

"If you want to do something and think you might be stopped, don't ask—just go ahead. You still might be stopped, but on the other hand, the *fait accompli* has a tendency to seem right and normal. Asking before-hand calls forth objections that need not materialize."

"I suppose you're right."

"On occasion I have been known to be right."

The opportunity to test his advice came along very soon. The Harlan Cyclones were having a hot basketball season, and the only team that stood between them and the state tournament in Des Moines was Carroll. A fleet of school buses was organized to transport nearly the whole student body to Carroll for the Friday night game. The departure time was during my working hours, but I remembered Sommer's advice and signed up for the trip before I discussed it with him. Tournament play being what it was, I had no time to give him notice in any case.

Usually I tried to look businesslike at work, but on Friday I came to the office dressed in my black sweater with the big red H that I earned in band. Sommer looked at me and raised one eyebrow. I had half an hour to inform him of my plans and get back to the bus, so I jumped right in and told him.

"Sit down," he said.

I sat, glancing at the wall clock nervously.

"Take a letter."

I snatched pad and pencil, hoping the letter would be a short one. It wasn't, and there was a second letter and a third. The minute hand of the big Seth Thomas moved inexorably toward the departure time, and when just five minutes remained, Sommer searched uncommonly long for the right phrase, staring at me above steepled fingers.

I stared back, hating him, and clutching my pencil so hard that my fingers whitened. The clock hand moved on, and he watched it, refusing to drop his voice in the customary rush of "Yoursverytruly" until I had missed the bus irrevocably. Then he disappeared into his inner office with a loud, "I want those to go out tonight."

I typed doggedly, making one mistake after another because I was crying too hard to see the page clearly. Just this once I had hoped to live completely within the excitement of tournament play. At most games, I stood outside of myself, viewing my black sweater with the big red H and my mouth opened wide to yell H, H, H-A-R, L, L, L-A-N as some kind of a disguise. Monica and Wyonne might be genuine high school girls caught up in the thrill of a basketball game, but I was there to play "Elmer's

Tune" and the school song set to the music of the "Notre Dame Fight Song." I couldn't use a reed cap, because Mr. Cooper was likely to give a frantic downbeat at any moment, so I had to be watchful of my instrument. I couldn't afford to buy a new reed at Weavers' every time somebody jumped around on the bleachers and knocked into my mouthpiece. Besides, reeds were hard to break in. A new one was the color of a pale canary, slightly rough to the tongue and balky—not worth much until it was blood-red with lipstick and soft enough to sing. When I wasn't watching out for my reed, I was sniffing the metallic scent of acne ointment and observing what sweat did to the sheen of the white satin uniforms the Cyclones wore at home. I took everything in—useless details that made no sense—and stored it all somewhere like Aunt Kam's upright Hoover vacuum cleaner. She let us use it now and then because she thought our broom and wire-carpet-beater maintenance was unsanitary.

As I typed and erased, pausing only to blow my nose, I was convinced that Mr. Sommer had deprived me of my one chance to be a genuine high school girl cheering her team on to victory. I'd been counting on the tournament to do what the slumber party at Monica's (our last social encounter before the commercial course–college prep split) had failed to do.

We had put aspirin tablets into bottles of Coke, holding the force of the fizz in with our thumbs as we shook them. We drank, expecting to feel high, and we did. Then Monica put on the Frank Sinatra records. The others swooned, sprawling dramatically on the bed and on the floor, but I just couldn't do it. I sat in the big chair where Monica always threw her underwear, crossed my legs under me, and waited for them to recover. When Mrs. Ryan looked in on us, her eyes met mine, and it was a communication between two grownups. She smiled, shrugged, and went away.

Monica was the first to surface. She looked slightly sheepish. "Jeez, I haven't done that since we were kids."

At the sound of her voice the others snapped out of it, and Wyonne said it wasn't quite the same as when Frankie first had them falling in the aisles. She just did it for old time's sake. I didn't remind them that I'd *never* done it. I just drank more of my doctored Coke and pretended I was Hedy Lamarr drinking champagne in Vienna. How did champagne taste? I certainly hoped it would live up to its promise better than Evening in Paris perfume had done.

According to the Seth Thomas, it was after six, and the letters weren't finished. The office had both phones, so I wouldn't inconvenience Mr. Sommer if he wanted to tell his wife he'd be late. I picked up the Farmers' Mutual.

"Number plee-uzh," said Lottie.

"I want to call home," I said, then wondered if she could recognize my tear-clotted voice. It wouldn't matter. The position of the switchboard light would tell Lottie that the call came from Sommer's office, and she knew I worked for him. She connected me.

"Hell-o?" If Grandma lived to be a hundred, she'd still sound faintly foreign.

"It's me. I'm going to be late because I have a bunch of letters to do."

"But, Margrethe." She said my name in Danish. "You're supposed to be in Carroll. We ate without you."

"I didn't go. Is there anything for me to eat?" I bit my lip to stifle a sob.

"Vegetable soup with dumplings. But why—"

"I'll tell you when I see you."

The thought of Mom and Grandma at a table set for two talking about how much fun I must be having at the game renewed my aggrieved outrage and further slowed my progress with the letters.

At half-past six Mr. Sommer came out to look over my shoulder. I tensed, willing every inch of my body surface to bombard him with arrows of hate. He went back to his inner office.

At five past seven I pulled the last letter from the typewriter. As I separated it from carbon paper and copy, a big tear fell on the onionskin, blistering its thin surface. I couldn't believe that I had a tear left, but I must have had a storage place for them as big as the hot water reservoir on our kitchen stove. Would some secretary in years to come pull that copy from the file and wonder about the wrinkled crater the tear had made? I left the copy unblotted, carrying the finished letters to my employer to be signed.

Mr. Sommer barely glanced at me before addressing himself to the job at hand. He used a fat fountain pen of an intense green with a marbled pattern. Wretched as I was, I registered the fact that the pen was new.

"Have you ever seen malachite, Margaret?"

It was pretty safe to say I hadn't, considering that I didn't know what it was. I shook my head, not wanting to risk a voice rusted by tears.

"This isn't the real thing, but it's a good imitation. Malachite is a semiprecious stone found in many copper-producing areas of the world. Some say that green is the color of eternity, a concept I find hard to grasp."

Why was he talking about malachite and eternity when both of us were late for supper? How could he toss out information in the usual way when the receiver was so unreceptive? I cleared my throat and suggested that Mrs. Sommer might be upset by his lateness.

"Mary does not live by the clock."

Mary. I finally knew her name, and that exclusive knowledge was a pinpoint of light in my black gloom.

"You think you've been ill-used, don't you?"

I lowered my eyes, refusing to answer. Jorgen women never let on when they were hurt.

"You've learned something today, Margaret."

I'd certainly learned not to take his advice, I thought, but I said nothing.

"From now on, you'll be more careful about taking anything or anyone for granted."

"But I didn't—"

"Come now, you were sure that Gregory Sommer would be indulgent of tournament fever and let you go to an out-of-town game with absolutely no notice regardless of what needed to be done in the office, right?"

I nodded, more tears welling.

"Margaret, I have learned one sure thing and learned it at great cost. In the end, only one thing can save us—work. Not religion, not love, not possessions, not friends, not diversions—only work."

"But what good has the work done? It's too late for these letters to go out tonight. The mail truck has gone."

"True. I'll drop them at the Post Office in the morning, and now I'll walk you home because it's dark."

"I'm used to walking alone in the dark."

"But I'm not used to being the cause of it. Get your coat."

He signed the remaining letters and threw them into a folder with their envelopes, turned off the lights, and joined me in the hall. I'd never been in the building this late before, and the cooking smells were a surprise—a reminder that people actually lived in this old building with no yard and no view.

We walked in silence along the south side of the Square past the Golden Rule, the dimestore, the bakery, the movie theater. Instead of turning left at the Saylor Hotel as I usually did, Sommer went straight on his own homeward route. This was a possible alternative for me. When we were well away from the bright lights of the Square, he said he was sorry he couldn't give me a ride.

"That's all right, I'm used to walking."

"No, it's not all right. I *should* be able to drive you home. You're very angry with me, aren't you?"

I admitted it but told him it was temporary. I'd been taught not to let the sun go down on my wrath, and while I was a little late this time, I was working on it.

"I pushed you to the limit, Margaret, and you maintained your dignity. I was happy to see that."

"But why did you have to do that? What difference does my dignity make to you?"

"I'm not sure I can answer that, but I would like to explain something else—if you'll keep it confidential."

I thought I could do that. After all, Mom never told what she heard at the switchboard. I promised.

"Eleven years ago on this day I swore I'd never drive a car again, and I haven't. There was an accident. Our child was killed, and Mary spent months in the hospital."

I pulled in my breath with shocked pity, standing still on the sidewalk, but he plunged his hands deeper into his coat pockets and went on.

"They recommended an institution for Mary, but I took her away and came here. I can take care of her, and I'm the one who should. Margaret, I'm telling you all this because I have to be honest about this afternoon. You didn't need a lesson—*I* needed the pretense of teaching one."

"I don't understand."

The cold wind sent a shiver through me, and I pulled the knot on my challis headscarf tighter. We were passing the jockey hitching post at the O'Neills' house, and Sommer came to a stop, running his gloved hand along the metal figure's extended arm. The jockey was given new racing colors every other year. His most recent red and white gleamed in the streetlight.

"This is a bad sort of anniversary for me, Margaret, especially bad around the hour when you come to work. I couldn't let you leave. Being alone in the office would have been unbearable, and going home to Mary would have been worse."

"If you'd just told me—I could have talked to you instead of—"

"You were a strongly felt presence."

We crossed the street to my corner, the revelation heavy between us, and he added to its weight by saying their daughter would have been almost my age by now. We had said good night and he had recrossed the street when I called after him.

"I was just doing what you told me—making a—what did you call it?"

The wind carried his voice back to me. "A *fait accompli*. Most of the time it works, so don't give up on it."

I dipped soup from the pot at the back of the stove and drank it straight from the bowl, not resorting to a spoon until the fluffy dumplings and vegetables were dry-docked.

"What exquisite manners!" Mom said. "Now would you care to tell us why you're not at the basketball game in Carroll?"

"Mr. Sommer had too much work to get out," I said, trowelling butter from the Kimballton creamery onto a thick slice of homemade bread. It seemed strange to keep anything back from Mom and Grandma, and Grandma especially seemed to know that I was doing it. As she took off her tiny, oval glasses and bent the gold earpieces to a more comfortable curve, the look in her eyes told me she knew.

The following day when I came to work in the morning rather than in the sad light of late afternoon, Mr. Sommer behaved as if nothing had passed between us, and so did I.

"Mrs. Sommer would like some Fitch shampoo. Will you get it at Pextons?"

No mention was made of the fact that the Cyclones were playing that night in the state tournament and all the genuine high school girls would be in Des Moines with the team. I put on my coat and went to the store for Mary.

2 6

MARY LOIS ENGLE played the piano accompaniment for my district music contest solo in Atlantic. Mr. Cooper told everybody not to wander around town, but we decided he couldn't mean us—we were seniors.

We found a drugstore where we could drink Cokes while we waited for the ratings. The high booths of dark wood covered with initials, arrow-pierced hearts, and raw rectangles where something indecent had been scratched out reminded me of grandma's sing-song phrase, "Fools' names and fools' faces are always seen in public places." I often had the mad urge to write my initials on the white, blank-eyed statues at the high school, but I never did, unwilling to be a fool. In a strange town, however, I felt the freedom of anonymity and scratched M.L. in the varnish with a bobby pin. The act gave me a wicked thrill.

"Too bad you don't have some initials to put with yours," Mary Lois said with a smirk. "They look kind of lonesome."

Leave it to Mary Lois to spoil things. I wanted to say something terrible to her, but I didn't dare until I knew whether we were going to the state contest. Accompanists were hard to find, and Mary Lois was playing for me only because her piano teacher made her do it as "such good experience." One reason why we played together as well as we did was our disinclination to waste time talking and giggling at practice sessions. We simply didn't like each other well enough for that. I almost wished for a second rating so I could smart off at her, but until I knew, it seemed best to follow Grandma's advice: "Don't sail out farther than you can row back." I concentrated on my Coke and didn't notice the white bits in Mary Lois's hair until a disembodied arm and hand dropped more confetti on her head.

"Ish!" she shrieked. "What *is* this?"

Two strange boys scrambled into our booth. One of them said his name was Tom and held out his hand to Mary Lois. She slapped it.

"I don't care what your name is. You're disgustingly juvenile."

"Yeah, but I'm cute. Hey, Ethel, bring us another round of Cokes."

"Come on, Margaret, let's get out of here."

The boy beside me slid out to let me pass, but Tom refused to budge. Ethel appeared with four Cokes and a smudgily-revised bill. Mary Lois relaxed her grip on her purse and sat back. It seemed that we were staying.

The quiet one said, "I guess you must be Margaret. They call me Speed."

"Why?"

He blushed beneath his freckles and shook his head. Speed didn't have much to say, but I did learn that he lived on a farm near Exira. I was surprised when he asked how to find me in the phone book.

Tom and Speed walked back to the school with us to check the bulletin board for my rating. It was a first, which made me glad I hadn't said anything snotty to Mary Lois, and Speed said he guessed I must be pretty good.

"Thanks to me," Mary Lois said.

In spite of her, I thought. She landed on the accompaniment as if she were playing a duet, and that was no way to accompany a solo.

"Get in gear, you two!" Mr. Cooper yelled. "You're holding two cars up. Congratulations, Margaret."

Mary Lois was waiting for him to say something nice to her, but he didn't. Piano players were no concern of his.

On the way home with a nervous and exhausted band mother at the wheel, we sang "There's a Hole in the Bottom of the Sea" until we ran out of objects to put into it. Then we switched to telling knock, knock jokes. If nobody groaned at a knock, knock, it was of poor quality.

"Knock, knock!"

"Who's there?"

"Tarzan."

"Tarzan who?"

"Tarzan Stripes Forever."

I leaned into my corner of the back seat and tuned out, thinking about Speed a little but mostly wondering how it would feel to get a second rating or worse. Mom and Grandma expected me to get a first rating, and I always did. I knew how it would be when I got home. They would smile and get that special light in their eyes, but right away they'd be talking about the next time. "Expectation is greater than realization," they said, and it must be true. What I expected was a man worthy of Hedy Lamarr, and what I got was Speed.

The rest of the trip was devoted to making the best of Speed. He was tall, and that was a plus, because I was tired of slumping and wearing flat shoes. Duane had been too short to allow me to obey Mom's orders to "stand straight and hold your stomach in." Albert had been taller, but I had continued to slump, unhappy to be seen with him.

Speed's glasses were a problem until I convinced myself that he wore them with a noble absence of vanity. I never wore the silver-framed spectacles prescribed for my near sightedness several years earlier in public.

His dark blond hair frustrated my yearning for a Tyrone Power–like black Irishman or a Latin lover type, but I had adored Leslie Howard as Ashley Wilkes in *Gone with the Wind* and thought I could make the adjustment. If Speed didn't have much to say for himself, so what? Neither did Gary Cooper. By the time we got home, Speed was a new man.

It was a soft spring, all violet and pale green. The high school chorus was practicing "All in the April Evening," and I sang it as I walked, alive to the vibrations of the good, the true, and the beautiful.

I stretched my arms wide and said, "My future is unknown and unlimited."

"You sound just like Kam," Mom said with a crooked smile, "and we all know that she doesn't live in the real world."

"She doesn't have to," Grandma pointed out, noting that Aunt Kam was the only Jorgen woman who had managed to keep a husband for any length of time. Grandpa, Daddy, Uncle Soren, and Uncle John all had died before their time from disease or disaster.

Uncle Karl and Aunt Kam called each other "sweetheart," and he kissed her good-bye—even when he took the garbage to the alley. When he came into the house, he always took the Bissell from its place near the back door to remove his footprints from the navy blue living-room rug.

Aunt Kam had something good to say about everybody, which made her blue and white kitchen a haven for anyone who needed a kind word. As long as Marianne lived at home, she resented the callers as much as she had resented me and my piano practice. She called them "cases." Uncle Karl was indulgent about all but one, a kid whose mother had named him Faye.

Faye, who lived down the block, took violin lessons and went into happy spasms over flowers. Nearly every day after school, Aunt Kam welcomed him with milk, cookies, and her observations on the good, the true, and the beautiful. He stayed until Uncle Karl came home from the store. He even came on Sundays until Aunt Kam was forced to tell him that was "family time."

On a day when I wanted to talk about *my* hopes and dreams—unformed as they were—Faye was hogging my aunt's attention. I willed him to leave, wondering how he could ignore a burning gaze that bored a hole in his forehead. I hadn't tried that for years—not since I did it to Vivian Corley and then wished I hadn't. It was childish, if not downright wicked, and besides, it wasn't working. I sat back with a sigh and gave it up.

That was when Uncle Karl came in carrying the Bissell. He kissed Aunt Kam's forehead, winked at me, and ignored Faye, who slid off his chair and headed for the door in a hurry.

"Good-bye, Faye," Aunt Kam said. "I know you'll do well in your test tomorrow."

Uncle Karl set the Bissell down and lit a cigarette. "That little sissy ought to wear a dress!" The s's shot into the room on a shaft of blue smoke.

"Hush, Karl, the window's open and he'll hear you."

"I hope he does. I'm sick of finding him here day after day."

"Now Karl, you don't make the slightest effort to appreciate Faye. He has the soul of an artist."

Uncle Karl snorted and left the room. The swipes he made with the Bissell had a savage sound.

"There's a letter from Marianne on the hall table, sweetheart," Aunt Kam called.

Marianne had decided not to marry Wayne Andrews, which surprised everyone but me. After all, I had read the dumb letters he wrote to her when he was in the service. Marianne became another Jorgen woman without a man, pursuing a career in Chicago. I wasn't quite sure what she did—something with money and banks—and she seldom came home, but when she did, she caused a lot of comment. She wore her red-gold hair in a smooth pageboy, and her expensive wool suits and silk blouses were such subtle colors that most people didn't know what to call them. Even when they asked, they weren't sure, because the answers sounded like a menu: shrimp, bisque, celery, banana. I still got most of her hand-me-downs, and when someone asked about a color, I'd make up something like "Vienna cinnamon" and offer it with authority. I had worn Marianne's clothes for so long that I didn't know what I'd choose if I could buy something just for me.

Aunt Kam was trying to give me her full attention, but I knew she was concerned about starting supper. She was a whiz at putting a meal together in a hurry, but she didn't want spectators. Good cooks never let the machinery show, she believed.

"Was there something special you wanted to talk to me about, Margaret?"

"Nothing special. Do you really think Faye has the soul of an artist?"

"Of course. He's sensitive."

"Am I?"

"I suppose so. It runs in the family."

"Then why is Aunt Val our only artist?"

"Margaret," she glanced at the clock and furtively opened a drawer, "artistry has many faces. If I bake a perfect loaf of bread, that's an art just as much as Val's paintings are."

"What's Mom's art?"

The question seemed to stump her at first. "Well, if she had been a man, she could have been an architect or a builder."

"But she's a woman."

"Honey, I really have to start supper." Her hand dipped into the drawer for a paring knife.

"I'm going. So Mom doesn't have an art?"

Aunt Kam dropped the knife to put both hands on my shoulders. "Of course she does. Petra has the art of survival. Every time life knocks her down, she gets up again."

I wanted to ask, "What about me?" but she was marching me to the door bodily. I walked home in a roundabout way to visit all the blooming lilac bushes in the neighborhood, breathing their fragrance as I wondered about it all. When I started to school, I had believed that I had a talent for drawing, but the episode of the black tree trunks had put an end to that. I worked hard at music, dreaming of Juilliard, but there was no money for that. Despite my admiration for Hedy, the stage and screen didn't attract me, so what was left? Maybe I could be a poet.

Supper was vegetable soup with barley, a menu more attractive on a cold winter night than in April when the whole universe breathed perfume. The slippery bits of barley were hard to capture and chew; as elusive as my unfixed ambitions.

I looked across the table at Grandma. As long as I could remember, she had been old, but she looked even older now. The bones at the hinges of her jaw stood out, and her thin mouth was rimmed with tiny wrinkles like stitches around a buttonhole. An old picture tucked into her Danish Bible had fallen out one day. She covered it with her hand, but not before I caught a glimpse of smooth, full lips, high cheekbones, and proud eyes with a steady gaze—the same eyes that looked at me now through the oval windows of her glasses. Had she wondered what to do with her life when she was my age?

"You're awfully quiet," Mom said. "Are you catching something?"

I shook my head, ate my canned pears, and wiped the supper dishes without being asked. Then I went to the dining room and turned on the light that had a low-hanging shade that looked like melted green and pink lollipops. With three sheets of notebook paper, two sharp pencils, and space cleared between stacks of folded laundry, I was prepared to write a poem. Nothing happened for nearly an hour.

Then something came in a rush: "I am not close to anyone, I love the wind, the rain, the sun. The leaves in autumn, winter's snow, are all the passion that I know." Was that true? It felt true, but why snow and autumn leaves when April came in through the window screen and the warm sun was caught in the pile of line-dried sheets at my elbow?

Grandma walked in and scooped up the sheets. She didn't ask what I was doing, but I told her.

"I haven't read poetry since Peter was alive," she said, "but I'd like to read yours when it's finished."

I made a noise in my throat that could be taken for a response. When she was gone, I crumpled the page. It hurt me to do that, but the feeling that what I had written was no good forced me to squeeze the words into a tight ball that never could be smoothed out and read. Animals knew how to cull their defective offspring, and poets had to learn that same essential cruelty. What I had written was not a poem but a jump-rope jingle.

In the morning, Grandma looked up from stirring the oatmeal and handed me something from her apron pocket. "Here. I've written a poem, too."

Her curly script on the back of a pink sales slip from the Golden Rule read: "Last night I lay and thought, and the thought became a hope, and the hope became a boat that carried me to the land of my heart's desire."

When I raised my eyes, she had turned back to the stove. Her hair was freshly combed and knotted high on her head without one wisp escaping the tortoise-shell combs. Her shoulders were straight and tense with waiting.

"It's beautiful, Grandma. I'm putting it here in your Bible."

The foreign book I could not read fell open where she had tucked the photograph, and the morning sun bathed the face of the young Amalie with the pink reflection from the Golden Rule sales slip.

"Throw a few cobs into the stove, will you?" she said.

I did as she asked, and the tight ball of my own rejected words flamed with the cobs.

2 7

THE EASTER SEASON always had a profound effect on me.
When we were younger, I had envied the Catholic observances of Monica
and Wyonne, borrowing whatever I could from them. My Lenten sacri-
fices this year were candy, chocolate Cokes, and movies.

I was sitting on the school steps with Merrilee when I refused her
kind offer to share a Mounds bar.

"Don't you like coconut?"

"I love it, but I'm giving up candy for Lent."

"Jeez, I didn't know you were Catholic."

"I'm not, but I might be if it didn't mean you had to have a million
kids. They've got a lot of good stuff—nuns, candles, incense, Latin. If
Baptists had nuns, I might be one."

"You're kidding!"

I shook my head. "The trouble is, Baptist nuns probably would wear
cotton dresses and Red Cross shoes."

Merrilee said she didn't believe in God anymore, and I told her that
was pretty dangerous. Reverend Harper, the minister of my early years,
had been succeeded by Reverend Spengler, who emphasized the im-
portance of snatching one's unsaved friends from the jaws of hell. It was
time that I went to work on Merrilee.

"What have you got against God?"

"He didn't do a damned thing for Donny, and it wasn't because I
didn't ask!" Merrilee popped the second half of the Mounds bar into her
mouth, looking as if she were eating a harmonica.

"Then there's a reason for it."

The bell rang, and I had no time to elaborate, drawing on a sermon
Reverend Spengler had delivered after playing "Trust and Obey" on his
musical saw. It was a marvel that I remembered anything about his sermon on God's purposes after watching his leg jiggle as if he had St.
Vitus's dance to produce a ghostly moan from the saw. Several of the
church ladies said it embarrassed them to watch.

It did seem unfair that Donny Adams had to suffer an operation in
Iowa City, miss a lot of school, and be no better off in the end, but according to Reverend Spengler, God had a reason for wanting Donny's
arm to stay withered. I couldn't imagine what that reason could be, but,
as Grandma said, "God is the boss."

Reverend Spengler also talked a great deal about leading souls to

Christ. I viewed this undertaking as the churchly equivalent of selling Girl Scout cookies, and I couldn't sell a Coke to a person lost in the Sahara. The hymn "Will There Be Any Stars in My Crown?" filled me with guilt. Not one soul, not one star.

The very thought of my starless crown produced a sense of urgency that stayed with me all afternoon. When I reported for work after school, I looked at Mr. Sommer speculatively, wondering about the condition of his soul. He seemed preoccupied and not at all open to a discussion of such matters, but that didn't let me off the hook.

"You seem to be in a ferment about something," he said, giving me a perfect opening.

I denied it, instantly remembering Peter and the crowing cock.

Walking home through the lilac and green April evening, I visualized Hedy Lamarr in a nun's habit. She always did favor black and white, according to the movie magazines. Looking holy surely must make it easier to *be* holy, but my church had to do it the hard way. Reverend Spengler looked like an insurance salesman.

After supper I washed my hair with rainwater and rolled it up with strips torn from an old sheet. I had just put my clarinet together to practice when the doorbell rang. It was Speed, sunburned from spring plowing and wearing a stiff jacket that stood away from his body.

"Wait!" I said, leaving him outside as I ran into the Farley bedroom to snatch the rags from my hair and rake my fingers through the damp corkscrews. I invited him into the parlor, where the light from the small, peach bulbs was dim. He sat on the horsehair sofa with the lion armrests, looking ill at ease.

"I guess I should have called," he said, "but I just took a chance. Have you seen the show that's on?"

I said that I hadn't, but I couldn't because I was giving up movies for Lent.

"I didn't know you were Catholic."

"There's a lot you don't know about me—almost everything."

"Then—you are?"

"Are what?"

"Catholic?"

"No."

He exhaled noisily. "That's good, because I'm Lutheran. Well, if you can't go to a movie, let's drive to Denison and get something to eat at Cronk's."

I explained the situation to Mom, and she brought Grandma into the parlor to meet Speed. He didn't get up for the introductions, and they didn't like that, but I was allowed to go out. I put my clarinet away and changed my clothes. Mom made me tie a scarf over my damp hair, but I took it off as soon as we were in the car.

Speed drove an old Chevy. It made a knocking sound that seemed abnormal, even to my untrained ears, but he said it was nothing serious.

155

We had little to say to each other. I might have done better if I hadn't felt so ugly, but it's hard to pour on the charm when you smell like a jar of pickles after rinsing your hair in vinegar.

"You'll be graduating soon, huh?" he said.

"In a few weeks."

"Then what, college?"

The question hurt. Lotus, Monica, and Wyonne had definite college plans, and Mary Lois would be going to school as soon as she finished her term as Rainbow Worthy Advisor. I'd never been offered the hope of college, and I was shocked at how jealous and deprived I felt when the college prep crowd started to talk about it in earnest.

Speed turned to look at me in the ghostly green light from the dashboard, still waiting for an answer.

"Maybe I'll join the WAVES."

The notion surprised even me. Maybe it arose from the fact that we were on our way to Denison, Duane's hometown. Where had he gone after the Navy? Did he have a girl? A wife?

Speed edged his hand across the expanse of upholstery between us, touching mine. "I was kind of hoping you'd stick around here."

I broke the contact by fishing in my purse for lipstick, not that another layer of Revlon's Cherries in the Snow would do much for my looks. My hair was drying straight as a stick.

The bright lights at Cronk's made everyone look like triumphs of the mortician's art. We found a booth right away, and Speed fed the jukebox without asking me what I wanted to hear, but "All The Things You Are" was fine with me. After my experience with Bardell, I wasn't saving that song for anything special.

We ordered hamburgers, and he said, "Without onions." The waitress cocked an eyebrow at me, and I asked for the works. Speed looked hurt. I was so pleased with him for picking up the signal that I said, "Wait a minute—hold the onions."

Billy Mullenger, the brother of Donna Reed the movie actress, came in. I pointed him out to Speed.

"How do you know him?"

"A friend of a friend introduced us," I said airily, remembering the night when Gene, Wyonne's date, had stopped at Billy's booth to make hasty introductions. Wyonne insisted. Billy wouldn't know me from Adam's off ox if I spoke to him now. Speed asked if I wanted to go over and say hello to Billy.

"No, I'd rather talk to you." That sounded like more of a come-on than I'd intended, but I was stuck with it. I encouraged Speed to tell me about his farming operation and smiled brightly at the ensuing rush of information on feeder pigs. Finally, he reminded me that we had met in a booth.

"How could I forget? It was only two weeks ago."

"I like booths," he said. "They're private."

156

"Unless somebody hangs over the top and bothers you."

He blushed through his sunburn, and I thought it was a pity that I couldn't feel more for him. He rated higher than Albert Rettig on my feeling scale, but that wasn't saying much.

I was frowning at the Cherries in the Snow semicircle on my coffee cup when a jukebox strain reminded me of Reverend Spengler's musical saw. Suddenly I perceived the purpose of this semisatisfactory date.

"Speed, are you a Christian?"

"I *told* you I was a Lutheran."

"That doesn't cut any ice," I said, remembering Reverend Spengler's remark about pagans in the pews. "I mean, do you really believe? Are your sins forgiven?"

Speed squirmed, looking highly uncomfortable. "I sure hope so."

"You should *know* so!"

"Well, I—"

"Let's get out of here."

He scooped up the check and fell over his own feet getting to the cash register. I reapplied the Revlon, and when I passed Billy Mullenger's booth, I smiled at him. He looked puzzled for a second, but he grinned back. Donna Reed's many siblings were reputed to be good-natured.

Speed put me into the car politely, and we headed south in silence. I could feel that his silence was apprehensive, but mine was active. I was working out the message that would win a star for my crown.

At length he said, "I didn't know you were so religious."

"It's important."

"Sure, but—" He turned the wheel suddenly, and the car bumped onto the shoulder of the road. We were near Dead Man's Curve at Defiance, and I suggested that we might be rear-ended into eternity. I asked if he considered himself ready for such an eventuality.

"God, Margaret, I thought we'd just go out and have a good time. I've been thinking about that ever since we met in Atlantic."

" 'Thou shalt not take the name of the Lord thy God in vain.' "

"Sorry." He pulled back onto the pavement and drove on. His jawline suggested that he was clenching his teeth.

It occurred to me that I was sounding like Jeannette Johnson, all preachy and snotty and holier than thou. I would do well to back off and start over.

"There are safer places to pull off the road," I suggested pleasantly.

The jawline relaxed, and soon we were bumping onto the gravelled shoulder of a flat stretch of the highway. Speed turned off the motor but not the lights. I smiled encouragingly in the green glow that was straining the battery.

"This is more like it," he said, cutting the lights and sliding out from under the wheel. He smelled of Brilliantine and laundry soap.

If kisses came in flavors, this one was vanilla, but he seemed to enjoy it. Bent on evangelism, I ran my fingers through his hair and wondered where to wipe the Brilliantine. Digging into my purse for a handkerchief would destroy whatever useful illusion I had managed to create. I splayed my fingers in the air while his moved to forbidden territory.

"All right, Speed, no fair."

"Oh, Margaret, you feel so good."

What he was doing felt good too, but I knew I'd feel pretty bad about the whole thing later if I let it go on. The Jorgen women had worked together to equip me with a Cadillac of a conscience. I told him he'd better take me home.

The motor wouldn't start. During the first few tries I wasn't concerned, but when even the growling and grinding stopped, I knew we were in trouble.

"How far from town are we?"

"A couple of miles."

"Let's walk, then."

The moon helped a little, but the terrain was treacherous, and we had to hold hands for mutual support. The few cars that came along didn't slow or stop to ask if we needed help. When we finally reached town, it was late, and all the gas stations were closed.

"Why don't you stay at my house tonight? You can call your folks, and in the morning somebody can take care of your car."

Our house was dark and quiet. Mom had left a cinnamon roll on the kitchen table for me, and I found another one for Speed. I poured two glasses of milk, and we took everything to the Farley bedroom.

"I don't have any men's pajamas," I apologized.

"That's O.K., I always sleep in my—" he broke off, blushing. I was beginning to like his blushes.

I sat on the dresser bench, and he sat on the bed while we snacked and talked about salvation.

"Wait," I said. "I'll get a Bible and show you what I mean about how simple it is."

I grabbed my white Rainbow Bible from the parlor bookcase and flipped through it, looking for the verse that told about believing with the heart and confessing with the mouth. Speed waited patiently, obviously receptive to the revelation I was about to present. I couldn't find what I was looking for immediately, but when I passed the verse in Galatians that speaks of crucifying the flesh and the lusts thereof, I sat close to Speed on the bed to share it with him. The print in the Rainbow Bible was very small, and the ceiling light in the Farley bedroom was not meant for reading. Our heads touched as I pointed out the passage.

"Margaret!"

Both of us jumped at the sound of Mom's voice and jumped again when she gave the sliding door of the Farley bedroom a shove that jarred it to the end of its track and bounced it back again. She was wearing the old cotton flannel bathrobe that was on loan every Christmas to the Wise Men in the Sunday school program.

"Mom, I'm just showing Speed something in the Bible."

"This is not the time nor the place."

Speed jumped to his feet, ready to run, but I clutched his arm while I explained the misfortune with the car.

"All right," she said, "he can stay the night, but you go straight to my room."

"Mom, I was just—"

"Never mind what you were just. Go!"

"Good night, Speed, I had a nice time."

"Yeah, me, too. Honest, Mrs. Langelund, we weren't doing anything."

Her response to that was the firm closing of the sliding door. She sat on the edge of the bathtub while I washed and brushed my teeth, telling me that I must be like Caesar's wife, above suspicion and beyond reproach. I listened dutifully and went to bed feeling much misunderstood and bereft of the star in my crown that had seemed a sure thing.

Speed was gone when I got up in the morning. Grandma said she had given him breakfast.

"He seemed like a nice enough young fellow," she said, "but he isn't for you."

"How do you know? You just saw him for a minute."

"If he were, you wouldn't have dared to take him into a bedroom."

That's when *I* blushed.

2 8

COMMENCEMENT might be the beginning for some, but for me, it seemed to be the end. Caps and gowns had been ordered, Mary Lois Engle was preparing her valedictorian speech, and I was practicing with the woodwind quintet for baccalaureate. The whole business seemed downright funereal.

The senior prom committee was making crepe paper orchids for a south seas theme that thrilled me about as much as it did the local veterans of the war in the Pacific. They said it gave them "a pain in the ass." I didn't object to the theme, but I didn't have a date and wanted to forget the whole thing.

"Just take one little look at the gym," Merrilee urged. "It's gorgeous!"

"I'd rather imagine it."

"Come on down and see my formal, at least. I hung it from the light fixture with a sheet around it so the kids wouldn't wallow all over it."

Merrilee, who had turned so tough so young, had reverted to girlishness when Jim Rasmussen asked her to the prom, and she had spent a month's salary on the dress. How could I refuse to look at her dress? After I left Mr. Sommer's office that night, I stopped at the Adamses'.

Donny was reading *Popular Mechanics* in the living room, using the withered hand to hold the magazine open while he turned pages with his good hand. When Mrs. Adams came out of the kitchen with a beer and a cigarette, I was horrified to see that she was pregnant.

"In here," Merrilee called from behind the curtains.

The dress looked like a huge flower suspended from the ceiling. I gasped in true admiration, as awed by its beauty as the open-mouthed, enraptured Delsey was.

"It's seafoam green," Merrilee said proudly, "and I had the silk shoes dyed to match. I had to get a strapless bra, too, so this little party is costing me plenty."

"You'll have a wonderful time," I said, swallowing a large lump of envy.

"Jim nearly dropped dead when I said I'd go. What he doesn't know is that I would have said yes to the devil himself. I figure I've got the right to remember a prom."

Delsey said, "Do I get that dress someday?"

"If I don't wear it out in one night and if you don't get any uglier. Now get out of here!"

Rid of Delsey, we sat on the stacked mattresses to talk. I asked if I had assessed Mrs. Adams' condition correctly.

Merrilee nodded, staring at the green gown swaying in a breeze from the open window. "Can you believe it? The old man was home for one week—just one week. As soon as they put that diploma in my hand, I'm getting out of here. I can't take any more kids!"

"If you go, I won't have a friend left. Everybody else is going to college."

"Why don't you leave, too? We could go to a city and get jobs—do all the things we've talked about."

The idea was alluring, but it also gave me a cold feeling in the pit of my stomach. Leave Mom and Grandma? If I were going to college, I could do it, but simply picking up my life and putting it down in another place was something different. I told Merrilee I'd have to think about it.

"Hey, Margaret, lots of people are going to the prom without dates. Why can't you?"

"Who wants to be like Jeannette Johnson? She thinks it's wicked to dance, so she'll be sitting in a corner with her nose in the air."

"You won't have to do that. I'll have Jim dance with you, and some other guys are coming alone."

"No thanks, and besides, I don't have a dress."

"I'll bet that aunt of yours could find something your cousin used to wear."

"Look, Merrilee, I don't want to remember a prom I went to alone in a borrowed dress, so let's forget it."

As I walked home, I remembered a shrimp-colored gown of Marianne's that now hung in Aunt Kam's attic, but I put it out of my mind.

Mom was lying back on the kitchen couch when I came in. She hadn't changed from her working clothes and said she was too tired to move after putting through dozens of calls to Gregory's Greenhouse—boys ordering corsages for their prom dates. One look at my face told her she shouldn't have mentioned it, and she apologized.

"That's O.K.," I said wearily. "By the way, all the girls are getting corsages for their graduation gowns. May I have one?"

"Corsages on academic robes are Dutchy," she said.

"But everybody—"

"Besides, it's an unnecessary expense."

I fled to the bedroom in tears. Was I to be denied everything? Even funeral flowers for the commencement that was the end for me? I cried for some time, soaking the bright squares of the patchwork quilt. I thought I heard a man's voice in the kitchen, but I knew that couldn't be, so I rolled over and dampened more quilt squares.

When hunger got the best of me, I blew my nose, wiped my eyes, and went to the kitchen. I *had* heard a male voice, and it belonged to a huge, young, and reasonably good-looking man.

"Margaret," Mom said, "this is your cousin Davy, Aunt Val's son."

I stared at the smiling giant in khaki shirt and pants. Had he really been the boy whose snapshot I'd punctured with a sharp pencil? I croaked a greeting, wishing to heaven that I hadn't wept myself into puffy-eyed ugliness.

When we sat down to supper, Mom and Grandma gave him such loving attention that I would have pierced his picture all over again, and yet I found myself listening to his tales of the building of the Alcan Highway with intense interest. When I was a kid, he was struggling against swamps, mountains, rushing rivers, forests, and giant mosquitoes.

"Of course it doesn't go much of anywhere," he said with a grin, "and they don't let tourists on it. That's the story of my life."

"What do you mean—that's the story of your life?" Mom looked at him with such love that I turned green.

He sighed. "I should have educated myself. All I have right now is these two hands and a strong back. I build something and move on to build another thing. You see a lot of the country that way, but sometimes I get the yearning to settle down. If my back ever goes, I've had it!"

They talked about Aunt Val, and Davy said she was planning to marry a man with a fair amount of money.

"He has something besides money, I hope," Grandma said.

"Yeah, he likes her paintings."

"Then he'll do."

Davy planned to stay for a week before going on to the next construction site, and when I heard Mom ask if he'd brought any decent clothes, I supposed she wanted him to go to church. On Thursday, the day before the prom, she told me that Davy would be my escort and steered me into the Farley bedroom to show me Marianne's shrimp-colored gown altered to my size.

I swallowed hard and asked, "Does he hate having to take me?"

"Of course not! Davy likes a surprise as well as the next person. He didn't want to tell you until tomorrow, but I knew you'd want to do something about your hair."

Davy washed and polished his green Ford. At the appointed hour, he went out the back door and walked around to the front to ring the bell. Dressed in a dark suit and holding a box from Gregory's Greenhouse, he asked for me, and Grandma told him to come right in. I watched the whole scene from the Farley parlor and thought it was well staged.

Davy told me how fine I looked and carefully pinned two gardenias tied with silver ribbon to the strapless bodice of the shrimp gown. Obviously he'd done such things before. Mom insisted that I'd catch cold with bare shoulders in the night air, and Grandma was ready for that with a lacy shawl she had worn to a dance before Mom was born. I hadn't even noticed that it was airing in the grape arbor for two days to get rid of the smell of mothballs.

1 6 2

The high school was only three blocks away, but we took the car, arriving at the same time as Mary Lois Engle and her date, a "better than nothing" escort.

It occurred to me that I hadn't mentioned our house guest to anyone, and I asked Davy, "Do you mind if I don't say you're my cousin?"

He laughed. "Tell 'em anything you please. I don't know a soul in this town anymore, so you'll never get caught."

Merrilee rushed over to greet us as we came into the gym, and I said, "This is Dave." Lotus, Monica, and Wyonne got the same cryptic introduction.

"Your dress is gorgeous," Wyonne whispered, "and so is he."

Davy was an excellent dancer—good enough to make me seem better than I was. He swept me through trellises of paper orchids, close to the bandstand, and past the mystified but smiling chaperones. It seemed that everyone was looking at us.

"Having a good time?" he asked.

"For once I *really* feel like Hedy Lamarr, but I suppose it isn't much fun for you."

"Sure it is. It takes me back. Maybe I should have married that girl I took to the senior prom."

We danced until the band played "Good-Night Sweetheart," but Davy drew the line at the postprom dinner in another town followed by an all-night party at the field club. I was perfectly willing to disappear like Cinderella before I was found out.

"I'll never forget this," I told him.

"Good," he said. "That's the idea."

"Whose idea was this?"

He laughed. "You know the Jorgen girls. They might seem as practical as bacon and eggs, but they're romantics—every one of 'em. Come to think of it, that's a pretty good description of a Dane."

We sat in the car under the streetlight talking for awhile before we went in, and I confessed what I had done to Davy's snapshot image. Considering what he had done for me, I was sorry.

"Think nothing of it, kid. I'm not sure I'd want *my* mother to love anybody else the way Aunt Pete loved me—Uncle Lauritz, too. I owe a lot to both of them. Your dad was quite a man, Margaret. Too bad you lost him so soon."

"If we hadn't, maybe I'd be going to college."

"Don't let that stop you." He smacked a fist into his palm. "Get there, do you hear?"

"We don't have the money."

"Then beg, borrow, or steal it! Don't be like me—thinking you'll make some money first and then go. I've said that for years, but I never get around to it."

We found Mom and Grandma at the kitchen table drinking tea and waiting to hear all. Their eyes shone as we talked, and Davy laughed, saying, "What did I tell you? Romantics."

"Pshaw!" said Grandma, but she wasn't displeased.

We stayed up later than I'd ever been awake, even on New Year's Eve, and when we finally rose from the table yawning, Davy leaned down and kissed my forehead.

"Don't forget what I told you," he said.

The next day he climbed into the green Ford and headed for New Mexico. Mom and Grandma turned away well before the car was out of sight, but I took the risk of watching until only a sliver of green roof was visible above the Willow Street hill.

"What was it that Davy didn't want you to forget?" Mom asked.

"How much you and Daddy did for him," I said, not wanting to worry her with his expensive recommendation. No matter what Davy said, college was out of the question for me.

"We did love him like our own," she said, "and then you came along." She put her arm around me and gave me a hug.

I was watching Grandma, thinking that Davy and I had the same blood relationship with her, but he hadn't lived with her for as many years as I had. Now that he was gone, she was all mine again.

She caught my look and said, "Grandchildren are like books of the Bible—all precious and each special."

Even the begats?" I said.

"Even the begats."

2 9

I WALKED to the law office humming "It Might As Well Be Spring," and it was. After a Friday night rain, the May morning glittered and dazzled. The lawns were as green as Easter basket grass. Rain had pooled in the waxy cups of late tulips, lapping at the dark anthers I had thought of as little people sitting around a table until a science teacher dashed my fancy.

This was the first day I had been allowed to leave the house in a cotton dress (the prom didn't count), and I felt reborn. My friends had been out of their winter cocoons all week, but Mom stepped outside every morning to test the air and said, "Wait another day." This was the day. It was nearly as glorious as those grade-school spring mornings when I was allowed to exchange long stockings for anklets. May was the time to sniff and touch flowers, roll in the grass, listen to Schubert on the radio, and profess undying love.

Of course, May had its dark side too. Grandma said that kittens born in May nearly always died before they became cats. She spoke of something that didn't work out as a "May cat." Suddenly I felt sorry for myself because I had to get up early and go to work while most of my friends slept deep into a Saturday morning. Those same friends would spend the summer collecting a college wardrobe while I typed letters and legal documents. In September, they would go off to unimaginable delights while I labored on.

In contrast with the brightness of the morning, the windowless law office seemed gloomier than usual. Volumes of the *Iowa Code Annotated* on the shelves looked like maroon tombstones. I looked years into the future and saw a woman in a drab skirt and what Grandma called a waist seated at the typewriter. Her tightly laced brown oxfords were planted in precise parallels, her hair was pulled back in a knot, and her fingers were ringless. She was me.

"Good morning, Margaret."

I saw the shoes first. Mr. Sommer always wore black shoes made in England, and the two-toned brown and white footgear startled me.

He flexed one foot and laughed. "My salute to the season, and speaking of that, I'll have to be looking for another girl. Can you recommend someone?"

My heart lurched as I realized what he was saying. I had taken my job for granted, going so far as to despise it, and now it was being snatched away? The somber office suddenly became dear to me. I loved the smell of the bookbindings and the carbon paper. I appreciated the rich wine shade of the law books. I wanted to wrap my arms around the old L.C. Smith typewriter and never let go. I was afraid.

Mr. Sommer watched me closely with the bright, quizzical look that usually signalled that a lesson was about to be taught, but I was too disturbed to interpret his expression. Tears welled in my eyes.

"Margaret, Margaret," he said, "when will you ever learn not to react until all the facts are in?"

"Wh-what facts?"

He sighed. "You're forcing me to reveal a carefully kept secret. Oh, well, it's probably better than having you break down and blubber during a public event."

"I always thought I'd go on working for you—I—" My voice quavered embarrassingly, and I fell silent.

He looked at me, and I remembered the feeling of leaving the Beekman farm in disgrace and of hearing the detasseling foreman say, "Don't come back." Now this: "I'll have to be looking for another girl." How could I ever tell Mom and Grandma? If I left the house every morning and spent the day somewhere, they wouldn't have to know for awhile, but where could I go in a town this size? How could I explain the absence of a paycheck indefinitely?

"Margaret," he finally said, "I don't see how you can work for me and go to college at the same time."

"But I'm not—I can't. I mean, I can't go to college."

"Not even with the Garner scholarship?"

Each year, as a memorial to a son who died in the war, the Garner family awarded to a graduating senior enough money for books and tuition at the State University of Iowa. I *couldn't* be getting it, because it always went to somebody in college prep. I shook my head in disbelief.

"I'm on the selection committee," he said.

This was another unbelievable piece of information. The Garners never revealed the number or identities of their selectors, but Sommer seemed an unlikely choice. He was nodding and telling me that his reputation for truth and veracity in the community was excellent.

"But I took the commercial course. They never—"

"I flatter myself that your association with me has been a liberal education."

I began to believe him—enough to make a timid inquiry about costs above and beyond the scholarship items.

He waved his hand airily. "That's where your typing and shorthand come in. You can get a part-time job. Margaret, do you want to go to college so much that you'd sleep in a culvert and raid garbage cans if you had to?"

I nodded with a trace of doubt, hearing Davy say, "Beg, borrow, or steal!"

"Then it's all settled. I'll talk to your mother if you think that will help. Just promise me one thing—"

"Anything!" Joy was bubbling up from my toes.

"When they make the announcement at commencement—Joe Garner will do it—for the love of God, act surprised. Carry on the way young girls are supposed to when you give them the moon. You might as well go home now, because I won't get any work out of you today, but I'll expect you Monday afternoon—and for the rest of the summer. And remember, this is a secret. Don't tell even your mother."

Taking the dim stairs three steps at a time, I was outside before I realized that I couldn't go home. Showing up when I should be working would raise all kinds of questions I couldn't answer without lying.

I started to run, feeling weightless in the cotton dress. It occurred to me that a prayer of thanks was in order. It should be offered in a church, but the blond woodwork and Palmolive odor of sanctity of my own church didn't seem right for the occasion. The quaint, old Episcopal church with the crimson doors was better. Two more blocks.

Nobody ever locked a church door in Harlan. I walked into soft, tawny light from mullioned windows and sank into a back pew to recover from the sideache I always got when I ran. The church had the same mysterious richness that had struck me in the Edelstein house. This was what I craved—decoration, complication, highlights, and shadows—more than could be seen with one swift glance. Without the familiar Jesus picture to focus my prayer, I simply said, "Thank You!" over and over.

Then I tried to imagine what the State University of Iowa might be like. I'd never been there and hadn't even looked at the catalogs, not wanting to see what I couldn't have. For the first time, I dared to think of myself as a college girl: carrying books, going to dances, sitting in a stadium. The backdrop was hazy, but Margaret Langelund, college girl, was well defined. This time, I would be the real thing, caught up in my college existence rather than standing aside to watch myself go through the motions.

My reverie was interrupted by the janitor (the Episcopalians call him a sexton), who was Mary Lois Engle's uncle. He knew me and looked so surprised that I felt guilty about being where I didn't belong. I hurried out and headed back toward the Square.

A new dress shop had opened in the space where Fern's Fashion had been. Usually I turned away when I passed it, fighting the memory of the day when Fern and Chet were carried through the front door. This time happiness was my shield, and I looked.

The Frockery was owned by Mardee Kreutzer, the wife of the new sale barn auctioneer. Rumor had it that Mardee had been a dancer in a Council Bluffs nightclub, but Mom thought people just jumped to that conclusion because she peroxided her hair and smoked cigarettes.

It could have been the May morning, my marvelously reopened future, the mere fact of being seventeen, or any combination of those factors, but I had to have the dress in the window. It was royal purple with a draped and swagged skirt further beautified with silver sequin butterflies.

I entered the shop in a trance, scarcely aware of the changes that had been made since Fern's day. Mardee herself asked if she could help me, and I simply pointed toward the window.

"The purple? You want to try it on?"

I nodded, not thinking to ask the size or the price, and Mardee climbed into the window where I had dressed mannequins in Fern's awful styles. One hand with long, red nails held the marvelous garment out to me while she used the other to cover the dummy's temporary nudity. I knew she didn't believe I'd come to buy. I was into the dress before she joined me in the fitting room and before I realized that remodeling had positioned the stall where Fern's bed had stood. When the thought struck me, I was glad for the sound of Mardee's voice.

"That looks good on you, honey, whyn't you come out and see yourself in the big mirror?"

I did, and the dress was beautiful. Never mind that I was wearing saddle shoes with it, never mind what it might cost, never mind anything at all. When I looked into the mirror, I saw Hedy Lamarr.

"Wouldn't have to do a thing to it," Mardee said. "Got a big occasion coming up?"

I nodded. The big occasion was my whole life. Then it occurred to me that I hadn't uttered a word since I entered the shop. Mardee would think I was (in the words of Mrs. Hess) "deef and dumb." I asked the price, and her answer shocked me into further silence.

"I could put it on lay-away."

"No, I want it today. Will you let me charge it? If you don't trust me, you can call Mr. Sommer."

"The lawyer on the east side of the Square?"

I nodded, terrified by my own audacity. I'd never charged anything in my life. Mom never bought anything until she could pay for it.

Mardee was willing to trust me. She folded the purple dress tenderly in tissue paper and put it into a big box distinguished by the name of the shop and the silhouette of a stylish lady. I didn't see how I could hide such a box and asked for a bag instead. Then I signed my name on the slip that said *Chg.*, feeling that I had made a pact with the devil.

The purple dress was my secret until just before the commencement ceremonies. It came to light when Mom spilled Lady Esther powder on her white gloves and went into the Farley bedroom to look for another pair.

The night was full of secrets. I was worrying about getting out of the house with the carnation corsage I'd bought at Gregory's Greenhouse to wear on my graduation robe. Mom had made it very clear that she disapproved of flowers on such garb, but everyone else was doing it, and I didn't want her to be embarrassed when I came down the aisle looking uncherished. She wasn't to know until the processional, and then it would be

1 6 8

a *fait accompli.* I was practicing holding the flower box beneath the carefully pressed robe draped on my arm when the trumpet of doom sounded from the Farley bedroom.

"Margaret, what *is* this?" She flung the double doors wide and held the dress between two fingers as if it were a distasteful object. Grandma, who was fastening her mother-of-pearl circle pin to her dress, turned to look and quickly covered her eyes with one hand.

What could I say? The dress was the token of something I couldn't tell her about—a celebration. In another hour I could explain, but not now.

"Can we talk about it later? We should start for the school right now."

She gave me a long, hard look and draped the purple glory over the back of a dining room chair.

Grandma said, "Remember when I found that dress of Else's? When she was trying to be somebody she wasn't?"

"Now that you mention it, I do," Mom said.

The three of us walked to the school in silence. Aunt Kam and Uncle Karl were waiting in the vestibule, and the four of them went to find seats in the auditorium while I headed for the girls' restroom to put on my cap and gown and affix the smuggled carnations.

Mary Lois Engle was moving her lips silently as she gave her valedictorian's speech to the mirror. Wyonne was trying to decide which end of her orchid was up and which was down. Monica was grousing about how hard it was to keep stocking seams straight when you had skinny legs. Merrilee breezed in with a shoulderful of pink roses and told me they were from Donny. "That kid has been scrounging pop bottles and taking them to the store for months to get the money," she said. "Can you beat it?"

We lined up in the hall, and with the opening bars of Elgar's "Pomp and Circumstance," Merrilee Adams and the long, double column of Andersens entered the auditorium. That marvelous, majestic music made me believe I could do anything—even walk past my mother wearing forbidden flowers.

Mom was on the aisle, and she turned expectantly as the first Ls passed. Her eyes met mine proudly, bounced to the flowers, and returned to my face with an ominous glitter. When Grandma saw the flowers, her lips curved in a tiny smile for an instant. Because she didn't understand the situation, Aunt Kam smiled guilelessly and poked Uncle Karl to be sure he didn't miss me.

I scarcely heard what Mary Lois had to say or what the bank president talked about, but when Joe Garner got up to speak, I came to rigid attention. He said his son Kevin was a brilliant boy whose flame was snuffed out too soon and that he and Mrs. Garner were determined to light a new flame to his memory each year by helping a young person with aspirations.

"This year," he said, "our selection committee has chosen a young woman from a pioneer family. When we speak of the pioneers, the image of a man breaking the prairie comes to mind, but in this case, we must think of strong women who struggled against harsh circumstances to raise worthy children."

Feeling most unworthy, I squirmed in my seat. Mr. Sommer was watching me, waiting to see how I would handle the big moment. When Joe Garner said my name, I threw my head back, dropping my mortar board into the lap of the Miller boy. He gave it back to me, and I smiled and even cried a little while everybody clapped. I hoped that I was carrying on the way young girls are supposed to when you give them the moon.

Somehow I managed to get through the rest of the ceremony, but I scarcely remembered walking across the stage to take my diploma from the hand of the high school principal. Mrs. Cooper repeated the Elgar piece for the recessional, and we rushed to return the caps and gowns to the rental people.

Merrilee said, "Well, it's all over for me, but not for you, I guess."

"I can't believe it."

Neither could my family, but Aunt Kam and Uncle Karl came to our house for lemonade and excited talk about what had to be done to get me into the University of Iowa. I listened quietly, preoccupied with the coming hour of reckoning. I wondered which Mom would tackle first, the corsage or the purple dress?

Was no joy ever pure? Here I was wearing my very first wristwatch (Mom's gift), a necklace with a single golden rose from Aunt Kam and Uncle Karl, and flowers on my shoulder. I was as festively adorned as I'd ever been, but I was miserable. The girl graduate in a white dress reflected in the dining room window was a whited sepulchre. Inside of her was a black-haired wench in a clinging purple dress.

When Aunt Kam and Uncle Karl left, I offered to wash the dishes, but Mom said, "Wait until morning. It's late."

I started to unpin the corsage, bracing myself for the worst, but she opened a drawer and handed me a cellophane bag that had been washed and reused repeatedly. "Put them in this, and they'll keep quite awhile in the Norge."

I felt uneasy, cheated of expiation, and I said, "I can take the dress back."

"No, keep it. In time, that dress will tell you something." She kissed my forehead. "Good night, Margaret, I'm very proud of you."

Tears smarted in my eyes as I put the flowers in the refrigerator between a jar of pickles and a covered bowl of fruit soup, my favorite Danish dish.

I was ready to turn out the light and climb into bed when I heard a tap at the door.

"Margrethe?"

Grandma stepped into my room in her long, muslin nightgown. The coiled braid of her hair had been released to hang down her back like a

Chinaman's pigtail. She said, "You probably thought I had no gift for you."

"I hadn't thought," I said honestly, because she wasn't in the habit of giving things.

"I want you to have this." She opened her hand, revealing a circle of gold.

"But that's your wedding ring—"

"Peter would approve." She pushed it on my ring finger, and it was too big, so she put it on the middle finger. "Such little hands! What will you do with those little hands?"

"I don't know, Grandma, but *something!*"

She nodded. "Sail out, Margaret, it's time."

I smiled. "But not farther than I can row back?"

She drew herself up with all the dignity of her eighty-seven years and slashed the air with a gnarled hand. "Don't worry about the rowing back, just *sail!*" With that, she left me.

I stared at the circlet of mellow, Danish gold for a moment before I pulled the purple dress from the closet. The ring on my hand made the dress look cheap. I climbed into bed and thought, and the thought became a hope, and the hope became a boat that carried me to the land of my heart's desire. Sailing out—sailing out at last.